THE AUTHORITY OF THE BIBLE

THE AUTHORITY OF THE BIBLE

BY

C. H. DODD

NORRIS-HULSE PROFESSOR OF DIVINITY
IN THE UNIVERSITY OF CAMBRIDGE.

London
NISBET & CO. LTD.
22 BERNERS STREET, W.1

First Published in November, 1928
Revised and Reprinted July, 1938
Reprinted . . January, 1941
Reprinted . . February, 1942

Then by Fontana 1960
Paperbacks

PRINTED IN GREAT BRITAIN
BY BRADFORD & DICKENS, DRAYTON HOUSE, LONDON, W.C.1

GENERAL INTRODUCTION

THE Editors of this series are convinced that the Christian Church as a whole is confronted with a great though largely silent crisis, and also with an unparalleled opportunity. They have a common mind concerning the way in which this crisis and opportunity should be met. The time has gone by when "apologetics" could be of any great value. Something more is needed than a defence of propositions already accepted on authority, for the present spiritual crisis is essentially a questioning of authority if not a revolt against it. It may be predicted that the number of people who are content simply to rest their religion on the authority of the Bible or the Church is steadily diminishing, and with the growing effectiveness of popular education will continue to diminish. We shall not therefore meet the need, if we have rightly diagnosed it, by dissertations, however learned, on the interpretation of the Bible or the history of Christian doctrine. Nothing less is required than a candid, courageous and well-informed effort to think out anew, in the light of modern knowledge, the foundation affirmations of our common Christianity. This is the aim of every writer in this series.

A further agreement is, we hope, characteristic of the books which will be published in the series. The authors have a common mind not only with regard to the problem but also with regard to the starting-point of reconstruction. They desire to lay stress upon the value and validity of religious experience and to develop their theology on the basis of the religious consciousness. In so doing they claim to be in harmony with modern thought. The massive achievements of the nineteenth and twentieth centuries have been built up on the method of observation and experiment, on experience, not on abstract *a priori* reasoning. Our contention is that the moral and spiritual experience of mankind has the right to be considered, and demands to be understood.

Many distinguished thinkers might be quoted in support of the assertion that philosophers are now prepared in a greater measure than formerly to consider religious experience as among the most significant of their data. One of the greatest has said, "There is nothing more real than what comes in religion. To compare facts such as these with what is given to us in outward existence would be to trifle with the subject. The man who demands a reality more solid than that of the religious consciousness, seeks he does not know what."[1] Nor does this estimate of religious experience come only from idealist thinkers. A philosopher who writes from the standpoint of mathematics and natural science has expressed the same thought in even more forcible language. "The fact of religious vision, and its history of persistent expansion, is our one ground for optimism. Apart from it, human life is a flash of occasional enjoyments lighting up a

[1] F. H. Bradley, *Appearance and Reality*, p. 449.

mass of pain and misery, a bagatelle of transient experience."[1]

The conviction that religious experience is to be taken as the starting-point of theological reconstruction does not, of course, imply that we are absolved from the labour of thought. On the contrary, it should serve as the stimulus to thought. No experience can be taken at its face value; it must be criticised and interpreted. Just as natural science could not exist without experience and the thought concerning experience, so theology cannot exist without the religious consciousness and reflection upon it. Nor do we mean by "experience" anything less than the whole experience of the human race, so far as it has shared in the Christian consciousness. As Mazzini finely said, "Tradition and conscience are the two wings given to the human soul to reach the truth."

It has been the aim of the writers and the Editors of the series to produce studies of the main aspects of Christianity which will be intelligible and interesting to the general reader and at the same time may be worthy of the attention of the specialist. After all, in religion we are dealing with a subject-matter which is open to all and the plan of the works does not require that they shall delve very deeply into questions of minute scholarship. We have had the ambition to produce volumes which might find a useful place on the shelves of the clergyman and minister, and no less on those of the intelligent layman. Perhaps we may have done something to bridge the gulf which too often separates the pulpit from the pew.

[1] A. N. Whitehead, *Science and the Modern World*, p. 275.

Naturally, the plan of our series has led us to give the utmost freedom to the authors of the books to work out their own lines of thought, and our part has been strictly confined to the invitation to contribute, and to suggestions concerning the mode of presentation. We hope that the series will contribute something useful to the great debate on religion which is proceeding in secret in the mind of our age, and we humbly pray that their endeavours and ours may be blessed by the Spirit of Truth for the building up of Christ's Universal Church.

PREFACE TO SECOND EDITION

THE call for a new edition of this book has given me an opportunity to make a number of corrections and alterations which do not affect its general form or character.

The question which is in view in Part IV, that of the meaning of history, has moved well into the foreground of thought during the decade since the book first appeared. I should like to add to what I have said some observations which may serve to bring it into the context of contemporary discussion, and at the same time may serve in some sort as *prolegomena* to the book as a whole, and as justification of its method.

Christianity is thoroughly committed to the view that God reveals Himself in and through history. It is no doubt paradoxical to affirm that our knowledge of eternal and necessary truths of religion depends upon contingent truths of history. Christianity accepts the paradox. Mysticism in its more extreme forms dismisses the historical order as irrelevant. Christianity cannot do so, while it uses as the symbol of its faith a creed which recites events "under Pontius Pilate," and includes among the objects of belief an historical society, the Catholic Church.

In some forms of Christian belief, the doctrine of the fall of man is held to imply that human nature has become so entirely corrupt that history as such, historians' history, as we might call it, does not in any degree disclose the truth of God, since it is the record of a fallen race. To this view I should raise the following objections : (i) It does violence to the continuity within which all historical events seem to lie, including those recited in the Creed. Pontius Pilate belongs both to the secular history of the Roman Empire and to the sacred history of the Bible and the Creed. (ii) It does less than justice to the fact that conceptions which originated in departments of history outside the biblical series (as for instance in primitive semitic religion, and in the religious thought of the Greeks) have been taken up into Christianity, even in the New Testament. They must therefore be in some sense of the same stuff as the biblical revelation. (iii) Our existence, including our thought, is historically conditioned. The thought of those to whom the biblical revelation first came was similarly conditioned. Unless, therefore, there is some disclosure of a divine meaning in history as such, it is difficult to see how that meaning could ever be apprehended in special events of history.

It is nevertheless true that mankind is a "fallen" race. The presence of evil in the human will, and of error in human thought, makes it inevitable that in long stretches of human history the divine meaning should be more or less completely obscured. If however there is an inner core of history in which the evil and error can be shown to be effectually dealt with, then we may believe that it discloses the divine meaning of all history; and therefore of the history which we are making, or which is being made through us; of our own experience as historically conditioned.

It is this inner core of history which is recorded, or reflected, in the Bible. We may call it sacred history, over against secular history, without implying discontinuity between the two, since the same events may belong to both, and without implying that the sacred history is exempt from evil and error. The sacred history, unlike secular history, is a finished series, for the coming of Christ is represented as "fulfilment" of the divine purpose. At the same time it is constantly re-lived in the Church, through the proclamation of the Gospel, in which the "saving facts" are rehearsed, and through the sacrament of the Eucharist, in which the Gospel history is recapitulated. The Church, however, simultaneously lives in the stream of secular history, setting upon it the seal of Gospel and Sacrament. It imposes upon the lives of its members, in their historical situations, the character which belongs to the sacred history, with its tensions and conflicts, and their ultimate resolution through the act of God in sending his Son.

It follows that as the actuality of our own historical experience is involved in our communion with God, so the actuality of the biblical history is vital to the process of revelation. The biblical story, therefore, though it plays the part which in some other religions is played by the sacred myths in which their beliefs are symbolically expressed, cannot be treated as a myth, whose truth to fact is irrelevant. The Gospel is not, in this sense, " truth embodied in a tale." That which happened, as well as what it means, is a part of revelation.

It is important to observe that these two elements, occurrence and meaning, are both essential to history as it is studied by the historian. An event capable of being regarded as historical includes both an occurrence and the meaning with which the occurrence entered into human experience, and so led on to subsequent occurrences. The events recorded in the Bible are rich in meaning. This meaning is declared to be nothing less than the " word " of the eternal God, itself transcending history as well as immanent in it. The record does not for this reason cease to be historical, for the events bore this meaning as they entered into experience, and became history. But the meaning which they bear leads to an interpretation of history according to which events in their actuality depend upon a supra-historical factor, the Word of God. The Christian interpretation of history therefore challenges other interpretations, which assign to purely intra-historical factors—biological, economic, " ideological ", or the like—

not only a real potency in history (which they undoubtedly possess, in the biblical history no less than in any other), but the sufficient explanation and meaning of the whole movement of history. Christianity does not either deny the potency of such factors or admit their potency in secular history while reserving to itself the field of sacred history. It affirms that history cannot be finally understood except as it is brought into the context of the sacred history which is completed by the coming of Christ, his death and resurrection.

In studying the Bible, then, we are dealing with actual history, disclosing a meaning which reaches beyond history, and not with a myth whose factual content is negligible. But if so, then the record must be studied by rational and critical methods applicable to historical records as such. It is in this way that I have tried to approach the documents in this book, upon the assumption that they will yield their meaning for religion to a strictly historical treatment, as they should, if the relation between history and the Word of God is such as Christianity affirms it to be. In this treatment the Canon of Scripture is taken for granted, and from this follows a certain perspective in the view taken of the history which it contains. This might appear as a limitation upon the strict objectivity of the method. But the Canon was not arbitrarily fixed. It shaped itself out of the course of events, and the perspective which it imposes is inherent in the nature of the process to which the documents testify.

The limitations of the historical method are manifest. It raises many questions which pass over into the field of theology or philosophy. Such a book as this can at best provide no more than an introduction to a doctrine of revelation, with which the whole question of authority in religion is bound up.

C. H. D.

CAMBRIDGE,
May 14, 1938.

PREFACE TO THE FIRST EDITION

APART from the general revolt against authority (to which reference is made in the General Introduction to this series), modern criticism, by destroying belief in the infallibility of the Bible, has undermined the traditional doctrine of its authority. Thus any general re-examination of the nature and seat of religious authority involves the special question of the authority of the Bible. I have here tried to deal with it inductively rather than *a priori*. We have before us a literature for which a high degree of authority has been claimed, and which does clearly exercise authority over many minds. Of what nature is that authority, and does it rightly command respect? I assume that the function of authority is to secure assent to truth; that for us the measure of any authority which the Bible may possess must lie in its direct religious value, open to discovery in experience; and that this value in turn will be related to the experience out of which the Scriptures came. (Thus the approach conforms to the maxim laid down in the General Introduction, "that religious experience is to be taken as the starting-point of theological reconstruction.")

Without any deeper analysis of the idea of authority as such, I have set out to study the specific religious value of the Bible in various aspects, laying emphasis everywhere less upon the word than upon the life behind the word, and upon that life as part of an historical context whose meaning is determined by "the fact of Christ." Such a study may, I hope, disclose lines of approach to a doctrine of authority tenable in the face of rational criticism. The four parts into which the main body of the work is divided will indicate the kind of doctrine to which I intend to point. That it raises many underlying questions of a philosophical kind I am aware. I have felt the more free to leave such questions outside my province since they form part of the subject-matter of other volumes in the series.

In citing passages from the Bible I have not scrupled to alter the current versions where they seem mistaken or obscure, or to make use of good modern translations, whether of the whole Bible (by Dr. James Moffatt), or of portions of the Bible (such as the translations of Jeremiah by John Skinner in his *Prophecy and Religion*, or of Isaiah, by G. B. Gray in the *I.C.C.* and by Principal G. A. Smith in the *Expositor's Bible*). In such cases I have indicated the source of the translation. Sometimes I have rendered short passages directly from the original. One liberty I have regularly allowed myself in citing any translation of the Old Testament: I have deliberately substituted the form "Jehovah" for "the Lord" or "the Eternal" as a rendering of the divine Name. A *vox nihili* it may be; but it has a literary tradition in English long and respectable enough to secure its place in the language.

I am greatly indebted to Dr. H. Wheeler Robinson, one of the editors of this series, for advice at various stages of the work, and for reading and criticizing the proofs with a friendly interest that went beyond mere editorial duty; to Professor N. Micklem, of Kingston, Ontario, for reading the proofs and making many valuable suggestions; and to the Rev. L. W. Grensted, of University College, Oxford (University Lecturer in the Psychology of Religion), for reading certain portions of the book which I submitted to his judgment. To these friends I would express my sincere thanks.

C. H. D.

OXFORD.

CONTENTS

INTRODUCTION

CHAPTER I

The literary value of the Bible is beyond controversy; yet it can be fully appreciated as literature only if its religious content is rightly understood. The traditional use of the Bible in public worship and private devotion is disturbed by modern criticism; only a more complete assimilation of the results of criticism can satisfactorily restore it. The use of the Bible as a dogmatic authority is the point at which criticism most radically challenges tradition. The notion of an external infallible authority is beset with difficulties. The ultimate authority is truth as it reveals itself in experience and compels assent. In religion such acceptance of authority is a matter of dependence on God, whose Mind is truth. The Bible as "Word of God." Equivocation of the phrase. In religion, as in science and art, the personal authority of the master carries weight, for sufficient reasons. Thus the authority of the Bible is a question (in the first place) of the authority of men of religious genius who speak in it.

PART I

THE AUTHORITY OF INDIVIDUAL INSPIRATION

CHAPTER II

Useless to discuss inspiration in the abstract or *a priori*. The inspiration of the prophets and their N.T. successors may be taken as a *datum*. From a study of their writings we seek an answer to the questions, what inspiration is, and how it carries authority. This demands a study of the religious conditions out of which biblical prophecy arose. Leading traits of the pre-

Contents

prophetic religion of Israel. The *nabi* or prophet began as an ecstatic (cf. the psychic " medium " of to-day). How far is the condition of the " medium " an essential property of inspiration ? Moral and religious influence of the *nabis ;* their success and failure.

CHAPTER III

The classical prophets to be distinguished from the ecstatics, whom they often stigmatize as " false prophets," without denying their psychic powers. Thus so far as they shared such powers they regarded them as secondary. Examination of prophetic " vision " ; the " word of the Lord." The distinctive gift of most of the classical prophets seems more closely analogous with poetic imagination than with psychic automatism. No criterion of truth can be found in the psychological mode of its apprehension or expression. We cannot therefore assess the authority of the prophets apart from the content of their teaching.

CHAPTER IV

The prophets radically transformed the religious conceptions of their day, particularly (a) in giving an ethical and rational value to " holiness," (b) in declaring that God is good in a sense analogous to human goodness, and (c) in assigning a universal scope to His concern and activity. They are thus the founders of ethical monotheism. Taking this as a whole, we find it so difficult to explain as a mere growth out of contemporary ideas (however continuous with them) that we are prepared to believe the prophets that it was " given " to them from a region beyond normal consciousness—from God.

CHAPTER V

The teaching of the prophets so public and so historically conditioned that personal religion in the modern sense is mostly in the background. Yet they founded a distinctive type of piety which runs through all subsequent history. They were individuals, playing a part in particular situations, and their universality lies in the truth of their response to those situations (truth being inherently universal) ; the truth to be apprehended not by abstracting from the particularity of the situations, but in and through it. This involves allowing for manifest error mingled with the truth. Inspiration does not carry inerrancy.

PART II

THE AUTHORITY OF CORPORATE EXPERIENCE

CHAPTER VI

Much of the Bible not the direct product of religious genius: wherein does its authority lie? In enlarging and enriching for us the area of experience within which truth reveals itself (see Chap. I), and so giving us something more than transient and individual "religious experiences" as the basis of faith. The Bible reflects the actual life of men in many stages of development, and shows religion as part of the stuff of it. This is illustrated from (*a*) primitive legends, (*b*) passages which illuminate the spiritual side of secular movements in history, and (*c*) pictures of common life in diverse aspects.

CHAPTER VII

The O.T. as we have it is the religious literature of the community which resulted from the work of the prophets. Formation of the Canon in the Jewish community. The Law represents the institutional framework of its life. In the Psalter we have the distinctive piety of the prophets made the possession of a whole society, in Proverbs and other "Wisdom" books its everyday morality.

CHAPTER VIII

The varying fortunes of post-exilic Judaism brought to light certain tensions within the accepted scheme, due partly to deficiencies in the prophetic religion and partly to its imperfect assimilation. The conflict between cultus and spiritual religion, between universalism and separatism, between transcendence and immanence. The challenge of wider experience to the prophetic theodicy, and the rise of apocalyptic as a partial reply.

PART III

THE AUTHORITY OF THE INCARNATION

CHAPTER IX

The New Testament represents a fresh outbreak of religious genius. Character of the N.T. Canon. Its witness to an experi-

PAGE

ence which its writers describe in terms of the "New Age" of apocalyptic—a description justified by reference to history. Spiritual factors in the Hellenistic world. The Christian Church the centre of a new spiritual movement. Hellenistic elements in the N.T. and their significance.

CHAPTER X

THE NEW TESTAMENT AS THE "FULFILMENT" OF THE OLD . 205–223

The N.T. estimated in relation to its direct historical antecedents. It meets the problems left open by Judaism out of a direct experience of spiritual things of which Christ is the centre. This illustrated with reference to (*a*) universalism and nationalism, (*b*) righteousness and grace, (*c*) the problem of suffering, (*d*) the future life, and (*e*) transcendence and immanence.

CHAPTER XI

JESUS CHRIST AND THE GOSPELS 224–241

The Synoptic Gospels a product of the experience of the early Church; yet enable us to go behind that experience to the events which created it. The authority of Jesus as Teacher. Useless to attempt to find in His words the last refuge of infallible external authority. They come to us with possibilities of erroneous transmission, and were in any case historically conditioned, and therefore demand some spiritual insight for their recognition and interpretation. Yet the eternal truth in His words makes direct impact on the mind through its temporal expression. The authority of the Personality behind the teaching.

PART IV

THE AUTHORITY OF HISTORY

CHAPTER XII

PROGRESS IN RELIGION 245–268

We now make explicit what has emerged in the discussion since Chap. VI. Revelation is inherent in the process as an historically continuous whole. The continuity is not merely intellectual (like the development in a philosophical "school"), but is in the life of a society self-identical in its various stages. Viewing it as a whole we are bound to report that it is the field of progress, though not of a uniform evolution.

CHAPTER XIII

"PROGRESSIVE REVELATION" 269–285

The idea of "progressive revelation" examined. Revelation and discovery. God as self-revealing under the conditions im-

PAGE

posed by human nature and the stages of its development. The part of illusion in the attainment of truth. God reveals Himself to a man through what the man is; and that he is by grace of God. Both progress and revelation are real. The consummation of the process in Jesus Christ. The interweaving of two factors in the authority of the Bible—inward vision and outward fact.

CONCLUSION

CHAPTER XIV

THE BIBLE AS "THE WORD OF GOD" 289–300

Jesus Christ is the key to the biblical revelation; ask therefore how He revealed God. Not by uttering dogmas to be accepted without question, but by leading men into such an attitude to life that they could see that certain things must be true—by bringing into play a spirit in man whereby God is truly known. This is the function of the Bible as a whole: it is the instrument of a Spirit in creating an experience of divine things. The "Word of God" is not the "last word," but the "seminal word."

INDEX 301–310

THE AUTHORITY OF THE BIBLE

CHAPTER I

INTRODUCTION: LITERATURE AND AUTHORITY

NOT long ago a distinguished biblical scholar published a "New Translation" of the Old Testament. It was not to be expected that so bold an undertaking should escape criticism, how far justified is not here the question. Many of the critics took exception not to this or that particular rendering, but to the whole attempt to give a precise rendering of the Old Testament in current speech. Among them could be discerned an alliance of forces not commonly found in the same camp. There were the pious devotees of the Holy Book, who missed in the crudity of modern English those hallowed words that brought their souls a sense of awe. There were the literary men, who, too emancipated to care for the religious meaning of Hebrew scriptures, hastened to the defence of King James's Version, that "well of English pure and undefiled". If a palpable mistranslation, they seemed to say, makes a piece of fine English, then it should not be meddled with. Both seemed agreed that the precise meaning intended by the original writers was not a primary consideration. The assumption made in this book is that this meaning is of deep and lasting import, and that to understand the Bible is worth more than, without understanding it, to be charmed by its beauty or impressed by its sanctity.

All the more it is necessary to say at the outset that the two judgments mentioned, though they miss the point, have their basis in standards of valuation which are true and important. The Bible (or most of it), *is* great literature, to be appreciated æsthetically ; and the value of its solemn language for liturgical or devotional purposes is very high. If modern criticism of its documents ever seems to imperil its appreciation in either aspect, something is wrong.

The widespread appreciation of the Bible as literature is, indeed, one of the most salutary results of the general change of outlook in the last two generations. There was a time when you either held the Book in superstitious reverence or repudiated it with scorn. The religious in general would have felt it trifling if not actually impious to enjoy the poetry of Holy Writ as poetry, or to read its splendid stories with the pleasure to be derived from consummate narrative prose. The humanist, on the other hand, rarely thought to look for literary charm in the book he regarded as the bulwark of superstition. But to-day the Bible is sufficiently emancipated from dogmatic schemes for the humanist to feel perfectly free to claim his rights in it. It causes no astonishment when a Professor of English Literature at an ancient university lectures on the English Bible,[1] or a Poet Laureate includes extracts from it in an anthology.[2] This is very much to the gain of the study of the Bible. Only we shall claim that a truly humanist approach cannot narrowly regard the virtues of style and form to the neglect of the matter ; that as dramatic literature cannot be estimated without reference to its value for the theatre, so a religious literature cannot be finally appreciated, even in an æsthetic sense, without reference to its value for

[1] A. Quiller-Couch, *On the Art of Reading ;* Lectures VIII–X.

[2] *The Spirit of Man,* by Robert Bridges.

religion, and therefore to the truth and elevation of its religious content. It is not necessary to pursue this theme further here, seeing that the aim of this book is to approach the Bible not as a collection of dogmatic texts, but as literature in the full humanist sense, in the belief that such an approach will most surely lead to the discovery of its unique qualities as religious literature.

Of the use of the Bible for devotional or liturgical reading it will be well to speak rather more fully at this point.

From the time of Ezra, in the fifth century before Christ, the reading of portions of the sacred Canon has formed part of public worship in the Jewish and Christian churches. Long before the Canon of the New Testament was formed, early Christian congregations read the Old Testament at their most solemn assemblies. Already its writings had acquired the dignity of antiquity, and were the centre of sacred associations. When the books of the New Testament came to be added to the ancient Canon, they had ceased to be modern. We still possess a list of books to be read in church, which was compiled for the Church of Rome in the second century. In rejecting the *Shepherd* of Hermas, it observes slightingly that Hermas wrote " quite recently, in our own times ".[1] His work could not serve the whole purpose of a sacred book because (apart from other defects) it had not yet entered deeply enough into the corporate experience. The writings which actually found a place in the Canon were those which were closely bound up with the creative period of Christianity. They were laden with suggestion, because those who heard them read in church were in the succession of their writers and their first readers, and were keenly conscious of sharing with them a corporate life and experience. To-day we have behind us many centuries during which the Scriptures of the Old and New

[1] Muratorian Canon: *Pastorem vero nuperrime temporibus nostris in urbe Roma Herma conscripsit.*

Testaments have been bound up with the life of the Christian people. Most of us in this country to-day could say that whatever stands for religion to us has from our earliest days found expression in the speech of the Bible. No wonder that when we hear it read at the solemn assembly its words carry "overtones" of association. Their precise meaning may not be present to us. They stir half-forgotten things in our subconscious minds, bred there partly by our explicit experience, partly by that which we have absorbed from our religious environment and tradition. Given certain conditions, religious feelings of real value may be evoked by such a use of the Scriptures even without clear understanding. In the same way the half-understood words of a liturgy may be means of grace, like all the symbolic ornaments, acts and gestures of the service.[1] "If you've niver had no church", said Dolly Winthrop to Silas Marner, "there's no telling the good it'll do you. For I feel so set up and comfortable as niver was, when I've been and heard the prayers, and the singing to the praise and glory o' God, as Mr. Macey gives out, and Mr. Crackenthorpe saying good words". That is genuine religious experience, of an elementary order. In those forms of Protestant worship where the liturgical element is relatively small, the "good words" of Scripture are (along with hymns) the principal vehicle of suggestion. They owe their effect, not in the first place to their intelligible meaning, but to the "aura" of sacred association surrounding them.

But the psychological disposition to which such experience is possible is easily disturbed. When the mind is awakened, a discomforting sense may arise that the whole mass of suggestion of which the service is the vehicle is not truly related to reality. The mind then enquires into the meaning of the "good words", perhaps misses the meaning, or finds it to be apparently out of harmony with its own

[1] Cf. W. B. Selbie, *Psychology of Religion*, pp. 72–73.

accepted attitude to life. In the presence of such inward criticism the words and symbols alike lose their power, or retain it only at the cost of intellectual integrity. In our own time this is what happens to very many awakened minds. All such minds are inevitably affected by the characteristic tendencies of modern thought. They think in terms of the new universe which natural science has revealed. Under its influence they come to think of human nature and history in an evolutionary scheme. Material and economic factors bulk largely in their interpretation of life. The genial and humanitarian optimism of the last age still holds influence over their less deliberate thinking at least, in spite of the War and its sequel. The tradition of the Christian Church meanwhile has lost its unquestioned authority, and the sense of sharing its historic corporate life grows dim even among people who still " go to church ". In these circumstances the more formal and traditional sides of the Church's services become less and less real, and the Bible, to come to that with which we are more immediately concerned, seems bound up with a scheme of unreal things. It reads " as if it all happened on Sunday ". Some are content to let religion and all its concerns rest in a watertight compartment of their minds. They are in grave danger of superstition. The rest can only regain the power to be helped religiously by the liturgical use of the Bible after they have resolutely forgotten for a time that the Bible is a holy book, and given it a place in their minds alongside all the things that make up their real world. There is no other way, and biblical criticism is the discipline of learning to read the Bible in that way.

Much the same may be said of what is called the " devotional " reading of the Bible. As commonly practised and recommended by religious persons it may be described thus. The reader takes a portion of the Bible, long or short, but usually short, chosen more or less arbitrarily, and not necessarily related to any context. Bringing himself into a contemplative frame of mind, he reads the verses at leisure, and lets his mind dwell meditatively upon them. After a time there arises in his mind a sense of truth revealed. He is warned, judged, comforted, stimulated, guided, blessed. It may be that the "message" he "received" has but little relation to the intention of the original writer or the precise meaning of his words. Of some of the classics of devotional literature this would be true, such as Bernard's meditations on the Song of Songs—that sequence of amorous lyrics so strangely alien in intention from the spiritual raptures of an ascetic. This is an extreme example, explained by a long-established exegetical tradition. But something of the kind occurs very frequently. The words of the Bible are in fact again serving not so much to convey a clear intellectual content as to awaken suggestions largely due to association.

What happens is probably something like this. The reader is familiar with the Bible. He has it, as we say, at his fingers' ends. To read one verse calls into his memory without deliberate effort other passages which provide a context—not always the context given by the writer, but one supplied by links of association in the reader's mind. Behind all this is the extensive background of experience and tradition. Here again the Bible is serving as the organ of a religious life lived by a continuous community in its various historical forms. Its words are laden with power to recall that which has passed out of this corporate life into the subconscious mind of the reader. That the Divine Spirit is at work in this pyschological process we may not deny. Under proper conditions it is a valuable function of the religious life. But again those conditions are not easily secured and they are very easily upset. If a person has but a slender stock of religious experience of his own, and if he is in no vital touch with the tradition of the Christian people, he is not likely to find much profit in reading the Bible thus. The words awake no echoes in his mind, and if he has not sufficient knowledge to be sure of their actual meaning in their own context, he will not make much of his reading. Certainly if his mind is awake and enquiring he will resent being expected to be moved by "holy" words whose meaning is quite uncertain to him, and may, he suspects, be untrue. It is fatal to make a separation between religious feeling and the sense of truth, as truth is understood in other departments of life. In this respect our reading of the Bible must be on the same footing with all our reading. Suppose, for example, I read a leading article in *The Times*, a new work on biology, a novel by Galsworthy, or a poem by John Masefield. In each case the relation between the written word and my ultimate estimate of its truth is different. But in all cases I ask, naturally, what the author meant to say, and how this stands to my general experience of the world. The same questions must be asked of any biblical writer. To answer the first question is difficult because of the gulf that separates us in history from these ancient writers. Biblical criticism is there to help us over the gulf. To answer the second question leads us into the depths, and all manner of factors enter in which are not there when we are reading books of lesser import. But the question must be asked with the same frankness and realism.

It is upon this basis of frank clarity that our devotional use of the Bible must be reconstructed. This is not to be taken as a prosaic insistence on the face value of every passage in its historical setting. We *start* with the original writer, what he said, what he had in mind, and what his contemporaries understood him to mean. But to stop there is the part of a pedant. No great literature will stand such treatment. All great writers meant more than they knew. They all welcome the imagination of their readers. But it must be instructed imagination, not fantasy. The imagination of the Christian reader of the Bible should be controlled by intelligent study, and it may then safely be inspired by the rich experience of the Christian centuries in their use of the sacred Canon. We stand at a point where the actual outlook of religious people has changed more than the expressed beliefs and practices of the Christian communions explicitly admit. Some things that are no longer real must go. New aspects of life and thought must be admitted. Among other things, the new knowledge of the Bible must be assimilated and given its rightful place. Then we shall be more free to open our minds again to all influences of the Christian tradition, and the Bible, more reasonably understood, will once again serve as the organ of a profound corporate experience.

Traditionally, however, the Bible has been regarded in the Christian Church as a great deal more than a collection of religious literature or of liturgical matter. It has been regarded as the supreme doctrinal authority in faith and morals, divine in origin and consequently infallible. Historic Christianity has been a religion of revelation. This has been held to mean that the ultimate truths of religion are not discoverable by the unaided faculties of the human mind, but must have been directly communicated by God in a "supernatural" way, and that the Bible is the "Word of God" in this unique sense. The change of outlook over the whole field of thought which began with the "Illumination" of the eighteenth century and was completed by the scientific movement of the nineteenth, raised difficulties about the idea of authority as such. Again the critical study of the Bible itself on scientific and historical principles has made the traditional doctrine of its authority untenable for those who are not willing to keep their religious beliefs isolated from the rest of their thinking. It is here that our problem arises. No one wishes to deny that the Bible contains literature of the highest order. All Christians, and many who would not so describe themselves, acknowledge what we may call its devotional value. The question is whether we can still regard it as possessing religious authority in any sense whatever.

The use of the Bible as an exclusive dogmatic authority is specially characteristic of those Christian communions which accepted more or less completely the Reformation of the sixteenth century. The authority of the Church in its councils and its hierarchy had scarcely been effectively questioned in the Middle Ages. The Renaissance brought the questioning spirit into play, and all authority stood on its trial. The Protestant movement appealed to the right of private judgment, but its leaders shrank from the full consequences of that appeal. They went behind the Church to the classical documents of Christianity in the Scriptures, and found a final authority in them. All doctrines necessary to salvation were held to be found there, and all dogmatic statements were presumed either to be derived from the Bible, or at least to be proved from the Bible, so that it constituted the final court of appeal. The infallibility denied to the Pope and the Councils was attributed to the Bible in all its parts. The view taken of the Scriptures themselves did not differ widely from that of the Catholic Church in its unreformed branches, but a documentary authority is in its effect something quite different from an institutional authority. Prophets and apostles may have written the final truth, but in their writings are "some things hard to be understood", as the latest of the canonical writers confesses.[1] Who is to say what they meant? The Church through its hierarchy, said the Catholics; the reason and conscience of the Christian man, guided by the Holy Spirit within, said the Protestants. The result for the reformed communions was on the one hand greatly to enhance the

[1] 2 Peter iii. 16.

importance of the documents, and on the other hand to leave the way open to free discussion of their meaning, and consequent variety of interpretation.

In its extreme form the dogma of the Infallibility of Scripture should mean that all parts of the Canon are directly and equally inspired by God, so that its every statement, whether concerning the mysteries of the divine Being, the processes of nature, or the facts of history, past or future, should be exactly and literally true. Many people think they believe this; no balanced mind has ever really tried to carry it through with complete logic. There is always an instinctive or arbitrary process of selection and distribution of emphasis, and it is always possible to reconcile contradictions and smooth away difficulties by allegorical or non-natural exegesis. Nor have instructed Christians in the great historic communions ever bound themselves in practice to a mechanical conception of inspiration which would make the genealogies of Chronicles as vital a divine revelation as the Gospel according to John. The most determined "Fundamentalists" do not show any strong desire to force into general acceptance *every* statement of Scripture. They are rather concerned either to maintain the dogma of infallibility for its own sake, because it seems to them a part of Christianity, or to protect certain cherished beliefs which they would not leave at the mercy of an irreligious criticism. The latter motive is the more formidable.

All religious readers in fact go to the Bible with some sort of presupposition. However firmly they may believe that they accept "the Word of God" without question, they have certain prior beliefs which determine their interpretation. The orthodox believer has accepted from the tradition of his Church a scheme of belief, or a "plan of salvation", which in a measure satisfactory to himself he has tested in experience. It is a part of this belief that God has revealed Himself in the Bible. He therefore goes to the

Bible convinced that the " plan of salvation " is given there. Passages of uncertain meaning he understands in the light of his accepted beliefs. Passages which seem to bear no relation to them he tacitly ignores, assuming that if he could understand them they would agree with what he holds as truth. If, however, a statement of Scripture is challenged, he is troubled and feels bound to protest ; for if the Bible can be wrong in a matter of fact, who knows but it may be wrong on a matter affecting his eternal salvation ? And if the Bible is wrong here, to what authority can he trust ?

We shall come back to this difficulty. Meanwhile we observe that in spite of his dogmatic belief that the biblical writers infallibly set forth the truth, the reader has not in fact let them speak for themselves. He has assumed that they must be saying the thing he has been taught to believe. Now there is indeed so large a measure of continuity between all vital Christian belief and the main stream of biblical teaching that within limits his assumption justifies itself. But as a matter of fact the biblical writers have lost incalculably because their writings have been forced into a dogmatic scheme alien from their thought.

The prophets, for example, were pioneers in a radical reformation of religion, belonging to a particular period of history. In Christian tradition they came to be regarded as men who had " foretold the Messiah ", and without knowing it gave testimony in advance to the truth of Christian doctrine. However much that view has been shaken, the tendency still remains in wide circles for those parts only of the prophets to be read with attention which can without much difficulty be given a dogmatic interpretation, and this means that whole reaches of their writings are passed over with no appreciation of their immense and independent religious import. Worst of all, under the influence of the prejudice that the main business of prophecy was to give a forecast of the future, they have often been studied as though they were only concerned to write "reversed history". Where that is so, those portions of prophecy which seem to offer most precise data bulk most largely.[1] But such portions are usually quite definitely second-rate in their religious value; while the great epoch-making utterances of an Isaiah or a Jeremiah take only a minor place in the scheme. Again, the method of reading the Pauline epistles as a set of documentary proofs for a fixed scheme of theology has resulted in giving a quite erroneous idea of Paul's real thought, and still more in effectually concealing Paul the man behind a theological lay-figure. In consequence, the present generation, disliking what passed for Pauline theology, misses the guidance and inspiration of one of the greatest religious teachers. As a matter of fact much teaching for which the authority of Paul is claimed has simply been read into his writings by a method which does scant justice to his striking individuality. Not least have the Synoptic Gospels suffered from the dogmatic approach to the Bible. The fresh, arresting presentation of the words and works of Jesus in these early writings becomes strangely dulled by a method which seeks in them simply the authentication of a doctrinal scheme. Indeed, it may fairly be said to be the strongest condemnation of the traditional attitude to the Scriptures that it is so much at a loss to know what to do with the Synoptic Gospels.

Thus our quarrel with the traditional way of reading the Bible is that actually it does less than justice to the Bible itself, in the interests of a theory about the Bible. That the Bible contains within it the materials for a well-articulated philosophy of life is certainly true, and its value in this respect will be examined in what follows. But in order that it may make its rightful contribution we need to find a truer method of approach than that of the old dogmatism. It will be a method which gives attention to the personal

[1] Such as the more prosaic portions of *Daniel* and *Revelation*.

and the historical element in the Scriptures. By this I mean that they should be read as the utterances of real individual men, who wrote out of their own intensely personal experience ; and they should be read as the record of an historic process of discovery or revelation, in which the cumulative experience of individuals through many generations built up a firm structure of faith and knowledge of God. But if they are so read, then all sorts of difficulties come to light, which the older method of Bible-reading covered up, and these must be recognized and dealt with before the true value of the Scriptures can be discerned.

It is unnecessary to enlarge on the process by which the old view of the infallibility of the Bible broke down under the successive attacks of scientific discovery and of historical criticism. It long ago became clear that in claiming for the Bible accuracy in matters of science and history its apologists had chosen a hopeless position to defend. Much more important is the fact that in matters of faith and morals an unprejudiced mind must needs recognize many things in the Bible which could not possibly be accepted by Christian people in anything approaching their clear and natural meaning. The harm that has been done to the general conscience by allowing the outworn morality of parts of the Old Testament to stand as authoritative declarations was startingly revealed during the War. The military representative who quoted " An eye for an eye and a tooth for a tooth " as a moral principle obviously binding on religious people, because it was " in the Bible ", provided a glaring instance. Many people found that the imprecatory psalms so perfectly expressed what they felt about the enemy that they could join in the services for certain days of the month with a fervour and reality they had never known. Yet as they look back upon that state of mind they probably do not regard it as the high-water mark of their religious life. It is high time to assert unambiguously that the Bible contains a good deal which if it is taken out of a temporary historical context and given general and permanent validity is simply pernicious. The old dogmatic view of the Bible therefore is not only open to attack from the standpoint of science and historical criticism, but if taken seriously it becomes a danger to religion and public morals. A revision of this view is therefore an imperative necessity.

The whole conception of an infallible external authority in any field of thought is open to criticism on the ground that it is difficult to state it without introducing two ultimate standards of truth. If his own observation or reasoning leads a man to one conclusion, while the external authority he recognises points to another, which is he to trust? If the latter, there would seem to be an end of intellectual adventure and discovery, to say nothing of moral responsibility. The advance of knowledge in modern times has come because thinkers in most fields have refused to allow absolute authority to any existing system of doctrine, and have taken observation and reason as their guides to truth. It may be held that religious knowledge is concerned with matters so inaccessible to observation and so transcending reason that in this field, if in no other, there is room for an absolute authority external to the mind. This raises large philosophical issues beyond our scope. But since we are dealing with one particular claimant to absolute authority it is relevant to ask the question, on what grounds does a man decide to trust such an outside authority; especially in a conflict of claims, on what grounds does he choose his allegiance? There must be some judgment of his own involved. Apparently in the last resort he must trust his own reason, or intuition, or mere inclination, in choosing to be guided by *this* authority rather than by *that*. It is difficult to avoid the conclusion that a man must accept responsibility for his choice. Yet in that case the external authority is no longer in the strict sense absolute.

Protestants in general accept such arguments when the authority of the Church is in question, but seek to find some way of maintaining an analogous authority for Scripture. Yet a book is as external as a church, or rather it is much more so. The act of faith which accepts the authority of the Bible is as purely individual a judgment as that which accepts the authority of the Church. What is the ground of it? The Bible itself does not make any claim to infallible authority for all its parts.[1] On the contrary, some of its greatest writers contemplate the possibility that they may be mistaken, or even confess that in some points they have been mistaken. Isaiah corrected his first sweeping predictions of complete disaster in favour of a faithful "remnant."[2] Jeremiah found his expectations in several points falsified, and at one time wondered if he had really been deceived.[3] Ezekiel withdrew his forecast of the fall of Tyre.[4] Paul some-

[1] The most downright claims to infallibility are made by the apocalyptists, as for example in the New Testament *Revelation* (see xxii. 6, 16, 18–19), a book which some of the wisest thinkers of the early Church wished to exclude from the Canon, and which as a whole is sub-Christian in tone and outlook. The oft-quoted passage 2 Tim. iii. 16 is probably to be rendered "Every inspired Scripture is also profitable . . .", but whether this or the A.V. rendering is taken, the passage leaves open the question whether inspired Scripture is infallible; that it is profitable, no one would deny. The other passage commonly quoted in this connection, 2 Peter i. 21, does seem to deny the human element in prophecy, and so perhaps by implication claims infallibility for it, though not necessarily for the entire Canon. Neither passage claims the rank of inspired Scripture for the writing in which it occurs, or defines the works to which it attributes inspiration.

[2] Isa. vi. 11 (about 740 B.C.), xxx. 19, xxxi. 4–9 (about 702 B.C.).

[3] Jer. xx. 7. He had apparently predicted that the Scythian raid of about 626 B.C. would bring disaster upon Judah (iv.), and "it is certain that Jeremiah was left in the end with a considerable margin of unfulfilled prediction on his hands" (J. Skinner, *Prophecy and Religion*, p. 45). He also seems to have changed his mind about Josiah's Reformation between xi. 1–8 and (the later) viii. 7–8.

[4] Ezek. xxvi.–xxviii. (586 B.C.), xxix. 18 (568 B.C.).

times claims to speak the word of the Lord, but at other times "gives his opinion" quite tentatively.[1] The Protestant who believes in the infallibility of the whole does so on some other grounds, such as the declaration of his own Church—which in this point he accepts as infallible, though he would reject the Roman doctrine of infallibility—or something personal to himself. Really—may we not say ?—he believes the Bible to be authoritive because of the effect it produces upon his own mind and spirit. For this as for all his beliefs he must accept personal responsibility.

It is often claimed that the Bible must be an infallible external authority, because it is "the Word of God". God certainly is the Author of truth; if He has spoken, His Word must possess absolute authority. Let us hold to that maxim: authority belongs to God, and what He says, and that alone, infallibly compels assent. But in the expression "the Word of God" lurks an equivocation. A word is properly a means of communicating thought, through vibrations of the vocal cords, peculiar to the human species. The Eternal has neither breath nor vocal cords; how should He speak words? Clearly enough the term "Word of God" is a metaphorical expression. We mean by it, a means whereby the "thought" of God, which is the truth, is mediated to the human mind. That the Bible as a whole is such a means will be maintained throughout this book. But in the literal sense the Bible consists of the "words" of men—or rather of their visible symbols in writing. It is not the utterance of God *in the same sense* in which it is the utterance of men. Not God but Paul is the author of the Epistle to the Romans, though in a transferred sense we may describe the Epistle to the Romans as a "Word of God", meaning that in some way it mediates to the reader the truth which is the thought of God. God is the Author not of the Bible, but of the life in which the

[1] 1 Cor. vii. 8, 10, 12, 25

authors of the Bible partake, and of which they tell in such imperfect human words as they could command.[1] The importance of this fairly obvious and elementary distinction is that it exposes the fallacy of arguing from an admission that the Bible is "the Word of God" to the conclusion that it must possess God's own infallibility. The words of a man, assuming that they are the deliberate expression of his meaning, command just that measure of authority which we recognize in the man himself. Thus the words of the Epistle to the Romans carry just as much weight as we are prepared to allow to Paul as a religious teacher. But the question, how far and in what way God "speaks" through Paul, is quite another question, which is in no sense answered by asserting that the Epistle to the Romans is "the Word of God". The mystery of revelation is not to be so lightly disposed of. It is the mystery of the way in which God uses the imperfect thoughts and feelings, words and deeds, of fallible men, to convey eternal truth, both to the men themselves and through them to others.

I do not propose here to attempt to set forth a philosophy of revelation. In so far as this book is to make any contribution to such a philosophy, it must be by way of studying the character of the biblical writings themselves, without any prior assumption other than the manifest fact that readers of these writings have actually found themselves brought nearer to God. My present purpose is simply to clear out of the way of the argument the chimerical idea that we may seek in the Bible, or indeed anywhere else, an expression of the mind of God so direct and so independent of human mediation that it could claim infallible authority over against all other means of apprehending truth. There is nothing in what we can know or surmise of the ways of God which would lead us to expect that in any field of exper-

[1] Cf. H. Wheeler Robinson, *The Christian Experience of the Holy Spirit*, p 170.

ience we should be dispensed from the task of proving all things for ourselves that we may hold fast that which is good. No unprejudiced mind could fail to recognize in the Bible manifest signs of the limitation and imperfection of the human authors which call for such critical approach. Only in the interest of a theory could they have been denied. If the Bible has authority as a revelation of truth it is in some sense which is not incompatible with its human imperfection.

The reluctance to assert full private judgment and to abandon all appeal to external authority is by no means ill-grounded. Are we then to say that "man is the measure of all things", as the ancient sophists said? Are we to say there is no standard of truth beyond what an individual thinks to be true—or more precisely what he thinks to be true to-day, though to-morrow he may think differently?

We do rightly to distrust such pure "subjectivism" in religion. Suppose we consider the problem in another sphere of enquiry, that of natural science. Here no one supposes that truth is established by appeal to authority. The days are long past when what Ptolemy said on astronomy or Galen on medicine passed for the incontrovertible basis of all knowledge of those subjects. The enquirer proceeds by observation and experiment. Yet in natural science no one supposes that the abandonment of the appeal to external authority means that there is no standard beyond the opinion of individuals. "The village that voted the earth was flat" made a fool of itself. It set itself up not against authoritative declarations, but against facts of the real world. You cannot make sense of our experience of the world, at the stage at which we have arrived, on the hypothesis that the earth is flat. This is not to say that any scientific dogma is final. Some doctrines which in the school-days of many of us seemed most absolute, such as the Newtonian theory of gravitation and the ultimacy of the atom, are to-day no longer believed. Any and every scientific statement is subject to the principle of relativity. Nevertheless, the man of science is aware that there is something in the real world that *compels* him to certain conclusions. It is there and he must accept it. He may never be perfectly sure that he is fully in touch with this reality; it still evades him. But it is solid enough for him never to cherish the illusion that he may think as he pleases, and that if he is but sincere his opinion is as good as any other opinion.

Now with many differences there is a real analogy here to our knowledge of spiritual things. The spiritual world is real. Like the world that science studies, it is *there:* we do not make it by our desires or opinions. We are more intimately involved in it and yet it is more elusive than the world of the scientist. It is as much more recalcitrant to experiment as the subject-matter of biology is more recalcitrant than that of chemistry. It is even more obviously the field of the principle of relativity. Yet withal we know it is *there*. What we believe, we believe in the end not because august authority bids us so believe, but, like the men of science, because there is something that compels us so to believe—something in the world of our experience.

All that is implied in the expression, "the world of our experience" is a matter to which we shall need to return.[1] But for the moment we are concerned to put on record this similarity between science and faith. In each sphere a man believes because he can do no other. He may hold a great deal more as hypothesis in science or pious opinion in religion; but there is a point at which compulsion comes in. The point is that at which it becomes impossible to make sense of the world of his experience unless a certain proposition is

[1] See ch. VI.

accepted as true (within the limits of the principle of relativity). Thus the point comes in biology at which you cannot make sense of the known facts of organic existence without believing that species have evolved in conformity with certain laws. Darwin never supposed (though some of his more ignorant followers seemed to claim) that his precise formulation of these laws was infallible. But evolution is a term that stands for something real, embedded in the nature of things, and however the formulation of it may need to be revised (as it is being revised to-day), we shall never go back on it. We have not gone back upon the discoveries of Newton because of Einstein. We find his formulation inadequate, but we know he called our attention to something real.

Similarly the point comes in our investigation of the spiritual world at which we are bound to say that we cannot make sense of the facts of experience as a whole without taking the view that there is a righteous God who stands behind all life and calls men into relations with Himself. The religious man does not hold that belief, any more than the man of science holds *his* beliefs, because it is so written. There is something in the nature of things that compels him to it. His belief is not any more " subjective " than that of the man of science. It is indeed even more than scientific propositions subject to relativity. The religious man, like the man of science, should be aware that the best statement he can make to himself is nothing more than a very inadequate and remote symbol of ultimate reality. Yet what it means is real, is in the nature of things. There is here no appeal to external authority ; yet we are far from " man the measure of all things ". Truth in religion is not what John Smith chooses to think, however sincere John Smith may be. It is the truth of things as they are, in a scheme of things which puts John Smith in his place.

In drawing this parallel between science and faith I do not

mean to suggest that their processes are identical, but only that there is an analogy between them in so far that in both fields belief is grounded neither on absolute authority nor on individual opinion, but upon something in the very nature of that with which we are dealing, which leaves the individual no choice, if he is to make sense of the world of his experience. In both fields complete scepticism is a theoretically possible attitude, but in both the assumption that things do make sense is the nobler hypothesis, if it be nothing more, and it is certainly the hypothesis on which all science proceeds.

Here we have authority in its primary form—the authority of the truth itself, compelling and subduing. The freedom to investigate passes into a bondservice to truth which is more perfect freedom. There are those to whom it will appear meaningless sublety to distinguish between having your own opinion and submitting to the truth as it comes to you. But somewhere thereabouts lies the difference between an irreligious and a religious attitude to life—and men of science are often in this sense more religious than theologians. For it is fundamental to religion to make a distinction between the self and God, and to acknowledge the complete dependence of the self upon God. And since God is the source or ground of truth, as of all value, we can know the truth only in dependence on Him.

There is, however, a secondary sense of the term "authority" which we must distinguish. Granted that the primary authority is that of truth itself, is there not such a thing as the authority of persons who being presumed to know the truth communicate it to others? In speaking of the man of science we have had mainly in view one who pursues research and adds to the sum of knowledge. But for the ordinary student of natural science the range of original research is strictly limited, and human authority comes into play in a very definite way. Even the original investigator cannot safely ignore the weight which must attach to the conclusions of acknowledged experts in his science. Still more must the ordinary student follow the experts, recognizing that their knowledge claims respect from his ignorance. He accepts what they say, on the understanding that if he had opportunity he could verify their results, but knowing also that he will never become competent to do so in any exhaustive way. He is therefore content to be guided by them in his practice, verifying what they say as occasion offers. This process of acceptance and verification is carried on unthinkingly by us all in a "scientific" age. I accept on authority, for instance, the abstruse laws which lie behind the wireless transmission of sound; but every time I "listen in" with success I am helping to verify those laws for myself. Because by obeying precepts founded upon the investigations of experts I find that the real world responds to my demands upon it, I am content to believe. Authority, therefore, not in the sense of dictation, but in a sense nearer to that of the original Latin *auctoritas*, has after all a considerable place in science. We respect the experts and are willing to be guided by them beyond the limits of our experience, on the constantly tested assumption that they know what they are talking about.

We may recognize a somewhat similar kind of authority in the arts. Artists are constantly experimenting in new forms, and those who do not create but appreciate are also exploring new ways. Art can never be bound to the past without becoming barren. Yet no person of sense despises the "authority" of Pheidias in sculpture or of Shakespeare in drama or of Beethoven in music. Their works represent permanent achievements of the human spirit. They revealed new possibilities in their various arts, and set a standard or norm for others who work in those fields. The creative artist, who would scorn slavish imitation, yet finds inspiration and direction in the masters. The layman to whom the arts bring enjoyment and understanding of beauty does not feel obliged to confine his appreciation in the strait bounds of classical precedent; but his taste is informed, tested and corrected by reference to the classics. In contemplating a work of art the judgment he forms is his own: he believes it to be beautiful or significant because he "feels in his bones" that it is so, and not because he has been told so. He is aware at the same time that if his judgment were simply an individual whim he would deserve the name of Philistine. He is trying to apprehend for himself something which is real beyond himself, and he is willing to accept the guidance, though not the dictation, of those who have seen farther than he can see; believing that as his own vision becomes wider and deeper he will be able to take up the experience of the masters into his own experience.

It will conduce to clearness if we say at this point that when we speak of the place of authority in science we are not thinking of the purely mechanical communication of facts, or in art, of the communication of technique. It goes without saying that for these things every beginner must be dependent on someone else; and no doubt in so far as religious education involves the imparting of facts of history, or training in the technique of worship and devotion, there must be similar dependence. But for the question of authority in religion this is of small importance. In scientific and artistic education something more than facts or technique must be conveyed—an outlook, a point of view, a method, none of which the beginner can attain wholly independently. And the field within which authority in religion is a matter of importance finds its analogy here. In religion few of us would deny that we are *in statu pupillari*, and have need of guidance, however strongly we should repudiate dictation in spiritual affairs.[1] We may therefore usefully observe that in science and in art authority has a definite place which is not inconsistent with the responsibility of the individual for his own judgments. In religion there is similarly a place for the authority of the expert, not as a dictatorial or coercive authority, but by way of stimulus, support and direction. The expert in religion is the saint or the prophet —the man of inspired character or the man of inspired vision.

Clearly the way in which authority works in science and in art respectively is only roughly the same. Their aims are different. Yet not after all so different as appears. The man of science may seem to be concerned solely with recording that such and such a thing is so. But the greater scientists give us imaginative generalizations which are in some sort works of art. Again, though the artist may seem to be doing no more than bring into being a particular concrete thing which is beautiful, yet in doing so he is telling us something about what *is*. For amid all the fluctuations of taste which often seem to rule out anything like objectivity in æsthetic judgments, we cannot but believe that there is a real and objective worth which all art is seeking to express. Thus in each case there is an appeal to something in the nature of things, and we respect authority in so far as it seems to represent independent insight into that nature of things. But when we come to compare these fields of human experience with religion it is instructive to observe certain differences between them in which religious experience has closer analogy with art than with science.

[1] The idea that in religion the individual soul is making a solitary adventure into unexplored regions, in which there is something contemptible about accepting help or guidance, is popular at present, but will not, if it is regarded as the whole truth, bear investigation in the light of history or of psychology. The element of originality, of adventure, is of course present in any religious experience worth the name, but the element of continuity or solidarity with the spiritual life of others is equally a part of it.

Thus while it is characteristic of science to describe and explain, though not without an element of imaginative construction, art is characteristically creative; and the saint, like the artist, creates something which expresses what he sees of reality: he creates a religious life, which is a work of art and something more. Rather, as he would say, such a life is created in him by the Reality he apprehends. Here therefore as in art authority authenticates itself in power to create. Further, whereas the ordinary man in his daily life can profit by the discoveries of science without sharing in the scientific experience to any appreciable degree, it is impossible so to separate the most elementary sense of beauty in daily things from the artistic experience. So in religion the attainment of truth imperatively calls for the sharing of a personal experience.

In this sense we find a religious authority in the Bible—the authority of experts in the knowledge of God, masters in the art of living; the authority of religious genius. Through its pages saints and prophets speak to us with convincing plainness of the things they have seen and heard with the senses of the spirit. All that they say would be so much gibberish to us if we did not in some measure share their experience. We know that they are dealing with a real inner world whose landmarks we recognize from afar, though its intimate features may be dim to us. This implies that there are men who by reason of some innate spiritual faculty, and by reason of the faithfulness with which they have followed its impulse, have attained experience of divine things fuller, deeper and more compelling than comes to the ordinary run of men. In religion, as in science, there is the sciolism that refuses to learn. In religion, as in art, there is the Philistinism that confuses originality with impertinence and independence with vulgarity. Democracy is perhaps loth to admit that there are fundamental differences in spiritual capacity. Yet such differences are undeniable. We cannot by taking thought add one cubit to our spiritual stature, though we may become as serviceable as little men can be. The truly religious man knows his betters when he meets them. What they say he will hold worthy of respect, and he will follow on to see if it can be verified in his own experience. He will not submit to them blindly, or expect them to be infallible. But he will expect to find himself in a world of growing experience where what they say is more and more relevant to him as it becomes more and more clear that they and he are moving among the same realities, and dealing with the same truth—or rather being dealt with by the one living Truth that is greater than he or they.

The emergence of genius in any sphere is an incalculable phenomenon. It appears at various stages of historical development, among primitive communities and in advanced civilizations alike. The forms in which it expresses itself naturally depend on the thought-forms current at the time, but there is something behind the forms which seems to be independent of such limitations. A sudden outcrop of men of genius may appear " like a root out of a dry ground ". They may glorify a single period of history, and then disappear, leaving no successors. It is of course always possible to be wise after the event, and to point to certain discoverable factors which may have been favourable to this sudden outcrop, but it is difficult to show why these conditions and no others should have had this effect, or why apparently similar conditions at other times have had no such result.

This is true of religious genius, in the saint or prophet. We may study the antecedents and environment of the prophet, and account for the direction his genius took; but just that unique quality that makes him a prophet evades our definition. Akhnaton, Zarathustra, Gautama, are in no intelligible sense merely the product of their age, though no one of them would have done and said the particular things recorded of him in any other age. Each is an individual, with the incalculable originality which is the inseparable mark of genius.

The dominant personalities of the Bible are of this order. That is not to say that all its writers are on the level of the highest genius. There is, indeed, very little in the Canon which does not possess distinction. It is in the fullest sense a classical literature. But as the Greek classics include a Hesiod as well as a Homer, a Xenophon as well as a Thucydides, so the quality of the Bible is on different levels, and not only on different literary levels, but on different levels of religious significance. Within the range of the biblical writings there are three epochs at which the highest type of religious genius appears. First, there is the almost prehistoric period of Moses. We have no literature which can with any probability be attributed to that period. Moses has left us no writings, and we know little of him with certainty. But it is scarcely questionable that the Hebrew religion, before the time when its literature begins, had felt the impulse of some tremendous personality. Tradition calls him Moses, and so may we. We are not, however, in direct touch with him, but only with men who drew their inspiration from the impulse he communicated. Next we have the period from the eighth to the sixth centuries before Christ, which threw up religious genius in a succession probably without parallel in the history of the world. To this age belong Amos, Hosea, Isaiah[1], Jeremiah, and the anonymous author who for convenience is called the "Second Isaiah[2]", as well

[1] Isaiah of Jerusalem, who lived in the latter half of the eighth century, is the author of the nucleus of that collection of prophecies which forms chaps. i.–xxxix. of our Book of Isaiah.

[2] This name is given to the prophecies preserved in chaps. xl.–lv. of the Book of Isaiah, most if not all of which are attributed to an anonymous prophet of the sixth century.

as some men of the second rank who would have adorned a duller age—Micah, Zephaniah, Ezekiel and a few others, some of whose names are no longer known to us because their writings came to pass current under greater names.[1] Lastly, the first century of our era was distinguished by the appearance of the Founder of Christianity, in whom religious genius reached its highest point and passed into something greater still. We know Him only in the writings of His followers. He dominates the whole New Testament in a unique way, making all else in it appear only derivative. Yet in Paul and the unknown author of the Fourth Gospel we recognize types of religious genius of the same high order as the prophets themselves.

These three widely separated epochs provide the personalities whose influence made the Bible what it is. They were flowering times of the spirit, when genius in the sphere of religion asserted itself after its own incalculable fashion. So far as the actual writers are concerned, we have to take into account here only the prophets of the great age, with Paul and John. No other writers reach quite their level, unless we should add the author of the Book of Job, who for sheer literary quality perhaps surpasses every other biblical writer.

We may distinguish from these major lights of the firmament those other writers whose main significance lies not in individual originality, but in the way in which they reflect and record the influence of greater personalities or of historical movements. In them we recognize something short of religious genius, but none the less something personal which makes its own impression upon us. They exhibit sincerity, insight, personal devotion, sensitiveness to spiritual values—in short, all the faculties necessary to make them the

[1] The books of Isaiah, Jeremiah, Micah and others have been enlarged by the incorporation of material not originating with the prophets whose names they bear, but often belonging to the classical period.

vehicles of a religious influence which did not originate in them.

Thus the narrators of the ancient stories of the Pentateuch and of the historical books of the Old Testament not only show high literary skill, but often reveal a sensitiveness to the religious significance of what they relate, which clearly arises from a personal religious life. Particularly when they have to describe the religious experience of a Moses or an Elijah they convince the reader that they are writing of that which they know for themselves. Yet we cannot attribute to them "inspiration" in the same sense as to the great prophets.

In the New Testament we have the first three evangelists, who come before us not as independent religious teachers, but as witnesses to the life and words of Jesus Christ. Their sincerity, their devotion to the Lord of whom they write, and their personal experience of the religious effects of faith in Him, are patent. One of them, the third, is, besides, a consummate literary artist. But they suppress their own personalities so successfully that it is a task of considerable delicacy to recover the "personal equation" in the record. The early Church in forming the Canon of the New Testament, rightly distinguished between writings whose authority was that of the authors themselves, as "spiritual men", and those whose authority resided in the contents of their works[1]. It is not "inspiration" in any specific sense that we seek in the latter class. It is fidelity and essential truthfulness.

This distinction is not without importance. It has sometimes been obscured by apologists for the "inspiration of the Scriptures". The story of Joseph and his Brethren is splendid narrative, with essential truth in its representation of human life, and a deep religious meaning inherent in it; but to call it "inspired" is to leave no term adequate

[1] Harnack, *Entstehung des N.T.'s*, pp. 7–9, 15.

to describe the altogether distinct quality that one perceives in Isaiah or Paul. Again to ask whether the Synoptic Gospels are "inspired" is to ask the wrong question; we want to know whether they are veracious. That the words which they report from the Master are inspired is another matter.

What the "inspiration" of the prophets meant as a matter of experience we shall enquire presently. Its patent effect is a quality in their writings which can be felt rather than defined. Perhaps we might describe it as the quality of being "first-hand"—of being in some immeasurably more direct touch with the sources of truth than most of us achieve. The "inspired" writer produces a masterpiece in the field of religious utterance, to be recognized as such by all who have the sense for such things. The reader who does not see that Amos or Isaiah is a master in the religious life, is as little to be considered as the person who cannot see that the Parthenon or *King Lear* is a masterpiece. The prophets have the timelessness which belongs to genius. Their age was rude, their knowledge of the world severely limited, their modes of expression and even their perceptions in a measure bound by contemporary forms of thought. Yet what they said has the quality of permanence. Age does not stale it. Our wider knowledge in many fields does not antiquate it, any more than Dante is antiquated because it has been discovered that there is no Mount Purgatory at the Antipodes to Jerusalem.

Whatever else we may have to say of their "inspiration", it is clear that it is something intensely personal in themselves. It is not their *words* that are inspired—as one might say perhaps of "automatic writing"—it is the *men* who are inspired. Their powers of mind, heart and will are heightened beyond the common measure. They dwell on austere heights of communion with God, and habitually subject themselves to the awful discipline of such communion.

Morally they stand far above their contemporaries. They are men great in character as in spiritual insight. They have passed through experiences which make life for them something vastly more significant than it is for most of us. Thus they will best make their effect upon us if our study of them has something of personal communion. A mathematical treatise convinces by the pure logic of its argument. It is not in that way that we appreciate the *Divine Comedy*. There the personal element is all important. So with the prophets. Their words convey a personal experience of reality, and our aim is to participate in it, rather than merely to assess the logic of their arguments. If they can make us do that in any measure, then their authority has established itself. It is the only sort of authority they need claim.

The first stage, then, of our enquiry leads to the proposition that in the Bible we must acknowledge the authority which belongs intrinsically to genius. Such genius is unquestionably before us in the outstanding personalities who give to the whole literature its distinctive character, though not all of its writers fall themselves within that category. What authority, if any, can be recognized in the literature as a whole, even where it cannot rank as the direct manifestation of religious genius, is a question which must occupy us at a later stage.[1] For the present we shall fix our attention upon certain outstanding portions of it, where the marks of genius are undeniable, and consider them more narrowly, having in mind particularly the question in what sense such scriptures may be regarded as "revelation", that is, as mediating through their personal quality that thought of God which is eternal truth.

[1] See chaps. VI–VIII.

Part I

THE AUTHORITY OF INDIVIDUAL INSPIRATION

CHAPTER II

INSPIRATION AND PROPHECY

WE have already used the term "inspiration". This concept has had so prominent a place in the traditional doctrine of the Scriptures that we must now examine it with some care. The authority of the Bible is in fact often treated as the simple correlate of its inspiration. The question "whether the Bible is inspired" figured largely in the controversies of the last generation. For us, it is difficult to give any precise meaning to the question, so vague and fluctuating is the usage of the word "inspiration" itself, and so uncertain its implications. The theory which is commonly described as that of "verbal inspiration" is fairly precise. It maintains that the entire corpus of Scripture consists of writings every word of which (presumably in the original autographs, for ever inaccessible to us) was directly "dictated" by the Deity, in a sense not applicable to any other known writings. They consequently convey absolute truth with no trace of error or relativity. What such a process of "dictation" might be, it is naturally impossible to say, since *ex hypothesi* no living man has experience of it, though some advocates of the theory have incautiously adduced as a parallel the phenomena of "control" in the practice of spiritualists. Any attempt to confront this theory of inspiration with the actual facts which meet us in the study of the biblical documents leads at once to such patent confusions and contradictions that it is unprofitable to discuss it.

No attempt will here be made to formulate an alternative

definition of inspiration and then to enquire whether in the light of such definition the Bible is to be regarded as inspired. That I believe to be a false method. There is indeed no question about the original implications of the term: for primitive religious thought the "inspired" person was under the control of a supernatural influence which inhibited the use of his normal faculties. The phenomena which led to such a belief are now studied for their bearing on abnormal psychology. But when people to-day speak of "inspiration" in literature and the arts, they are not thinking of the mechanism of artistic production, but of a quality in the product which has a certain effect upon those who appreciate it. It is in a similar sense that the term has been used in the preceding chapter with reference to the biblical writings. If the term "inspiration" is to retain any place in our vocabulary, then it is certain that the Bible contains inspired writings. That is the starting point; it is not a proposition that needs discussion. The question "Is the Bible inspired?" is the wrong question to ask. We want to ask, granted that these writings are inspired, what is the specific value of their inspiration for religion? Is there in fact for us any sense in speaking of these writings, because they are inspired, as "the Word of God"? The only way to approach such questions is to look at the writings themselves and ask what it is they give us.

We have seen that there are two groups of writings in the Bible which exhibit the marks of religious genius at its highest, the writings of the classical Hebrew prophets, and certain books of the New Testament. It is in these writings that we should naturally seek materials for the study of inspiration. In the New Testament, however, there are certain factors which complicate the question, notably the unique influence of Jesus Christ upon all its writers. This influence seems to have been exerted partly through the abiding effect of personal intercourse with a supreme

Teacher, partly through a tradition in the community He founded, and partly through what we can only describe as mystical experience. Thus the operations of religious genius in such a man as Paul, at once intensely original and consciously derivative, are far from simple. The Old Testament prophets present less difficulty, and it will be convenient to make them the principal object of our study, though there are points at which a comparison with the "prophets" of the New Testament may prove illuminating.

We have before us, then, the writings of the Hebrew prophets of the eighth to sixth centuries before Christ. We must take their texts in the form in which the most scientific criticism has restored it to us. For the prophetic books as they stand in the Canon are the result of an extensive process of editing at a period long after the classical prophets lived, when prophecy had died out or profoundly changed its character, and much of the material they contain originated at this late period. To determine with precision the limits of the original prophecies and of later supplements is a task of great difficulty, in which few critics would claim to be able to attain complete certainty. Indeed there are wide differences of opinion in many cases. I shall attempt here to make use primarily of such passages as seem to command a fairly wide consensus of moderate opinion as belonging to known authors or at least to authors of the classical period, leaving aside passages where great uncertainty exists.

We are considering therefore a definite body of literature, with an unmistakable character of its own, having known historical relations, and attributable for the most part to known authors. If we can form some precise estimate of the "inspiration" of the classical prophets, then we may hope to see the whole question of inspiration in an illuminating perspective. But the prophets cannot be studied in independence of their historical context. Prophecy represents a phase of the religious history of Israel, and for its understanding it is necessary to have in view its spiritual antecedents and the circumstances in which it occurred. Our study, therefore, of prophetic inspiration must be introduced by some short discussion of the distinctive character of the religion within which it arose.

All religion seems to carry within it a certain rhythm of movement between two poles of feeling—the feeling of the utter remoteness and strangeness of God, and the feeling of His nearness to men. He is the unknown, the mysterious, the " completely other " than man ; and man must " fear " Him. Yet there is an irresistible impulse to " seek God "—to experience His power, to come into communion with Him. Religious rites both impress upon the mind the unapproachableness of the Deity, and offer a way of approach to Him. Some appreciation of the form which this twofold rhythm took in the historic religion of Israel is necessary to an understanding of the prophetic experience.

Professor Rudolf Otto[1] has offered to us a term to describe that element in religion (according to him the most essential and universal element) which is related to the " otherness " of God—namely, the " numinous ". This word was invented to denote a unique mode of feeling, which cannot be described in terms of other feelings without the loss of some of its content. In its crudest form this feeling is simply a sense of the uncanny. It has, like other instinctive feelings, a characteristic physical symptom. As anger is accompanied by a flow of blood to the face, and fear by its ebb, so the " numinous " feeling in its crudest form is accompanied by " gooseflesh ". There must be many of us not yet too civilized to feel a " grue " among the gaunt triliths of Stonehenge or by the gloomy shores of Llyn Idwal. We say they are " haunted ". To us that is

[1] In his book *Das Heilige* (Eng. trans. *The Idea of the Holy*).

metaphor ; to the primitive it is stark truth, though who or what " haunts " or what " haunting " may mean he cannot tell. The feeling is akin to fear ; yet it is not fear of that which reason knows to be dangerous. It is a shuddering dread of something altogether unknown and unknowable. A child was terrified in the dark. Questioned, he said he was afraid of a great bear. The questioner tried to comfort him by the assurance that it was not a real bear. " I know ", replied the child ; " that's why I am afraid of it ". There is a classical description in a well-known passage of Wordsworth's Prelude.

> " I dipped my oars into the silent lake,
> And, as I rose upon the stroke, my boat
> Went heaving through the water like a swan ;
> When, from behind that craggy steep till then
> The horizon's bound, a huge peak, black and huge,
> As if with voluntary power instinct
> Upreared its head. I struck and struck again,
> And growing still in stature the grim shape
> Towered up between me and the stars, and still,
> For so it seemed, with purpose of its own,
> And measured motion like a living thing,
> Strode after me. With trembling oars I turned,
> And through the silent water stole my way
> Back to the covert of the willow tree ;
> There in her mooring-place I left my bark—
> And through the meadows homeward went, in grave
> And serious mood ; but after I had seen
> That spectacle, for many days my brain
> Worked with a dim and undetermined sense
> Of unknown modes of being ; o'er my thoughts
> There hung a darkness, call it solitude
> Or blank desertion. No familiar shapes
> Remained, no pleasant images of trees,
> Of sea or sky, no colours of green fields ;
> But huge and mighty forms, that do not live
> Like living men, moved slowly through the mind
> By day, and were a trouble to my dreams."

In this experience we can trace most of the various features which Otto records as marks of the " numinous ". There is the sense of mystery—" a dim and undetermined sense of unknown modes of being ". There is the feeling of the power or energy of the unknown object, and of its " complete otherness ". There is the haunting terror, with its universal symbols of darkness and solitude. There is the fascination that keeps the boy looking at the black peak and afterwards keeps him thinking about it to the exclusion of all else. This childish experience is, in fact, very close to primitive religious experience, and Otto seems to be right in holding that as religion advances it still retains features corresponding to these characteristic marks of the numinous, transformed and sublimated. " Religion within the bounds of mere reason " (in the Kantian phrase) is a chimera. There is no real religion without " awe " in the presence of the " completely other " than ourselves—the *mysterium tremendum et fascinans*. Such awe is not rational in its origin, though capable of being rationalized. The " development " of religion is partly a deepening of the numinous feeling itself from a mere " grue " to a moral obeisance of the spirit in the presence of the Highest. It is partly a re-interpretation of the Object of that feeling, in which rational and moral processes play a large part, so that what is at first merely uncanny becomes in the fullest sense " holy ", as Christianity uses that word. For " holiness " is never merely goodness ; it is the moral absolute as the object of awe.

The Bible is, as Otto recognizes, rich in the numinous element, throughout almost the whole range of its varied manifestation, from the crudest to the most elevated. The folk-tales of ancient Israel are full of it, in crude forms, hardly disguised by the prophetic writers who gave these narratives their literary shape. Jacob, waking terror-stricken from a dream amid the desolate uplands of central Palestine, cries " How awe-inspiring this place is ! It is a dwelling of *Elohim !* "[1] At the haunted ford, alone and in

[1] Gen. xxviii. 17.

the dark, he meets a nameless Being in desperate conflict. Dawn comes, when all ghosts and goblins flee, and Jacob, surprised at finding himself alive after that night of terror, names the place *Peniel*—presence of *El.*[1] To the writers of the narratives as we have them, *El* and *Elohim* no doubt meant "God", in something like our own sense of the word, but in the old tales they used we are at a more primitive level. When Laban and Jacob take mutual pledges before the *Elohim* of their fathers, Jacob swears by "The *Fear* of his father Isaac".[2] These men are aware of an undefined Somewhat, belonging to a different order of being from themselves, before which they shudder in dread. Nor is this confined to the patriarchal narratives. In the days of the Judges a stranger came to Manoah. Manoah asked his name. He replied, "Why do you ask after my name? It is mystery", and presently he vanished in flames. "We are doomed to die", cried the terrified Manoah, "because we have seen *Elohim!*"[3]

At the stage where the numinous Object is no longer a vague *El*, but the definite personality of Jehovah, the same sense of mystery and dread is there. Sinai flamed and thundered with the Presence. Fascination drew the people to "break through unto Jehovah to gaze", but terror held them back "lest he break forth upon them".[4] A mysterious, incalculable, immensely powerful Being, one perceives, quite different from ourselves. Out of this sheer terror the faith of Moses soars. Longing to see God, he stands in a cleft of the Sinai crags. The glory of Jehovah passes by, but the cleft is wrapped in darkness. Jehovah's

[1] Gen. xxxii. 24–32.

[2] Gen. xxxi. 53. Cf. also that usage of the word *El* in which it means simply "strength," "power," e.g. Gen. xxxi. 29 (E), "it is according to the *El* of my hand," Deut. xxviii. 32. This looks like a reduced survival of a primitive use of the term for supernatural power or *mana.*

[3] Judges xiii. 22. The story as we have it describes the *Elohim* as "the angel of Jehovah": the author of Judges belongs to a more advanced age than the primitive tale he used.

[4] Exod. xix. 21–22.

face may not be seen, even by the "man of God". But as the darkness disperses, he catches a glimpse of Jehovah's retreating glory.[1] Whether this classical description be a record transmitted in some strange way from the almost prehistoric leader himself, or a transcript from the experience of a prophetic writer of later days, it bears its essential authenticity on its face. Scarcely anything even of the symbolism needs to be "written off" in order to make it immediately intelligible to ourselves as an actual experience. So Goethe writes:

> "Wenn der uralte
> heilige Vater
> mit gelassener Hand
> aus rollenden Wolken
> segnende Blitze
> über die Erde saet,
> küss' ich den letzen
> Saum seines Kleides,
> kindliche Schauer
> treu in der Brust."

The essential being of the Godhead remains a mystery, for which the only symbol is the "numinous" darkness. But something of God can be "seen", without diminishing the awe He must command. The half-seen "glory" is the "goodness" of Jehovah—and if this is not to be read in a fully ethical sense, at least it means that an element of rational valuation has entered into the "numinous" feeling. The growth of this element is reflected in the development of meaning of the Hebrew term which is nearly the equivalent of "numinous"—the word *qadhosh*. In the story of Sinai to which we have just alluded Moses is directed to make the mountain of the Presence *qadhosh*, so that no one may approach it.[2] At this level the word connotes merely that which is uncanny, haunted, *tabu*, as the South Sea Islanders say. When Isaiah[3] heard the word sung thrice

[1] Exod. xxxiii. 20–23. [2] Exod. xix. 23. [3] Isa. vi. 3–5.

by Jehovah's unearthly attendants, it certainly carried with it the sense of awful and unapproachable majesty, for Isaiah groaned, "Alas! I am undone! My eyes have seen the King!" But equally certainly it has a deeply ethical meaning. The majesty is not that of mere mystery or terror; it is the majesty of sheer goodness compelling the reverence of sinful man. Here is the first note of the prophetic experience—an overwhelming sense of God's majesty as the supremely ethical Being.

But while religion may start with sheer awe before the "completely other" than ourselves, it carries within it the necessity for finding some ground of communion with the Mystery. Indeed we might say that the whole practice of religion means the overcoming of the sense of separation from the God before whom we bow in awe, for its end is "to glorify God and to enjoy Him for ever". It is characteristic of biblical religion that it always assumes that the bridging of the gulf of separation must begin from the side of God. It is He who reveals himself—at first in manifestations of crude power in nature, in thunder and fire, in the giving of rain and of water-springs, in the increase of cattle and flocks, or in more mysterious psychical effects upon the mind of man in dream or ecstasy, or the "berserk" fury of battle. The primitive Israelite, like his contemporaries among other peoples, went to "seek the face of God" at places where His power had been manifested—the sacred well, the holy tree, or the high place, or best of all, the awe-inspiring highlands of Sinai. How far the "*El*" or "*Baal*" of the spot had for him distinct "personality", as we say; how far he felt a plurality of *Elohim* or *Baalim*, or how far he thought of the "powers" inhabiting the sacred sites as varying manifestations of a vague Divine, it would be hard to say, nor indeed is it really profitable to enquire. At a later stage it became a matter of intense conflict, and a conflict with decisive results for human history, whether or no the local baals might be worshipped alongside of the great God, but at first such a distinction is hardly present. Yet in the patriarchial narratives we seem to discern the emergence of belief in a God whose true "personality" is symbolized in a certain naive anthropomorphism. Abraham entertains three strangers—and one of them is the God whom he worships. "Behold", he cries, "I have taken upon me to speak unto the Lord, which am but dust and ashes". No words could more clearly express the sense of "complete otherness"; and yet by grace of God Himself Abraham has held converse with Him as man to man.[1]

It is yet an open question how far the piety distinctive of the patriarchal narratives represents a genuinely pre-Mosaic phase of religion, and how far it is an ideal construction of early prophetic teachers projecting upon a golden age in the past a conception of religion higher than that which was common in their own day. In any case there is no doubt that the narratives have been much worked over at an advanced stage of religious thought; yet there are features in the relations of the patriarchs to their God which do not appear in the earlier stages of the religion of Jehovah; and the very names by which the patriarchs know the Object of their worship—El Elyon, El Shaddai, and so forth—are of a different type from the titles of Jehovah or of His rivals the baals. The northern or Ephraimite tradition that the God of the patriarchs was later revealed as Jehovah may have some historical basis.[2]

With the emergence under Moses of the religion of Jehovah we come to more clear-cut conceptions of the approach of the divine Mystery to man. Jehovah, the stormy God of Sinai, is conceived in strongly personal terms. Though He may carry over some of the features of a nature God, yet He is very distinctly a Person, a "Man of war"[3] on the grand scale. He is essentially a "living God", who of His

[1] Gen. xviii. [2] Exod. iii. 13–15. [3] Exod. xv. 3.

own will revealed himself in mighty acts to the Hebrew clans because he loved them, and chose them for his people. He arrested Moses by a powerful experience of His majesty and " holiness ".[1] He made of him the heaven-sent leader at whose command the serfs of the Egyptian Pharaoh rose and left their habitual servile duties and burdens and went out into the desert to seek the face of God. They recognized in him a " man of God "[2]—a man possessed of something of the " numinous " quality, of something of the mysterious power—*mana*, to use the term which the comparative study of religion has adopted from the South Sea Islanders—which is the mark of Deity. In and through him the power of the great God of Sinai was at work. He was a magician, a medicine-man, whose magic wand wrought wonders of deliverance and destruction.[3] That was how the people regarded him. To separate history from legend in the stories of his career is impossible, and the attempt is not very profitable. What is certainly historical is the commanding sense of divine power and authority he aroused and the unshakable conviction he was able to implant in the minds of the Israelites that Jehovah Himself had taken control of their tribal life and was shaping it to his own mighty ends. It was a signal experience of the divine initiative in history. " I am Jehovah thy God, who brought thee up out of the land of Egypt ".[4] No Israelite ever really doubted the truth of that watchword. Jehovah by His own mighty acts had made Himself the God of Israel, had made Israel His people.

[1] Exod. iii. 1–6.

[2] The phrase " man of God " has acquired such a conventional meaning that it needs an effort of imagination to " feel " its original significance. A mountain or hill of *El* or *Elohim* is a " haunted mountain " (Exod. xviii. 5, 1 Sam. x. 5, Ps. xxxvi. 6). Cedars of *El* (Ps. lxxx. 10) are originally trees that give the " numinous " feeling. So an " *Elohim* man " is a " Shaman." The ghost of Samuel is *Elohim*, 1 Sam. xxviii. 13. Manoah's wife (see above) took the *Elohim* who appeared to her for an " *Elohim*-man."

[3] Exod. iv. 1–9 (J), vii. 20 (E), ix. 22–34 (JE).

[4] Exod. xx 2.

Henceforward an inseparable bond linked the people to their deliverer. The Mystery had declared Itself in acts having a human, a moral significance. In that lies already the germ of the faith of the prophets.

Crude enough indeed is the early conception of the character of this mighty God of Israel. Yet it is a great thing that He *has* a character, in a true sense. He is not just power, or holiness (" numinousness "), not just a presence or a " haunting ". He feels, chooses, wills. He loves His people, and His love knows jealousy; He can be terribly angry, and He can forgive. He chooses to act this way and not that, and He is free to alter His mind. Crudely anthropomorphic ; and yet it is upon such a conception of the Deity that a truly ethical monotheism can be built, and not upon a remote heavenly " Creator-god " (*Urheber-gott*) like the Chinese Shang-ti, or a metaphysical abstraction like Brahma, beyond good and evil. And withal even the most ancient worshippers of Jehovah were well aware that at bottom He was " completely other " than man. He could not even be represented in an image. When all was said and done, He was God and not man, Spirit and not flesh.[1] Yet they knew from the way He dealt with them that He had character and demanded character in them.

His character was indeed implied in the nature of the call He had given to His people through Moses. That call had made them a free people, with an ideal of solidarity that overrode the instinctive selfishness of individual and clan, with an ideal of self-sacrificing courage and heroic endurance in battle. This ideal developed itself through the austere, ascetic virtues of desert life. Jehovah hated the soft, licentious, self-indulgent ways of the worshippers of the fertility-gods, the *Baalim* whom Israel found in Canaan and tried to fit into the religion of the desert-God. However widespread might be the influence of these enervating cults

[1] Cf. Isa. xxxi. 3.

upon the social and moral life of the people, there was always in the background a more austere ideal to appeal to. At times of crisis the emotional appeal for loyalty to Jehovah, the Lord of the Hosts of Israel, could express itself in poetry like the Song of Deborah,[1] and be sure of response. There at least was something about which a higher ethic could be built.

In fact, in the primitive revelation of Jehovah as the *El Gibbor*,[2] the "mighty God" of Israel—Leader, Deliverer, Law-giver—we have a creative force set free to work among men, the faith and experience of a God whose awful majesty is brought near to men in qualities of a personal and moral sort, operating in the development of a social ethic.

Into the obscure question of the beginnings of prophecy in the religion of Jehovah it is not necessary to enquire, nor to decide whether it belonged to the earliest stages of that religion or was the result of Canaanite influence. "Prophets" come into the clear light of history about the time of the beginning of the monarchy. They are then described in terms which set before us a perfectly recognizable religious type, common to many different cultures. All religions have their devotees, their "men of God", and so had the religion of Jehovah. Such personages are felt by the common man in more or less primitive communities to partake in some degree of that supernatural, "uncanny" or "holy" quality which he associates with divinity. The man of God may be the official priest of a tribe, and his divine character then derives from the "holiness" of the shrine at which he ministers. He wears the vestments of the God; he knows the sacred words and gestures by which divine *mana* is liberated, and the rites by which its dangers may be averted. Such priests formed in early Israel a kind of guild, tracing their descent from Levi, as in later Greece

[1] Judges v. [2] Deut. x. 17, Isa. x. 21, Jer. xxxii. 18.

the guild of physicians professed themselves the sons of Asklepios. They knew, better than priests outside the guild, the words of power; they could manipulate the sacred lots, Urim and Thummim; they could wear the sacred ephod and speak with the voice of God; at their shrines they gave *Torah*, authoritative divine decisions on points of ritual and *tabu*.

But beside the official priest may stand the "man of God" whose divine character derives from some mysterious personal endowment. Perhaps originally the priest was such a man who contrived to hand on to his successors or descendants the sacred character he had won. But the priest does not displace the psychic adept. He is clairvoyant (a "seer") or he is liable to trance and ecstasy in which he speaks strange things, more clearly "divine" even than the priest's spells. He behaves, without any conscious intent, so differently from the general run of men that no one can doubt that he is "possessed" by some supernatural influence. The "strong breath" (*ruach*, "spirit") of the God is upon him. Here we meet the original sense of the term "inspiration." Among such "men of God" were the persons whom the Hebrews called *nābi*, a word whose original and etymological sense is not quite certain, but is probably derived from the incoherent babblings of the ecstatic. It is translated "prophet", but the latter term has acquired such an entirely different meaning that it will be well for our present purpose to retain the Hebrew word for these prototypes of the dervish of to-day.[1] They wandered about the country in bands, worked themselves up into frenzy with music and dancing, and were regarded by the populace with that mingled awe and contempt which is often the lot of their

[1] The use of the terms "*nabi*" for the more primitive and "prophet" for the more developed type may offend purists in the Hebrew language, but we need to make a distinction which the Hebrews did not make. I owe the suggestion to Hans Duhm, *Verkehr Gottes mit dem M nschen im Alten Testament*.

kind.[1] Among them were doubtless idle vagabonds, who gladly lived upon the reluctant alms of the superstitious.[2] But many, perhaps most, of them must have been according to their lights genuine and ardent devotees of Jehovah. Certainly we find the body of *nabis* standing with fanatical fervour for the worship of the national God in times of widespread surrender to " strange gods ". If, to the vulgar, " crazy " and " inspired " were scarcely distinguishable ideas,[3] yet psychology prepares us to find that this peculiar psychic type, with its exceptional suggestibility, is capable under the right conditions of grasping ideas with exceptional force, and of acting in the moral sphere with a decision and an emotional intensity beyond the reach of common men. What the conditions are it is difficult to say. Partly they depend on the original spiritual endowment of the individual " as God made him ", partly upon the ideas and ideals accepted as dominant by his reason, and partly upon elements in the environment.

The age was not given to careful discrimination of spiritual states, and so it is not surprising that men are grouped according to striking similarities in outward behaviour without much regard to differences in the more inward aspects of personality. While we hear of *nabis* who are no more than strolling dervishes, we hear also of other *nabis* who display outstanding moral and intellectual qualities. It is true that our records come to us in a form extensively edited and revised at a late period, and that we must allow for a tendency to idealize earlier *nabis* in the light of what prophecy had become in the Deuteronomic age. Yet it seems impossible to deny that from the beginning of the Monarchy, that is, from the time at which authentic records of prophecy begin, the order included personalities, like Samuel

[1] 1 Sam. x. 5–6, 10–13 ; xix. 23–24.

[2] Such is the implication of passages like Micah iii. 5, 11 ; Amos vii. 12 ; 2 Kings v. 22.

[3] 2 Kings. ix. 4, 11.

and Nathan, of elevated character and great intellectual or executive power, who were natural leaders and reformers.

Samuel is represented in the oldest stories of his time as attached to the "high place" at Ramah, where we find him in his natural position as "man of God" presiding at a local religious festival.[1] He associates with the bands of *nabis*, and himself enjoys great repute as a "seer", or clairvoyant—so great that after his death he is invoked by necromancers to foretell the future.[2] He would "find" lost property for a quarter-shekel fee. Yet it is certain that his abilities qualified him to play an important though obscure rôle in the foundation of the monarchy. The story of his part in the important work of this epoch has been so completely rewritten by later prophetic authors that it is difficult to arrive at the truth. But the varying traditions that gathered about him can be accounted for only if he really was a man of outstanding character and influence. We are given to understand that it was in the interests of the religion of Jehovah, as he understood them, that he carried the prophetic order with him from the side of Saul to that of the rebel David. If so, the first dynastic revolution in Hebrew history was a religious revolution, and it was led by a *nabi*.

To Nathan is attributed a more definitely ethical witness to the character and claims of Jehovah. David was a "man after God's own heart" in that he embodied in a captivating way the heroic if savage purpose of the God of Armies. This purpose we can recognize not only in such ancient literature as the Song of Deborah, but equally in David's own Song of the Bow.[3] But it fell to Nathan to make him aware of a whole range of moral demands of Jehovah which he had ignored in his practice.[4] Perhaps the abnormal endowments

[1] 1 Sam. ix. [2] 1 Sam. xxviii. 11–20.

[3] 2 Sam. i. 19–27, probably an authentic composition of the poet-king.

[4] 2 Sam. xii. 1–9.

of the *nabi* gave Nathan the certainty and confidence without which he might not have dared to beard the king, and they may have clothed him with a majesty, as " man of God ", which commanded the king's respect. Yet in reality the truth he declared stands on its own bottom, and in the narrative as we have it the *nabi* puts the case for a higher ethic with perfect simplicity and reasonableness.

In the next age we are already on surer historical ground in marking the likeness and the difference between the gigantic figure of Elijah and the general order of *nabis*. The kind of men they were at this time we can gather from the curious story of Micaiah ben Imlah.[1] From this it appears that Ahab kept a band of *nabis* as a sort of court soothsayers. They still experienced the " fine frenzy " of the ecstatic, though, knowing on which side their bread was buttered, they readily accepted as the " word of Jehovah " unconscious " auto-suggestions " in accord with the royal wishes. The grotesque antics of Zedekiah ben Chenaanah, with his iron horns, were not deliberate play-acting; he was doubtless powerfully " inspired "; but there was no sort of moral ballast to it all. On the other hand Micaiah ben Imlah is a good type of the genuine and thoroughly honest clairvoyant. He is no religious genius, but his " inspiration " is of a kind which drives him to tell the truth as he sees it without fear or favour. " What Jehovah says to me, that will I speak ". It is illuminating to observe that he can explain the contrary utterance of his fellow-*nabis* only by the assumption, which presents itself to him in the form of a visual hallucination, that Jehovah sent a " spirit " to put lying words in their mouths.

We may take it that there were many like Micaiah among those " sons of the prophets " whom Elijah visited at such popular shrines as Jericho, Bethel and Gilgal. Their simple honesty and fidelity to the plain moral demands of the service of their God kept alive a sound religious influence in the

[1] 1 Kings xxii. 1–28.

midst of an order sadly exposed to corruption just because of its exceptional psychic gifts. Their ideal of the prophetic character is admirably set forth in the legendary figure of Balaam, created by prophetic authors of about this time. In the story of the blessing of Israel he plays the part of Micaiah to Balak's Ahab. He is a true clairvoyant: he sees the vision and hears the word[1]:

> "The oracle of Balaam son of Beor,
> the oracle of the seer,
> the oracle of him who hears God speak,
> who knows what the Most High knows,
> who sees a vision of the Almighty,
> sleeping but awake in soul!
> I see them in the future far,
> I mark them in the days to come;
> a star of a king has come from Jacob,
> a mace has risen from Israel,
> crushing in Moab's head,
> the skull of these proud creatures!"

He is naturally reluctant to utter a vision so little likely to please his royal patron; but a divine compulsion is upon him, and despising the wrath of the king he tells what he has seen and heard.

There is, of course, nothing in the content of such prophecies of any profound religious import; they are merely forecasts of weal or woe unrelated to moral conditions. But the ideal of the prophetic character which such stories convey is an elevated one. The *nabi* must be without personal bias or prepossession, open to the impact of truth as it comes to him in his moments of "inspiration." And he may not pervert or suppress the message. When a man arises in such an order who really has something of importance to say, he may well be a power among his fellows.

Here Elijah emerges. Through the mists of his legend he looms as the greatest of the *nabis*. On one side he is a "man of God" of a very primitive type. He is "possessed";

[1] Num. xxiv. 15–17 (Moffatt).

he can see visions, hear voices, and read the thoughts of the heart, and when the *ruach* is on him he can perform feats of abnormal endurance.[1] He is driven by influences entirely beyond his own control, and seems to appear and disappear like a wraith.[2] He is in great repute as a medicine-man and rain-maker.[3] Yet this man faces Ahab and Jezebel with the sanity of one who sees directly into the moral issues of things,[4] and his stand for the clear, straightforward logic of Jehovah-worship in an age of muddled syncretism marks him out as one of the great pioneers of rational and ethical religion.

The description of his vision on Horeb[5] seems to preserve an authentic piece of religious experience. Behind the zeal of the reformer lay this intense and immediate sense of the majestic Presence of God—a deeply "numinous" Something revealed in silence, which remains after the obvious terrors of wind, earthquake, and fire have passed. Whatever elements of abnormal psychology are here, clearly they are but the outer shell of an experience of God which authenticates itself in the attitude to life and its problems which it forces the man to take. Jehovah is such and such, and His will cannot be otherwise. It is the immediacy of this conviction, and its tremendous urgency for Elijah himself, that give him his real power, rather than the abnormal phenomena of "possession".

The *nabis* then of the eleventh to ninth centuries have as a class little in common beyond their abnormal psychic disposition and their attachment to the cult of the national God. In personal character as in religious insight they differ widely. Amid all corruptions the order must have included throughout the period a sound nucleus of men in whom the abnormal powers of the ecstatic were at the service of a

[1] 1 Kings xviii. 46. [2] 1 Kings xviii. 12; 2 Kings ii. 16.
[3] 1 Kings xvii. 1, xviii. 32–35, 41–45. [4] 1 Kings xxi.
[5] 1 Kings xix. 8–18.

religious life of some depth and richness, and from time to time it threw up men of real religious genius. These men, in whom the psychic mechanism of ecstasy, clairvoyance, and the rest became the vehicle of an exceptionally fine religious insight, based on a personal communion with God, were able down to the time of Elijah to keep the order of *nabis* in the main a force on the side of true and ethical religion. They believed profoundly in the power of Jehovah, in His special providence over the life of Israel from earliest times, and in His purpose for His people in the present and the future. They were entirely indifferent to the other deities whose cults from time to time allured their countrymen. They fought the *Baalim* tooth and nail, as devotees of the stern God of Sinai. They stood by the belief that their God demanded a certain austere, disciplined, heroic standard of conduct, and they sought to keep the social life of their people true to that standard, against self-indulgence, greed, dishonesty, cowardice, and injustice in king or commoner. In an age of material " progress " they were conservative, even to preserving old desert customs in dress and food. Their attitude to advancing civilization, secular and religious, was almost entirely negative. Being frequently in opposition to the ruling tendencies, they had no overweening respect for the throne, and were always ready at a crisis to be champions of the ancient rights and liberties of the free Israelite. Their religious outlook has deeply coloured the two narratives which in the northern and the southern kingdoms respectively embodied old traditions of the early history of Israel. These narratives can still be partially isolated in the composite writings of the Pentateuch. Taken as a whole they represent no mean achievement in religion, and it is the achievement of the *nabis*.[1]

[1] Opinion is still divided as to the extent to which even the JE narrative has been affected by the influence of the earlier classical prophets. In the main, however, this narrative, and particularly its J component, seems to be prior to the work of Amos and Hosea.

In spite, however, of all that they contributed to the religious life of Israel, the order held within it from the beginning dangerous possibilities of corruption. Even in what we may regard as its best days, such a story as that of Micaiah ben Imlah reflects the dubious repute into which the order might easily fall. Perhaps that repute was not ultimately improved by the part which the *nabis*, led by Elijah's successor Elisha, played in the dynastic revolution which dethroned the house of Ahab.[1] Elisha appears in his legend as a type much nearer the ordinary *nabi* than his master. Nothing is related of him which suggests any deep religious experience or any outstanding ethical insight. On the other hand he captured the vulgar imagination by his flamboyant wonder-working.[2] A patriot he certainly was. His religion was chiefly a fanatical and unscrupulous zeal for the exclusive cult of the national God, combined with a very limited appreciation of His ethical demands. He was popularly credited with having instigated the disreputable measures by which Jehu in Israel and Hazael in Syria[3] obtained their thrones, and the political ascendancy he clearly enjoyed under the dynasty of Jehu implicates him at least as an accessory in the atrocities with which the reign commenced—atrocities which a generation later called forth the indignant condemnation of Hosea.[4] In fact he has much of the character of a Court prophet—arrogant, imperious, vindictive when his dignity is touched. In one sense the triumph of Jehu by Elisha's support was the success for which the *nabis* had been fighting against odds for a century or more, for it was the triumph of a party fiercely nationalist, and committed to the exclusive worship of the national God. But in a deeper sense it marks the fall of prophecy from its best ideals. It had done its work of consolidating Israel's formal allegiance to Jehovah but

[1] 2 Kings ix.–x. [2] 2 Kings iv. 32–37, 38–44; vi. 1–7, 18–20.
[3] 2 Kings viii. 7–15. [4] Hosea i. 4.

it now found itself largely bankrupt of spiritual energy and ethical ideals. It was not an Elisha who could give life and reality to the now established national religion. From this time onwards the *nabis* as a body appear rather as a degrading than an elevating influence. They become the "false prophets" of the time of Isaiah and Jeremiah. Their "inspiration", in the formal sense, never fails; they see visions and dream dreams, but the word of the Lord has departed from them.

Our survey of the early history of prophecy suffices to show that the psychological phenomena which the people of the Bible identified with divine inspiration had no necessary connection with those moral and spiritual qualities which mark true religious genius. Where any of the early *nabis* became a real religious force it was by virtue of something in him which directed his abnormal gifts into fruitful ways. If therefore inspiration is to be considered as in any way a condition of the authority of the biblical writers it must be something more than a function of abnormal psychology as we meet it in the primitive ecstatic (or his modern analogue the psychic "medium").

CHAPTER III

THE FORMS OF PROPHETIC INSPIRATION

THE great prophets of the eighth and seventh centuries are a very different breed from their predecessors. They no doubt displayed certain characteristics which associated them in the general mind with the order of *nabis*, but clearly they did not like their company. Amos repudiates any connection with the professional prophets. "I was no prophet", says he, "neither was I a prophet's son (that is, a member of the "order"); but I was a herdman".[1] Amos, according to the note at the beginning of his book, was a *nōkēd*—a sheep-farmer, like Mesha, King of Moab[2]—and so a person of some substance. He resents Amaziah's imputation that he is prophesying for a living. Just as little, evidently, would Micah care to be classed with the *nabis* of his time,—"prophets divining for money".[3]

> "As for the prophets, Jehovah says,
> Who lead my folk astray,
> Who cry, 'All's well!' if they get food to eat,
> And open war on any who refuse them,
> It shall be night for you, devoid of vision,
> So dark that you cannot divine."

Isaiah, though he does not repudiate the title *nabi*, and shows more positive appreciation of the ideal value of the order, is scarcely less trenchant in criticism of its contemporary representatives.[4]

> "Prophets and priests are reeling drunk,
> Fuddled with liquor;
> They reel amid their revelations;
> They stumble as they give their charges."

[1] Amos vii. 14.
[2] Amos i. 1. Cf. 2 Kings iii 4.
[3] Micah iii. 5 sqq. (Moffatt).
[4] Isa. xxviii. 7 (Moffatt).

In the next century Jeremiah finds in the *nabis* the most bitter and constant opponents of everything for which he stands. He has not a good word to say for them.[1]

"In Samaria's prophets I saw unseemliness;
They prophesied by Baal and misled my people.
In Jerusalem's prophets I have seen a horror,
Adultery, walking in lies, and strengthening the hands of ill-doers.
They are all to me like Sodom,
As the inhabitants of Gomorrah."

Jeremiah's contemporary, Zephaniah, denounces the prophets as "light and treacherous persons."[2] Ezekiel is as emphatic in his condemnation:[3]

"Woe to the fools of prophets who only prophesy from what they feel, without a real vision. . . . You give 'the word of Jehovah', and Jehovah never sent you!"

We are not here so much concerned with the particular charges that these great religious teachers bring against the *nabis* of their day—charges of self-indulgence and immoral conduct, of venality, covetousness, and base flattery for gain, charges of misrepresentation and perversion of the truth of God. But what we observe is the cold and detached way in which they speak of "the prophets" as a body—certainly not in the tone of men who took a pride in belonging to that body, hardly in the tone of members of a profession jealous for its honour impugned by unworthy representatives. Some of them at least allowed themselves to bear the name of *nabi*, yet they were far more conscious of the differences between themselves and the professional bearers of the name than of what they had in common with them. It is of a piece with this attitude that the great prophets of the eighth and seventh centuries have little to say of the *ruach* or "spirit" which had seemed the distinguishing mark of the *nabi*. They use by preference expressions which imply a more personal kind of relation to God. They feel

[1] Jer. xxiii. 13, 14 (Skinner). [2] Zeph. iii. 4 (R.V.).
[3] Ezek. xiii. 3, 6 (Moffatt).

themselves to be an altogether new kind of "prophet", channels of a new religious impulse and a revolutionary message. This fact is of more real importance than any affinities they may have had with the "dervish" type of prophet.[1]

To what extent they are to be classed in a psychological sense with the ecstatic it is difficult to define. Ezekiel, who except Jeremiah himself is most bitter in his denunciations of the *nabis*, nevertheless displays traits which we can hardly help regarding as those of psychic abnormality. In him the "spirit" once again has a dominant part. He appears subject to trance and catalepsy.[2] He feels himself, like a psychic "medium", lifted into the air and transported to distant places.[3] He records at least one clear case of "telepathy", when he was aware in Babylonia of the beginning of the siege of Jerusalem on the day on which it occurred.[4] The strange episode of the death of Pelatiah may perhaps be interpreted as a case of clairvoyance,[5] and the "vision" of pagan worship in the Temple at Jerusalem is conceivably of the same kind.[6]

No other of the greater prophets appears to display such definite symptoms of abnormality. Isaiah, Amos, and others describe "visions" which may well be what psychology describes as "visual hallucinations". That is, when Isaiah says: "I saw Jehovah sitting on a throne",[7] or Amos says: "Behold the Lord stood beside a wall",[8] we must probably think not that they deliberately set to work to form a mental picture of their God out of their stock of intellectual ideas about Him, but that at the time

[1] The extent to which the classical prophets exhibit the abnormal psychology of the ecstatic is much discussed in recent literature. Two books representing the opposite extremes of opinion are T. H. Robinson's *Prophecy and the Prophets*, and N. Micklem's *Prophecy and Eschatology*.

[2] Ezek. iii. 23–27, iv. 4–8, viii. 1–2.

[3] Ezek. viii. 3, xi. 1, xxxvii. 1, xl. 1–2.

[4] Ezek. xxiv. 1–5.

[5] Ezek. xi. 1–13.

[6] Ezek. viii. 3–18.

[7] Isa. vi. 1.

[8] Amos vii. 7.

they had an immediate conviction that they actually saw Him before their eyes. Similarly there are expressions which seem naturally to imply that such prophets experienced "auditions", that is, they were convinced that they actually heard sounds which conveyed intelligible meaning to them, though no man spoke. Thus Amos compares the "speaking" of Jehovah to the roaring of a lion.[1] Isaiah says: "Jehovah spoke to me with a strong hand";[2] and again: "I have *heard* the Lord of Hosts decree doom fixed and final for the world".[3] Indeed, the very phrase, "Thus saith the Lord"—more properly, "Thus said Jehovah"—implies at least in form that the oracle which follows was "heard" by the prophet as an utterance of a divine voice.

Yet in all this we must bear in mind the limitations of language, and the influence of preconceived ideas not only upon the expression given to an experience but upon the actual form of the experience itself. Terms describing psychological processes necessarily conform to the general working theories assumed consciously or unconsciously by the subject, and the psychological theories of the prophets were not ours. Jeremiah seems to be wrestling with language for a clear expression of the difference he felt to exist between the *nabis* and himself. That they "saw" visions and "heard" voices, much as he did himself, he never thinks of denying. Yet he is aware of something in his own experience which stands over against the purely ecstatic and criticizes it, and in virtue of that something he gives the lie to the "inspired" vaticinations of his rivals.[4]

> "The prophet that has a dream
> Let him relate a dream;
> And he that has My word,
> Let him declare My word in truth.

[1] Amos iii. 8. [2] Isa. viii. 11 ("with overwhelming force," Moffatt).
[3] Isa. xxviii. 22 (Moffatt).
[4] Jer. xxiii. 28 sqq. (Skinner. See his *Prophecy and Religion*, chap. x.).

> What has the chaff to do with the wheat ?
> Is Jehovah's oracle.
> Is not My word like fire,
> Like a hammer that shatters the rock ? "

It is true that he does not succeed in establishing any psychological criterion of the difference between true and false prophecy, but we cannot doubt that he is aware of a profound contrast between the ecstasies of the *nabis* and his own inspiration. And Jeremiah speaks for his compeers. Their experience had more or less similarity to that of the popular *nabis* of the day, but the similarity was accidental, the difference essential. So they themselves were convinced, and no treatment of their experience which leaves this conviction out of account can do justice to them.

If we are to follow Jeremiah's lead we shall refuse to find the test of inspiration in the psychological mechanism by which it is mediated ; we shall seek it in the value of the inspired utterance itself. That in the last resort is the only test we can apply. But where value is concerned appeal must be made to the reason and to the moral interests of human society. Here the analysis which Jeremiah had attempted is carried further by Paul. He, like the Old Testament prophets, had experience of ecstatic conditions, and of the irrational utterance which was often its form of expression. Paul's " speaking with tongues " is the equivalent of the primitive " *hith-nabbe* " or " prophesying " at its lower level. He did not deny its " inspired " quality, in some sense ; one and the same Spirit produced it and the higher form of utterance for which he would reserve the honourable name of " prophecy ".[1] But " speaking with tongues " has small value, for two reasons : first, it has no intelligible content ; and, secondly, it makes no contribution to the moral development of a community : it does not " edify " in the fine Pauline sense of the word.[2] Prophecy in the true sense has rational content, and it edifies.

[1] 1 Cor. xii. 10–11. [2] 1 Cor. xiv.

Yet we should not therefore be justified in concluding that prophecy in the Pauline sense is no more than the result of a highly intelligent process of conscious reasoning. In his own writings we can distinguish various modes of thinking. Sometimes he is a Rabbi, drawing conclusions from accepted traditional authority, whether that of the Old Testament or that of Jesus and His apostles. Sometimes he is a philosopher, reasoning with more or less cogency, deducing from first principles or making an induction from experience. At other times he casts aside tradition and argument, and declares with an ardour of immediate conviction what he, no less than Isaiah or Jeremiah, holds to be the "word of the Lord": he speaks as a prophet, declaring "all mysteries and all knowledge".[1] What we do not find in him is any exploiting of his mystical experiences, or any attempt to interpret the "unutterable words" he "heard" in ecstasy, as specially authoritative divine messages.[2] We may here instructively contrast the attitude of Ignatius of Antioch, who will add weight to his arguments for the monarchical authority of the bishop by recalling words he uttered in ecstasy. "I shouted out when I was in your midst; I spoke with a great voice—the voice of God—'Give heed to the bishop, the presbyters, and the deacons!' Some suspected that I was speaking thus because I had previous knowledge of the dissensions of certain persons; but He in whom I am bound prisoner is my witness that I did not know it from any human or fleshly source. But it was the Spirit that proclaimed: 'Do nothing without the bishop'".[3] Here Ignatius appeals to an entirely automatic utterance, displaying apparently supernatural knowledge of things of which he was not informed, and claims that, just because it was an utterance of that kind, it is the voice of God. The more impersonal the utterance, the more divine. This is a view foreign to

[1] 1 Thess. iv. 15; 1 Cor. ii. 4–5, xiii. 2; 2 Cor. xiii. 3.
[2] 2 Cor. xii. 1–6.
[3] Ign. *ad Phil.* vii. 1–2.

Paul, and in essence to the greater prophets of the eighth and seventh centuries B.C. Quite otherwise is it with the Apocalyptists, who definitely exploit ecstatic visions of a wholly non-rational kind, and value them in proportion as they are outside the normal control of their human faculties. The Apocalypses are impersonal, and that is one reason why they are generally anonymous, or pseudonymous. They stand or fall by the objectivity of the trance-dreams upon which they are based. The findings of modern psychology, it is hardly necessary to say, support Jeremiah and Paul against Ignatius and the Apocalyptists.

We may perhaps estimate the difference between the prophet and the mere ecstatic by considering the relation between inspiration in the arts and the automatism of quasi-hypnotic states. I have been shown by a psycho-analyst a series of drawings done by one of his patients under such conditions. As the patient had some technical skill the drawings are striking products, but they express nothing but the morbid confusions and conflicts of the patient's mind. The guidance and control of the higher centres of consciousness were removed. Such productions could never take their place among the achievements of art. In much current work, indeed, the subconscious is deliberately exploited; but without entering into current controversy we may surely affirm that the enduring masterpieces display something more than automatic response to subliminal impulses. They are the product of a heightening and refining of the conscious powers of the mind. They display character, intelligence and controlled imagination. Yet in the very highest ranges of art there is a sense of something received from beyond the limits of conscious thought. It is indeed just this that seems to distinguish genius from talent. Two very well-known painters of the last generation, I have been told, met at a dinner party in their old age. Said the first: "As one grows old, the difficulty is to think of fresh subjects. Don't you find it so?"—"Yes, we're growing old ", replied the other ; then, turning to his neighbour, he added in a low voice : " They crowd upon me ! " The speakers were Millais and Burne-Jones. Most people probably would feel that the difference is characteristic of the artists. Yet the work of an artist of genius who feels that his subjects " come to " him is not on the same level as the automatic drawings of the psycho-analyst's patient.

In literature, again, we do not look to automatism for the most truly " inspired " work. *Kubla Khan* indeed is a notorious example of fine poetry written under conditions inhibiting the exercise of conscious control, and apparently some of the work of other great poets has been produced under somewhat similar psychological conditions. But in these cases we are dealing with men whose whole range of thought and imagination is of a high order, and the quality of the man comes out even where the higher centres of consciousness are asleep. It is at least clear that their inspiration does not consist in the mode in which it is conveyed. The value of automatism as such may better be tested by the mass of " scripts " recently given to the world as the product of the trances of spiritualist " mediums ". They would not appear to have added greatly to the literary heritage of our race. Yet the poet has his " fine frenzy " (like the lunatic and the lover), in which imagination " bodies forth the forms of things unknown ". Doubtless they stream from the subconscious region into the field of consciousness. They are, however, subject to some process of selection and control which is absent in the trance of the " medium ". To speak of control and selection is not to suggest that the writing of poetry is chiefly a matter of " workmanship ", or that genius is in this sphere merely a " capacity for taking pains ". We receive from the Press yearly many volumes of " thoughtful verse ", which any person of education and taste, with some facility in language, could produce, but which no one could mistake for the real thing.

The element of inspiration is essential to poetry, and it is recognizable however difficult it may be to define. But if we compare the poet with the "medium" we must say that the sources of imagination in the subconscious are in the former richer and in some way worthier than in common men, however psychically gifted they may be. The poet and the artist draw from deeper springs.

Now the poetic quality of the utterances of the great prophets is manifest.[1] Not only do they fall into the rhythmical form natural to poetry, but the processes of thought and imagination they embody recall those of the great poets. We may take as a first example Ezekiel's dirge over Tyre. The dirge was indeed somewhat "previous", for Tyre was a flourishing city, and it continued to flourish for centuries after the prophet had predicted its doom. But the form which the prediction takes is splendidly imaginative. The mercantile city is depicted as a gallant ship:

"Thou, O Tyre, hast said, I am perfect in beauty!
  In the heart of the seas is thy domain.
Thy builders have perfected thy beauty.
  Of fir-trees from Senir have they made all thy planks;
  Cedars from Lebanon have they taken to make a mast for thee;
  Of the oaks of Bashan have they made thine oars;
  Thy deck they have made of ivory inlaid with boxwood from the isles of Kittim.

. . . .

Thou wast replenished and made very glorious
  In the heart of the seas.
Thy rowers have brought thee into great waters;
  The east wind hath broken thee,
  In the heart of the seas.
Thy riches and thy wares,
  Thy merchandise, thy mariners and thy pilots,
Thy calkers and the exchangers of thy merchandise,
  And all thy men of war that are in thee,
  With all thy company which is in the midst of thee,
Shall sink into the heart of the seas,
  In the day of thy ruin.

[1] Cf. N. Micklem, *Prophecy and Eschatology*, ch. I.

F

At the sound of the cry of thy pilots
The coastlands shall shake.
And all that handle the oar shall come down from their ships;
The mariners and all the pilots of the sea shall stand upon the land.
And they shall cause their voice to be heard over thee,
And shall cry bitterly and cast dust upon their heads;
They shall wallow themselves in the ashes.
And they shall make themselves bald for thee and gird them with sackcloth;
And they shall weep for thee in bitterness of soul with bitter mourning.

And in their wailing they shall take up a lamentation for thee
And lament over thee, saying, Who is there like Tyre?
Like her that is brought to silence in the midst of the sea?
When thy wares went forth out of the seas, thou filledst many peoples;
Thou didst enrich the kings of the earth with the multitude of thy riches and of thy merchandise.
But now thou art broken by the seas in the depths of the waters;
Thy merchandise and all thy company are sunken in the midst of thee."[1]

There is nothing more abnormal about Ezekiel's mental processes here than there is about Æschylus singing the downfall of Persia or Virgil calling the roll of the Latin cities before their overthrow by the Trojans. There is appreciation of the beauty of ships and the pathos of a wreck; there is the sense of the romance of names; and behind the song lies deep and intense patriotic feeling, a longing for the downfall of an implacable enemy, which finds in the picture of disaster a "wish-fulfilment". There is nothing dream-like, ecstatic, or hypnoidal about it. It is pure imagination. In the comparisons suggested above the Hebrew must no doubt yield the palm to the Greek and the Roman. Ezekiel is not a poet of the very first rank. But I have chosen this particular prophecy because it can be judged simply as secular poetry, without any complication of religious motive or aim. But it is the same quality of

[1] Ezek. xxvii. 3–6, 25–34 (R.V. altered).

imagination that informs Ezekiel's definitely religious utterances. If among his prophecies there appear some bearing the marks of trance or automatism, this element is accidental, and no more relevant to a general estimate of his work than is the fact that Mr. Masefield once published a poem, certainly not one of his best, which had come to him in a dream.[1] As a matter of fact, Ezekiel is least poetical, least inspired in the true sense, where he shows most marks of the ecstatic.

On a higher level of inspiration stand the poems in which Jeremiah embodied his early forebodings of disaster :[2]

> "Hark ! a runner from Dan !
>   A herald of evil from Ephraim's hills :
> Warn the people : Behold they come !
>   Let Jerusalem hear !
> From a far land leopards are coming,
>   Against Judah's townships they roar ;
> Like sleepless field-watchers they prowl around.
>
> I looked to the earth—and behold a chaos !
>   To the heavens—and their light was gone.
> I looked to the hills—and lo ! they quivered,
>   And all the mountains shook.
> I looked—and behold no man was there,
>   And all the birds of heaven were flown.
> I looked to the cornland—and lo, a desert,
>   And all its cities were razed away.
>
> From the noise of horsemen and bowmen
>   All the land is in flight :
> They crawl into caverns, hide in the thickets,
>   And scale the crags.
> Every town is deserted,
>   None dwell therein.
>
> Hark ! a shriek like a travailing woman's
>   With her first child !
> 'Tis the voice of the daughter of Zion, gasping,
>   Stretching her hands, and crying
> 'Woe is me ! for my soul faints away
>   At the feet of the slayers.' "

[1] *The Woman Speaks ;* in the volume *King Cole and Other Poems*, 1923

[2] Jer. iv. 15–17, 23–26, 29, 31 (Skinner).

It is little worth while to enquire whether or no the prophet is here reproducing a series of "visual hallucinations". Whatever the psychological mechanism employed, the result is imaginative writing of a high order. In part its material is remembered experiences in war-time, possibly during a Scythian raid into Palestine. But the whole is dominated by an idea made incandescent by intense feeling. The idea is that of the certain doom of a people rotten with social evils, and the feeling is compounded of the misery, fear, indignation, pity, which are aroused within (as psychologists would say) the "sentiment" of love of country by the thought of disaster to that which one loves. When we have said that, we have not, of course, explained the specific quality which makes these songs great poetry, their "inspiration", but we have recorded the fact that whatever that quality may be it is not dependent on any ecstatic element in the prophecy. It is somewhere inherent in the elevation of the idea and the emotional strength of the sentiment as they exist in a mind essentially noble.

We recognize, then, in the prophets the truly poetic power of apprehending an idea imaginatively—not bit by bit, discursively, but synthetically, in a vivid picture. That which distinguishes them from other poets is not the manner of apprehension but the nature of the ideas which they so apprehend. They are religious ideas of remarkable sublimity and originality. They do not coldly assert such ideas as true, and they do not argue about them. They grasp them intuitively and hold them suffused with emotion, until the emotion breaks into lyric utterance. As Ezekiel apprehends with the intense primitive emotions of patriotism the idea of an enemy's downfall, until he *sees* it as the wreck of a gallant ship; as Jeremiah grasps the idea of national disaster with an intensity of feeling which makes him *see* the havoc of war—so they and their compeers apprehend such ideas as the holiness, power, righteousness, and grace of God, or the immutable moral principles of human life, or the spiritual possibilities of a situation, with the same imaginative directness and the same strength and simplicity of feeling.

We may select for the study of the imaginative expression of religious ideas a remarkable poem of Amos whose four stanzas (the last separated from the rest, probably by a later editor) describe four "visions" referring to Jehovah's dealings with Israel. Amos is contemplating the forbearance and the ultimate inexorableness of divine justice, and his thought comes out in these visionary pictures.[1]

"Then the Lord Jehovah showed me this,
showed me Himself forming a brood of locusts,
just as the spring crops were coming up,
when the royal crop had been mowed.
As they devoured all the green growth, I cried,
'Have mercy, Lord, have mercy!
How can Jacob recover?—he has so little!'
Then Jehovah did relent,
Jehovah said, 'This shall not be.'

The Lord Jehovah showed me this,
showed me Himself calling down fire
to burn up the great deep,
to burn up the tilled land.
'Cease, Lord, oh cease,' I cried.
'How can Jacob recover?—he has so little.'
Then Jehovah did relent,
Jehovah said, 'This shall not be.'

The Lord Jehovah showed me this,
showed me Himself standing beside a wall,
a plumb-line in His hand.
Jehovah said to me,
'Amos, what do you see?'
'A plumb-line,' I replied.
Jehovah said, 'With a plumb-line I test my people;
Never again will I pardon them,
but Isaac's heights shall be laid waste,
the shrines of Israel shall be ruined,
and I will attack Jeroboam's house with the sword.'

[1] Amos vii. 1–9; viii. 1–2 (Moffatt).

> The Lord Jehovah showed me this,
> a basket of ripe fruit.
> Then said He,
> 'Amos, what do you see ?'
> 'A basket of ripe fruit,' said I ;
> and Jehovah said to me,
> 'So is the doom ripe for my people Israel ;
> never again will I pardon them.'"

How these pictures came to Amos is a question on which it would be unwise to dogmatize. The vision of fire and the vision of the plumb-line may plausibly be regarded as instances of creative imagination become vivid to the point of visual hallucination, though in both cases it is possible or likely that things actually seen (in the real world) have helped to determine the form of the vision. Of these two more presently. The basket of fruit certainly may well have been an actual object which met the prophet's eye in contemplative mood and took significance from his thoughts. The ravages of locusts were an all too familiar sight, and Amos may well have experienced the horror of a specially devastating attack. But we must beware of the prosaic interpretation, into which commentators are easily betrayed, which assumes that Amos literally believed that this particular attack of locusts was destined to be the means of the final destruction of Israel, but for his intercession. Rather we must suppose that for reasons belonging to the state of the man's mind more than to the external world, this particular sight kindled emotion and clothed itself with symbolic meaning.

An old Oxfordshire villager, well known to me many years ago, told how in his youth he was much affected by apprehensions of the imminent "end of the world" which were stirred about that time. Standing in the fields at the close of a working day, he saw a cloud of rooks black against the sunset sky, flying into the west. It "came to him" that these birds were heralds of the Lord's coming. But thereupon a voice called him by name, and told him it was not the Lord's will that he should meddle with such matters; he must serve in his appointed place and the Lord would come in His own time. Peace fell upon him, and from that time he had never again been perturbed by eschatological fancies. The psychological process is closely similar in the Oxfordshire peasant and the Hebrew sheep-farmer. The differences between them are in the richness and coherence of the symbolism and in the universal import of the meaning divined. Amos' vision is imaginative, the other merely fanciful, with some resemblance to a dream.

All poets have something of this faculty of seizing symbolic meaning in common things, and the philosophic poet is aware that it is something inward and personal that gives, or at least releases, the meaning.

> "The clouds that gather round the setting sun
> Do take a sober colouring from the eye
> That hath kept watch o'er man's mortality;
> Another race hath been, and other palms are won.
> Thanks to the human heart by which we live,
> Thanks to its tenderness, its joys, and fears,
> To me the meanest flower that blows can give
> Thoughts that do often lie too deep for tears."

Now for the prophets all things take their "colouring" from an eye that has kept watch over God's ways with man. The predominant religious interest asserts itself in the prophetic apprehension even of common things, and clothes them with its own meanings.

We meet this symbolizing power in the prophets in differing degrees of intensity. Take Jeremiah's account of his visit to the potter's shop—literary ancestor of a numerous posterity, from Paul to Omar Khayyam.[1] The poetical element here is small. We have a plain story, whose truth to actual fact we need not question. "He found himself" (writes Skinner[2]) "one day in a potter's work-

[1] Jer. xviii. 1–4. [2] *Prophecy and Religion*, p. 162.

shop in the lower quarter of Jerusalem, intently watching the process by which he deftly fashioned on the wheel out of one clay different vessels just as he chose. He saw that the potter was not always immediately successful. Something would go wrong, and then he would squeeze the clay into a shapeless lump and start afresh, till he attained the result he sought. The prophet's thoughts were at this time occupied with the problem of his people's fate ; and a sudden inspiration revealed to him the analogy between the work of the potter and Yahwe's dealings with Israel. He realized that it was no chance impulse that had moved him to go down to the potter's house that day ; he had been led thither by the hand of God that he might receive the message enunciated : 'Can I not like this potter do with you, house of Israel ? Behold, like potter's clay are ye in my hand ' ". What we have here is the simple observation of an object, followed by the "sudden inspiration" which seizes the meaning of it. But the process is slower and more reflective than in the cases we have been considering. We are at a lower level of intensity. The perception of the object and the perception of the meaning are not yet fused into a simultaneous experience which deserves the name of vision.

On occasion Jeremiah too saw things and their meaning in that same rapid flash of vision. He saw a branch of almond —and who can see its lovely blossom clothing the bare boughs at the end of winter without some lightening of heart ? The Hebrews called it *shākēd*—"the waker", probably as the first tree to wake in the spring. This is how the prophet tells of it.[1] "The word of Jehovah came unto me, saying, 'Jeremiah, what seest thou ?' And I said, 'I see the rod of an almond-tree (*shākēd*).' Then said Jehovah unto me, 'Thou hast well seen, for I am wakeful (*shōkēd*) over my word to perform it ' ". Again, when the Scythian terror was on the horizon the prophet chanced to

[1] Jer. i. 11–12 (R.V. altered).

be watching a boiling pot. "The word of Jehovah came unto me the second time, saying, 'What seest thou ?' And I said, 'I see a seething cauldron, and the face thereof is from the north.' Then Jehovah said unto me, 'Out of the north evil shall come upon all the inhabitants of the land. For lo, I will call all the families of the Kingdoms of the North. . . . And I will utter my judgments against them (the Jews), touching all their wickedness'".

In all these cases what has happened is essentially the same: a religious idea has projected itself upon things seen and made them symbolic of a meaning. The difference lies in the intensity of the emotion with which the idea is suffused and the consequent measure of imagination evoked.

We now turn to the remaining two of Amos' visions, those of the fire and of the plumb-line, in which the element of sensible perception is at any rate much smaller, and the imagination is working more freely. It is, indeed, by no means impossible that while the mind of the prophet was concentrated on religious ideas, his eye subconsciously caught sight of a builder with a plumb-line—a most irrelevant object, one might have supposed—but the poetic imagination immediately worked it into the material of a vision substantially produced from within by the projection of ideas in a symbolic form. The mental process is familiar enough. Francis Thompson describes in a passage of rich imagery his dereliction in London, how he

> "Stood bound and helplessly
> For Time to shoot his barbèd minutes at me;
> Suffered the trampling hoof of every hour
> In night's slow-wheeled car;
> Until the tardy dawn dragged me at length
> From under those dread wheels."

His biographer[1] has shown with much probability how the

[1] F. Meynell, *Life of Francis Thompson*, p. 91. He speaks of Thompson's "habitual appropriation of things seen for his poetic images," and gives another example.

details of these images were supplied—hardly consciously —by the experiences of nights on the streets, amid "the heavy traffic of Covent Garden harassing the straggler in the gutter". Even the arrow-like hand of a neighbouring clock may have helped to mould the vision of Time the Archer. In some such way the imagination of Amos may have turned to account some accidental observation. But the spring of the whole vision is the inward thought. The prophet is brooding upon God and His inexorable righteousness. Instead of being moved to express his thoughts in arguments or theological propositions, he "sees" the Lord with his plumb-line, testing by His unerring judgment the ways of His sinful people.

A more notable example of this kind of imagination is Isaiah's inaugural vision, perhaps the most perfect expression in all literature of the idea of "holiness".[1] The young prophet is worshipping in the court of the Temple. Before his waking eyes are the smoking altar and the figures of winged serpents (seraphim) placed, as such symbolic figures are placed in Babylonian temples known to us, as guardians of the approach to the divine Presence. All this he sees with the bodily eye, but his mind is so possessed with the sense of God's majesty that it projects a vision in which the sensible objects before him are taken up into an imaginative picture (probably amounting to a visual hallucination) of Jehovah Himself enthroned in His temple and adored by supernatural beings. The idea creates the vision, but it does so only because it is powerfully suffused with "numinous" emotion.

There is no difference in principle between a vision of this type and one in which the mind works in complete independence of any immediate sense-stimulus, and creates its own picture out of its own store of imagery. Such image-material is of course ultimately derived

[1] Isa. vi. 1–8.

from sensible experience, but it can be used by the imagination with perfect freedom, as we all know from our dreams. This is indeed the most common form of prophetic vision, and it has many varieties. The freedom gained by detachment from any present outward stimulus makes it possible for the idea to develop itself in a sustained dramatic scene rather than a momentary picture. Hosea's representation of the history of Israel as the story of an unfaithful wife is in essence a visionary drama of this kind.[1] The creative idea is that of Jehovah's well-nigh incredible love for a sinful people, and the emotion with which it is entertained is sharpened by the prophet's own experience of his broken marriage. Ezekiel similarly, though with less deep feeling and obviously inferior imagination in its laboured detail, tells the story of Jehovah's relations with Jerusalem in a sustained narrative of a foundling child who proved ungrateful to her benefactor.[2]

As the past dealings of God are thus dramatically conceived, so His future dealings may be, and then we get the characteristic predictive vision. The poems of Jeremiah and Ezekiel, from which this discussion started, are of this kind. An earlier example is the finely imaginative poem (or series of poems) in Isaiah ii. 10—iii. 15. The whole is dominated by Isaiah's characteristic conception of God—the idea of His majesty, His holiness, His righteousness, in necessary and eternal reaction against human arrogance and presumptuous wickedness. We may compare the repeated theme of the Greek tragedians—the divine "jealousy" which breaks out against insolent pride (ὕβρις).

This is, indeed, the true character of predictive prophecy in its classical exponents. The *nabi* had a reputation as a "seer" of future events,[3] and this was inherited from him by the prophets. It is, indeed, possible that some of them possessed "second sight", whatever that may be—the

[1] Hosea ii. 2–23. [2] Ezek. xvi. [3] Cf. 1 Sam. ix. 6.

apparent power of foreseeing in hallucinatory form that which will shortly happen. But supposing this to be possible, it obviously has no more value than a vivid recollection of what has already happened, unless it be derived from some deeper insight into the tendencies of things and into the spiritual principles which govern them.[1] Jeremiah's count against the *nabis* to whom he was opposed was that they foresaw victory and prosperity for Israel apart from any moral or spiritual basis.[2] They were the successors of those whom Amos knew, who promised a "Day of Jehovah" bringing "light" and triumph over enemies to a people unashamed and unrepentant in their sin.[3] Jeremiah would have had to include in his condemnation many of those unknown writers who have interpolated among the sombre utterances of the great prophets optimistic promises of unconditioned bliss. Jeremiah's own visions of ultimate bliss (in chapters xxx–xxxi[4]) are as strictly the expression of moral principle as his earlier denunciations of woe. They are imaginative presentations of what God must do because of what He is, righteous and gracious, loving His own to the end.

The predictions of the great prophets then we must regard neither as mere "second-sight" nor as a deliberate presentation in mythical form of their logical inferences about the future from the present—after the manner of Mr. H. G. Wells' romances of the future. They are an imaginative and poetical form of apprehending certain ideas about God in relation to the movement of history. It is only in later apocalyptic that the predictive vision develops into a kind of pious fortune-telling, where a quasi-scientific method of dream-interpretation is made to yield precise data of time and place for future happenings.

[1] Cf. N. Micklem, *Prophecy and Eschatology*, p. 146.

[2] Jer. xxiii. 16–18.

[3] Amos v. 18.

[4] Some critics regard these chapters as the work of a later prophet, but probably without sufficient reason.

We have so far considered the prophetic form of experience chiefly as visual imagination. But many of the examples we have already studied include things "heard" as well as things "seen". Thus in Isaiah's inaugural vision the voices of Jehovah and His attendants, and the prophet's own responses, are essential to the drama. Similarly, in Ezekiel's vision of the Valley of Bones the "word of Jehovah" spoken at His bidding by the prophet, sets the whole scene in action.[1] Sometimes the whole drama falls into dialogue form, as in a fine anonymous fragment placed among the prophecies of the "Third Isaiah", full of the power, majesty, and terror of God:[2]

> "Who is this that cometh from Edom,
> With dyed garments from Bozrah?
> This that is glorious in his apparel,
> Marching in the greatness of his strength?
>
> '*I that speak in righteousness,*
> *Mighty to save*'.
>
> Wherefore art thou red in thine apparel,
> And thy garments like him that treadeth in the winefat?
>
> '*I have trodden the winepress alone,*
> *And of the peoples there was no man with me;*
> *Yea, I trod them in my anger,*
> *And trampled them in my fury;*
> *And their lifeblood is sprinkled on my garments,*
> *And I have stained all my raiment.*'"

—or in this sixth-century oracle on Edom;[3]

> "One calleth unto me out of Seir;
> '*Watchman, what of the night?*
> *Watchman, what of the night?*'

[1] Ezek. xxxvii.

[2] Isa. lxiii. 1–3 (R.V.). Duhm and others emend the proper names, and read, "Who is this that cometh stained red; redder in garments than a grape-gatherer?"

[3] Isa. xxi. 11–12 (R.V. corrected after G. B. Gray).

The watchman said ;
'*The morning hath come—*
And the night too ;
Would ye enquire, enquire,
Come back again !' "

Hallucination or not, the dialogue is clearly imaginative experience and not literary artifice.[1]

In Jeremiah's story of his call there is still less of imagery or dramatic setting. We have little but the pure colloquy of the soul with God :[2]

" Now the word of Jehovah came to me, saying,
'*Before I formed thee in the belly I knew thee,*
And before thou camest out of the womb I sanctified thee ;
I have appointed thee a prophet to the nations.'

Then said I,
'*Oh, Lord Jehovah ! Behold I cannot speak ; I am too young.*'

But Jehovah said unto me,
'*Say not, I am too young ;*
For to whomsoever I send thee thou shalt go,
And whatsoever I command thee thou shalt speak.
Be not afraid because of them ;
For I am with thee to deliver thee,
Saith Jehovah.'

Then Jehovah put forth his hand and touched my mouth ; and Jehovah said to me,
'*Behold I have put my words in thy mouth :*
See, I have this day set thee over the nations,
And over the kingdoms :
To pluck up and to break down,
To destroy and to overthrow ;
To build and to plant ' ".

[1] There is something curiously dream-like about this second passage in its combination of emotional vividness and intellectual inconclusiveness. It may or may not be, as the commentators suggest, that the seer had been consulted by a deputation of Edomites and had to put them off, but I refuse to accept the oracle as a mere extract from the day-book of an enquiry bureau. We may contrast with these the frigid conversations with the "*angelus interpretans*" in any apocalypse.

[2] Jer. i. 4–10 (R.V. slightly altered).

That this is direct imaginative experience does not admit of question. We may readily suppose that the words and the touch on the lips were actual hallucinations. The creative idea is simply the intense conviction of vocation, struggling against inhibitions in the prophet's mind. The struggle itself raises the accompanying emotion to a greater heat, and the conflict dramatizes itself in the imagination. The crisis takes the form of a vividly felt "touch" upon the lips—the touch of God himself. Parallels for such solution of a conflict could readily be supplied from dream-psychology; but here all that is fantastic or dream-like is refined away; the whole experience is rational and coherent. We must bear in mind that the expression "I have put my words in thy mouth"—pure metaphor to us—is in Hebrew psychology a realistic expression of fact.[1] For the Hebrew, man is not a compound of body and soul (as for the Greek), but an animated body, and each member may be separately animated and controlled. Thus an intense feeling of obligation to speak for God naturally enters consciousness as a sense of divine control of the lips, and this in turn takes the imaginative form of a supernatural touch upon that organ. Exactly in the same way, Isaiah's inward tension between the overwhelming sense of God's holiness and the sense of his own uncleanness is resolved by a touch of the holy fire upon his lips.[2] In each case, however, as with the prophets in general, the actual content of that which the prophet has to proclaim is given in the form of "hearing" God speak.

A simple and instructive passage where a "word" alone resolves the tension in the prophet's mind may be found in the sixth-century Habakkuk:[3]

[1] See H. Wheeler Robinson in *The People and the Book* (ed. by A. S. Peake), p. 365.

[2] Isa. vi. 7.

[3] Hab. ii. 1–3 (Moffatt).

"On my watchtower I will stand,
at my post on the turret,
watching to see what he will say to me,
what answer he will offer to my plea.
Then answered Jehovah,
'*Take this down on your tablets*
plainly, that one may read it at a glance.
the vision has its own appointed hour;
it is ripening, it will flower;
if it be long, then wait,
for it is sure and it will not be late.'"

It is no deliberate artifice but direct imagination that dramatizes the prophet's questioning and expectant attitude of mind, before he is sure that the Lord has spoken, and then reports the oracular voice that brings assurance and counsels patience. The contemporary "Second Isaiah" similarly tells how he "heard" the message he was to proclaim:[1]

"Hark, one saying, '*Call!*'

And I said,
'*What can I call?*
All flesh is grass,
And all its beauty like a wild-flower!
Withers grass, fades flower,
When the breath of Jehovah blows on it.
Surely grass is the people."

[The voice replies]
"*Withers grass, fades flower,*
But the word of our God endureth for ever."

The foregoing study should have prepared us to raise the question, What exactly lies behind the prophetic formula, "Thus saith the Lord"? More correctly it should be rendered "thus spoke Jehovah". In the classical prophets at least it means that the prophet had had an actual personal experience in which he "heard" the words he proclaims uttered by a divine voice, whether we are

[1] Isa. xl. 6–8 (G. A Smith).

prepared to suppose that the hearing took the form of an hallucination under trance conditions, or whether we find it more closely parallel to the creative imagination of the poet. The probability is that it covered a wide range of psychological form. What is essential to it is that an inward conviction accompanied by pure and intense emotion dramatized itself in the prophet's consciousness. He was persuaded of the truth, not by discursive reasoning, but intuitively. As the prophet emotionally possessed by the thought of God " saw " Him in forms created by his imagination, so also he " heard " God's voice, in forms of speech supplied from the like source.

It might seem that in bringing the prophets' apprehension of the " word of the Lord " under the category of " imagination ", we are somehow emptying it of that immediate reality which alone, it might be thought, could guarantee the truth of what they say. It will be well to make it clear, first, that the word " imagination " is here used in the sense which Wordsworth has fixed upon it, in which it is sharply distinguished from mere fancy. The word, he admits, has to be used only " through sad incompetence of human speech " ; it is in truth

> " But another name for absolute power
> And clearest insight, amplitude of mind,
> And Reason in her most exalted mood."

It is interesting to recall that Wordsworth himself names " the prophetic and lyrical parts of the Holy Scriptures, and the works of Milton " as " the grand storehouses of enthusiastic and meditative imagination ".[1] We should wish to add some of his own works to the list. When he speaks of imagination he speaks of that which he knows " from the inside ". To the poet and the prophet the Philistine's contrast of matter-of-fact and " mere imagination " is simply absurd. They are assured that only

[1] Preface to the 1815 edition of his poems.

through imagination can the highest truth be made subject to human comprehension. When, however, we ask whether what any particular poet or prophet says is true, we cannot find a criterion in the imaginative form in which he speaks. In the end we do not believe the prophet *because* he says, "Thus saith the Lord", with however great conviction and sincerity he says it, but for other reasons, to which we shall presently come.

We may, however, properly raise here the question, whether we are to consider it an advantage that the principal writers of the Bible are of this poetic cast, that they write not logically but imaginatively, that they think not discursively but intuitively. The question is part of the larger and more fundamental question of truth in religion. It was said above, in passing, that the truth of religion is more akin to that of art than of science. This point must here be made more definite. We are accustomed in these days to think of truth primarily in terms of scientific statement, with its logical precision and its reliance upon facts directly subject to test by experiment. But this way of knowledge is not the only way. It depends upon measurement of quantity. But reality has not only quantity but quality, or value. If science gives a representation of Reality in terms of quantity, religion, like art, gives it in terms of quality or value.[1]

Now while discursive reasoning is supreme in the quantitative representation of Reality, intuition and imagination play a larger part in the qualitative representation. That is not to say that religion is irrational, for imagination itself is a function of the Reason. It is not even to say that the strictest kind of logical ratiocination is out of place in theology. But the theologian would have nothing to reason about if it were not for the prophet—unless indeed he had himself something of the prophet's gift. The very

[1] See B. H. Streeter, *Reality*, chap. II.

ideas which we must reason about are in this sphere given and appropriated only in imaginative experience.[1] Moreover, religious ideas are to be communicated to any effect only if the person who has grasped them can make us share his own experience. But only the poet (or the artist in other fields) can make us sharers in his experience. This, indeed, is precisely what he *can* do. The famous complaint of the Cambridge mathematician who was induced to read Keats' *Ode to Autumn* is strictly true—"It doesn't prove anything". It would be equally true even of a "theological" poem like *Paradise Lost.* Few of Milton's admirers would have the hardihood to maintain that he reached his ostensible aim, "to justify the ways of God to men". But the poem makes the reader free of a world of the spirit, where power and wonder, beauty and terror abide, beyond the range of all our definitions. He who has lived with Milton awhile in that world knows that he has been on the heights where truth dwells. He may not be able to express in propositions what he has learned, but there is something new in his own experience which must enter into any account he is to give to himself of the ultimate Reality. In like manner we must say that Isaiah's vision of the holiness of God "does not prove anything". But it can make us sharers in an experience of awe which challenges all our workaday assumptions and denials.

The rudimentary psychological analysis here attempted shows that in the prophetic experience we have an elevated idea, suffused with intense emotion, entering consciousness in dramatic forms created by imagination, and uttering itself

[1] Cf. J. MacMurray in *Adventure*, by B. H. Streeter and others, p. 29. "In itself the mystic's experience is not knowledge, but rather a vision of what there is to be known. The vision itself is conditioned in many ways by the social influences, the traditions of thought and activity, the institutions and habits which press continuously upon the mystic's life and mould his consciousness. And if the vision is to issue in knowledge it must find expression and definition in thought and language."

in poetical language. Because of a certain capacity for association in the mind, the language has power to kindle in the hearer or reader the original emotion felt by the prophet, and so to recreate in some measure the whole experience in which the central idea became real and urgent for him.[1] Thus a channel is made through which that idea may enter the reader's mind with something of its original force. Where the idea came from is another question, and the reasons why it became the centre of emotions and stirred imagination to work in just these ways, could only be known if the "subconscious" mind of the prophet himself could be made to yield its secrets. In conscious experience the idea has no history until it emerges in its imaginative form, full-armed like Athena from the head of Zeus.

Psychology, then, can help us up to a point to understand the facts of inspiration. But if we ask how far the experiences it recognizes, and up to a point explains, provide a *valid* representation of Reality, we are out of the domain of psychology. Indeed, the explanation which psychology offers is at one important point so limited that it leaves us with an open question. It has to introduce the concept of the "subconscious" (or "subliminal consciousness", or "unconscious", or "co-conscious", according to the varying nomenclature of different schools). But there is no agreement on the true meaning of this enigmatic concept. The only thing which is clear and agreed is that there is an element in many kinds of imaginative experience which is not fully explicable within the limits of the field of conscious thought at the time of the experience. Some psychologists hold that given sufficient knowledge of all that the subject has passed through from (or even before) birth, it could be shown that everything in the subconscious is a memory

[1] See Lascelles Abercrombie, *The Idea of Great Poetry*, especially lectures I and III, where the analysis of what makes poetry, and great poetry, can in many points be directly and illuminatingly applied to the prophetic writings.

(in some sense) of former experience. Others find it necessary to bring in the experience of other minds, mediated through "telepathy" (another mere name for a process recognized but not understood). Others again speak of a "racial unconscious" upon which the individual draws. There is nothing here to rule out the religious hypothesis that the ultimate source is a Mind beyond the world, communicating with man through imagination, as It also communicates with him through sensible experience in the world of things. The psychologist as such may quite rightly not feel free to adopt any such hypothesis unless and until every other possible one has manifestly failed, since *entia non sunt multiplicanda praeter necessitatem*. But if on general grounds we are driven to hold that our experience as a whole best makes sense on the assumption that there is such a Mind beyond the world, then the simplest interpretation of imaginative experience is to suppose that its awareness of something "received" is not delusive.

But this does not lead to the conclusion that *because* imaginative experience involves an appeal to the unexplained "subconscious", *therefore* it has greater validity than other forms of experience. It only guards against the false conclusion that *because* such experience can be, up to a point, explained psychologically, *therefore* it is not to be accepted as being just as valid in its own sphere as the data of science in their sphere. The true conclusion is that our ultimate beliefs must express that which makes sense of our whole experience, and that the prophets make us sharers in an experience so pure and so elevated, with so urgent a sense of immediate reality in it, that it has the strongest claim to be heard before the court of Reason. But when it comes to be so heard, it is the ideas it embodies, not any longer the mere mode of apprehending them, that must engage our attention.

CHAPTER IV

THE CONTENT OF OLD TESTAMENT PROPHECY

THE idea of the "holy" (*qadhosh*), as we have seen, is in the early religion of Israel, as elsewhere, a non-rational idea. It is the idea of a Mystery, completely other than ourselves, which arouses a "numinous" feeling. Religious cultus is the natural outgrowth of this feeling, and the early cultus of the Hebrews bears clearly the marks of its originating impulse. Man expresses his sense of awe instinctively in solemn words and gestures, associated with places and objects which stimulate the numinous feeling. They constitute a ritual which, if the worshipper has confidence that it is rightly performed, may give to the feeling a joyous, serene, or enthusiastic colour. Thus the ancient Hebrews had their joyous festivals at "holy" sites, such as hill-tops ("high places"), spreading trees, and copious springs.

But the Mystery possesses enormous power (*mana*), incalculable in its incidence and its effects. It may be terribly hurtful; it may be marvellously beneficial. It is therefore very necessary to find out and practice such operations as will avert the hostile and promote the friendly activity of the Power. The Hebrews lived in terror that Jehovah might "break forth upon them". They handed down many stories showing how His "holiness" reacted in "wrath". For example, they related how once upon a time one Uzzah had, with the best intentions in the world, thoughtlessly touched the sacred box in which was the presence of Jehovah. The "holiness" in it had so powerfully "broken forth upon Uzzah" that he there and then fell dead: the name of the place "Breaking of Uzzah" stands "to witness if I lie".[1] That put the fear of the Lord into King David, and he was mightily cautious thereafter in all his dealings with the sacred box to do all the right and proper things. "When they that bore the ark of Jehovah had gone six paces he sacrificed an ox and a fatling; and David danced before Jehovah with all his might; and David was girded with a linen vestment . . . and they brought in the ark of Jehovah, and set it in its place inside the tent that David had pitched for it; and David sacrificed burnt-offerings and peace-offerings before Jehovah".[2] All in proper form, one sees; there must be no more playing with fire!

It behoved men therefore to know the rules of "holiness", so far as they could be known, and those were benefactors of the race, to whom was revealed what was "clean" and "unclean", and how to avert the "wrath" which was the reaction of "holiness" against a breach of the rules. Early Hebrew religion had a fairly elaborate system of rules of *tabu* and expiatory rites, whose origin was attributed to Moses, though many of them doubtless were much older than he, while others had grown up later, or had been learned from neighbouring peoples or from the priesthoods of shrines taken from earlier occupants.

It is interesting to observe that the earliest "Ten Commandments" known to us, a code which was authoritative in the southern kingdom at the beginning of the prophetic period, are almost entirely concerned with religious festivals and with rules of *tabu*.

I. Thou shalt worship no other god, for Jehovah, whose name is Jealous, is a jealous god.

II. Thou shalt make thee no molten gods.

III. The feast of unleavened bread shalt thou keep.

IV. All that openeth the womb is mine.

[1] 2 Sam. vi. 6–9. [2] 2 Sam. vi. 13–15, 17 (R.V. slightly altered).

V. Thou shalt observe the Feast of Weeks.

VI. Thou shalt observe the Feast of Ingathering at the year's end.

VII. Thou shalt not offer the blood of my sacrifice with leavened bread.

VIII. The fat of my feast shall not be left over until morning.

IX. The first of the firstfruits of thy ground shalt thou bring into the house of Jehovah thy God.

X. Thou shalt not seethe a kid in its mother's milk.[1]

This is in fact the code which according to the ancient Judaean narrative of the Pentateuch was inscribed by Moses on sacred stones at the dictation of Jehovah Himself.[2] Its relative simplicity suggests that it is very old, though it can scarcely antedate the beginnings of agricultural life in Palestine. It is wholly a ritual code, with no ethical element in it.

This was, however, only the traditional nucleus of a highly developed cult actually practised at this period. From the writings of the prophets, and from the ritual regulations preserved by the meticulous antiquarianism of the later Priestly Code, we can form an idea of the elaborate, costly, and impressive ceremonial which for the eighth-century Israelite expressed the awful holiness of his God. Imposing buildings, symbolic imagery, troops of priests and devotees, solemn processions and dances, music and liturgical speech, but above all the perpetual spectacle of ritual slaughter with its thrilling horror of newly shed blood (sometimes human blood)[3],— all nurtured a highly emotional "fear of Jehovah" devoid of any necessary rational or ethical

[1] Exod. xxxiv. 14–26. In the text as it stands there are more than ten commandments, the original list having been expanded by commentary and by interpolation from other codes. The above reconstruction is Wellhausen's.

[2] Exod. xxxiv. 27–28.

[3] Judges xi. 30–40; 2 Kings xvi. 3, xxiii. 10; Micah vi. 7; Jer. vii. 31; Ezek. xx. 26. The prophets discountenance the practice, but their claim that it had not been part of the early religion of Jehovah seems to be disproved by Exod. xxii. 29. An animal substitute is allowed in Exod. xxxiv. 20 (cf. Gen. xxii. 13), and human sacrifice is forbidden in Deut, xviii. 10.

element. More and more religion came to mean the impressive ritual celebrated at the "carved stones" of Gilgal, the sacred well of Beersheba, or, later, the awful splendour of Solomon's lordly fane at Jerusalem, or the bull-temples of Bethel and Dan. There the majesty of Jehovah was shown forth, and thither in times of popular excitement or danger the worshippers thronged to avert the wrath or to celebrate the favour of the national God.

Then Amos came to Bethel. Priests and worshippers heard him with incredulous astonishment.[1]

"Here is Jehovah's message for the house of Israel:

"Seek me and you shall live.
Seek not Bethel,
go not to Gilgal,
cross not to Beersheba. . . .
Seek Jehovah and live,
lest he set Joseph's house ablaze with fire
that none can quench in Israel.

Your sacred festivals? I hate them, scorn them;
your sacrifices? I will not smell their smoke;
you offer me your gifts? I will not take them;
you offer fatted cattle? I will not look at them.
No more of your hymns for me!
I will not listen to your lutes.

Go to Bethel, go on with your sins!
Pile sin on sin at Gilgal!
Aye, sacrifice in the morning,
and every third day pay your tithes,
burn your dough as a thankoffering,
announce your freewill gifts—
oh, make them public,
for you love all that, you Israelites!

I saw the Lord standing beside the altar;
'Strike the pillars on the top', said he,
'that the ceiling may be shaken,
break them on the heads of all the worshippers . . .
My eye will be upon them
for evil, not for good'".

[1] Amos v. 4–6, 21–23; iv. 4–5; x. 1, 4 (Moffatt).

In thus attacking the cult Amos believed himself to be harking back to an older and purer form of the religion of Jehovah[1]. He was probably justified in his belief, at least in a measure, and the tradition of the simpler worship of an earlier day was doubtless sufficiently alive for his denunciations to find some response in the popular conscience. But in relation to the religion officially practised at the time, his criticism was radical, and it is no wonder that Amaziah, the priest of the "royal chapel", sent him packing for a dangerous agitator[2]. Yet Amos was far from being the fanatical nihilist he appeared to the priest. Certainly he had no less keen a sense than Amaziah himself of the awful holiness of God. The true "numinous" note is heard all through his prophecies. But it is a holiness that reacts not against breaches of irrational *tabu*, but against definite and intelligible moral and social wrongs.[3]

"They trample down the poor like dust,
and humble souls they harry;
father and son go in to the same girl—
a profanation of my holy shrine!
They loll on garments seized in pledge
by every altar;
they drink the money taken in fines
in the temple of their God.

Listen to this, you men who crush the humble
and oppress the poor,
muttering, 'When will the new-moon be over,
that we may sell our grain?
When will the sabbath be done,
that our corn may be on sale?'
Small you make your measures,
large your weights,
you cheat by tampering with the scales—
and all to buy up innocent folk,
to buy the needy for a pair of shoes,
to sell the very refuse of your grain.
Jehovah has sworn by the pride of Jacob,
'Never will I forget what you have done.'"

[1] Amos v. 25. [2] Amos vii. 10–13. [3] Amos ii. 7–8; viii. 4–7 (Moffatt).

While this sort of thing goes on, in fact, the most gorgeous solemnities and the most appalling rites of expiation do nothing to protect men from the " wrath " of an outraged holiness. Jehovah demands not ritual, but simple justice :[1]

> " Let justice well up like fresh water,
> let honesty roll in full tide."

Like Amos in the north, Isaiah in the south scourged the futility of the sacred rites—the sacrifices of bulls and goats, the fasts and festivals, the solemn prayers, and all the weary " temple-tramping ".[2] Certainly there was never a man more possessed by the sense of " holiness ". His most habitual name for God is " the Holy One ", and his highest ideal for his people is that

> " They shall sanctify the Holy One of Jacob,
> and shall stand in awe of the God of Israel ".[3]

But the only true way to " sanctify " God is to yield Him moral obedience ; for

> " The Lord of Hosts is exalted in judgment,
> and God the Holy One is sanctified in righteousness."[4]

The trivialities of an artificial cult are irrelevant to the awful reality of such holiness, which demands a life of righteousness in men. " Profanity " (that is, the reverse of holiness) is not breach of *tabu*, but moral iniquity.[5]

This is the theme of all the great prophets. Hosea crystallizes the matter in a verse[6] :

> " I desire mercy and not sacrifice,
> And the knowledge of God more than burnt-offerings ",

and a century later an anonymous prophet of the south finds for the idea perfect and final expression :[7]

[1] Amos v. 24 (Moffatt). [2] Isa. i. 10–15 *et passim*. [3] *Id.* xxix. 23.
[4] *Id.* v. 16. [5] *Id.* ix. 17. [6] Hosea vi. 6. [7] Micah vi. 6–8

"Wherewith shall I come before Jehovah ?
and bow myself before the high God ?
Shall I come before him with offerings,
with calves of a year old ?
Will Jehovah be pleased with thousands of rams,
or with ten thousands of rivers of oil ?
Shall I give my firstborn for my transgression,
the fruit of my body for the sin of my soul ?

He hath shewed thee, O man, what is good,
and what doth Jehovah require of thee,
But to do justly and to love mercy,
and to walk humbly with thy God ?"

With that great utterance religion has taken a decisive turn. There is no going back on that.

It is to us so much a commonplace that religion involves morality that we can scarcely feel the force of this tremendous discovery. Ancient religion indeed regularly provides sanction for tribal custom, as it is the fullest expression of the corporate life of the tribe. And the religion of Jehovah, as we have seen, early formed a rallying centre for the more heroic and austere side of Hebrew life. But always in this religion as in other religions the centre lay elsewhere—in the mysterious, the irrational, the unethical. In classical Greece the moralists found religion their enemy. In India to-day no one looks to the temples as the strongholds of public morals. Confucius made "virtue" (*Te*) a power in China by dissociating his teaching from the superstitious religion of his time. It is the Hebrew prophets who most clearly and uncompromisingly asserted that the holy *is* the righteous, and worship itself a sham apart from the intention to be and to do good.

It is indeed not quite clear how far the denunciations of the cult are to be understood as a root-and-branch condemnation of any ritual whatever. It is certainly difficult to discover any kind of sympathy for ritual worship in Amos, Isaiah, Micah, or Jeremiah. Amos and Jeremiah even take the view that sacrifice was no part of the original worship of Jehovah.[1] Hosea on the other hand sometimes speaks (with doubtful consistency) as though the abolition of sacrifice, sacred pillar, oracular " ephod ", and household images were a punishment for the abuse of what might have been good things, and perhaps may be restored when Israel has learnt the true essence of religion.[2] The Deuteronomists, here as elsewhere more closely affiliated to Hosea than to any other prophet, believed themselves to be applying the main principles of prophetic teaching in a reformation which included the purifying of the cult from abuses. Not till Ezekiel, however, do we find a prophet whole-heartedly accepting a purified cult as an integral part of religion.

But even if we should allow that the greater prophets in general did not contemplate a purely spiritual worship divorced from any outward form, yet it remains true that they took the momentous step of making holiness a moral ideal. Once that was established, there was room for indefinite advance ; for it brought the fundamental religious idea within the field of reason and judgment. If religion means the stimulation and satisfaction of " numinous " emotion by thrilling ceremonial, or the averting of hostile *mana* by apotropaic rites, then it is something outside reason, not subject to value-judgment, and alien from the ordered life of human society. It can develop only by becoming ever more fantastic and appalling, ever less in touch with social and rational values, till we arrive at the level of Aztec religion or some of the Indian cults. But if the " numinous " feeling can be redirected or " sublimated " so that the most profound awe is felt for that which is morally perfect, then though the Object of worship remains in Its perfection beyond the reach of our apprehension, yet the social life of man, as ethically valued and guided, becomes the true field of religion, because it is " of one

[1] Amos v. 25 Jer. vii. 22–23. [2] Hosea ii. 11, iii. 4.

substance " with that which is most truly divine. We are then dealing with that which we can understand, criticize, and control by the orderly processes of reason. Religious emotion becomes a moral and social force, while it is itself elevated and deepened by being associated with man's noblest part. The more realistically and concretely the religious mind can envisage the ethical stuff of life, the more powerful is the ameliorating effect upon religion itself and upon social morals. The prophets are realist and concrete to the utmost in their religious valuation of the life of their time. Their descriptions enable us to form a vivid picture of their world, and their criticisms build up an intensely concrete and definite social ideal. What they condemn as an affront to God's holiness is inhumanity, arrogance, dishonesty, falsehood, self-indulgence, greed, disloyalty, and the like. What they demand as God's rightful service is kindness, justice, chivalry towards the weak and suffering, integrity in business and social relations, incorruptibility in the administration of the law, honour in politics, and such simple, reasonable, practical virtues as are the basis of a sound society.

Very striking is their insistence on fundamental truth and clear-sightedness in matters of morals. The virtue of a ritual religion is scrupulosity ; the virtues of ethical religion are intelligence and sincerity. Isaiah accuses his contemporaries of calling evil good and good evil.[1] They have made lies their refuge, and under falsehood they have hid themselves.[2] Hosea complains that Ephraim is like a silly dove, without understanding ; liquor and lust have deprived the people of their wits.[3] In " lack of knowledge " both these prophets find the cause of national downfall.[4] The knowledge they desiderate is, of course, quite other than that technique of ritual observance which Isaiah says the people

[1] Isa. v. 20.
[2] Isa. xxviii 15.
[3] Hos. viii. 11, iv. 11.
[4] Isa. v 13 ; Hos. iv. 6.

had learned by rote.[1] It is knowledge of God in terms of His moral and spiritual demands. Such knowledge, they hold, is natural to man if he is sincere and open-minded: ignorance of God is against nature.[2]

> "The ox knoweth his owner
> and the ass his master's crib;
> Israel doth not know,
> my people doth not consider."

Jeremiah pronounces this ethical understanding of God's nature the most precious of all attainments:[3]

> "Let not the wise man glory in his wisdom,
> neither let the mighty man glory in his might;
> let not the rich man glory in his riches,
> but let him that glorieth glory in this,
> that he understandeth and knoweth me—
> that I am Jehovah,
> which exercise lovingkindness, judgment, and righteousness in the earth;
> for in these things I delight, saith Jehovah."

When once men begin to think of God in terms of their own highest values, superstition is vanquished.

Enough has been said to suggest how tremendous a step in human development was taken by the prophets who reinterpreted the holy in terms of the morally excellent. It was a new, a creative idea. It must be repeated that the idea of holiness in itself could not have brought forth this conception. In itself it is more apt to develop a religion like that of ancient Mexico—a religion of blood, terror, and slavery. Nor again do the prophets come to it by argument from step to step. Indeed it is hard to see how so fundamental an idea could be reached by argument (that it can be defended by argument is another matter). The prophets themselves say that they *saw* that Jehovah, the Holy One, is a God of righteousness; that they *heard* Him say that

[1] Isa. xxix. 13 (R.V. mg.). [2] Isa. i. 3 (R.V.). [3] Jer. ix. 23–24 (R.V.).

He desires mercy and not sacrifice. It is clear that the idea *came* to them; and if we believe in God at all, we may well accept their conviction that it came to them from God, not because of the imaginative form in which so lofty an idea could not but come, but because of its inherent truth and worthiness.

We have seen that the prophetic reinterpretation of religion called for insight into the moral demands of God, and this opened the way for an understanding of God Himself in terms of moral values. This leads to the second of the great ideas by which the prophets were inspired—a new and worthier idea of the character of God Himself.

It may perhaps be thought that in following this order of thought we are putting the cart before the horse. Is it not true that men's ideas of the demands of religion depend on their conception of the character of God? In a broad way, yes; but perhaps not so directly as is commonly supposed. On the one hand many backward peoples believe in a remote Supreme Being who is vaguely good, while their actual religious practice is full of abominations. On the other hand it is quite possible for the moral standards of a people, supported up to a point by religious sanctions, to be in advance of the character of the God to whom they appeal. If God, as the object of the "numinous" feeling, is Mystery, "completely other" than ourselves, it may be precisely in this that He is other—that He may act in ways which human morality would repudiate. It is thus that the moral standards of Homer's heroes are an improvement on those of Olympus, and that there must be thousands of worshippers of Krishna who would never stoop to the conduct they attribute to him. Is there not a story of a Calvinist preacher who explained that "the Almighty is compelled to do many things in his official capacity which He would scorn in His private capacity"? Indeed the question might be raised whether at the present time the next step in human morals is not being hindered, particularly in regard to the penal system and to war, by a lingering belief among Christians that God treats His enemies in ways in which we are already ashamed of treating our own?[1] The necessary condition of wholesome development in religion and ethics is that the idea of God which is central to worship should be kept in close and constant touch with rational morals.

It may often be that a higher conception of God comes by following out the implications of moral demands of which the conscience has already become aware. It was partly so in Israel. Jehovah, as we have seen, started with the inestimable advantage of having a decided character of his own. The naïve anthropomorphism of early ideas about Him was of great value and significance for subsequent development. Though He had the "numinous" qualities of mystery and terror in a high degree, yet Jehovah the God of Armies was always personal enough, individual enough, to challenge comparison between His ways and the ways of men. In early nomadic days the conception of Jehovah as a heroic warrior gave sanction to the martial virtues of desert tribes. In Canaan He all but lost His personal identity. He inherited cults quite alien from the spirit of His religion. He was identified or confused with local Els and Baals whose "personality" was a fluctuating quantity, till no one knew whether there was one Jehovah among a multitude of Baals, or a multitude of Jehovahs who were also Baals. (That is why the Deuteronomic reformers laid down the fundamental article of belief in the form, "Jehovah thy God is *one* Jehovah".[2]) In the midst of such disintegration His faithful devotees could only hold on with obstinate conservatism to the antique ideas of the desert. *Nabis*,

[1] See Lily Dougall, *God's Way with Man*, Essay IV

[2] Deut. vi. 4.

Nazirites,[1] Rechabites[2] all have reactionary or atavistic traits, and the Jehovah whom they pitted against the more civilized deities of farm, market, and city has something of the uncouth look of a fighting squire from an older time, scorning the softness of courtiers and the wiliness of prosperous hucksters, yet a little awkward and self-conscious in their presence. Civilization was divorced from the traditional religion, and religion suffered as well as civilization. That is one reason why the conception of the character of Jehovah in the ninth-century prophets shows so little advance on that of the period of the Judges, if it does not show actual decline. In the ninth century Jehovah is still cruel, capricious, irritable, unjust (by human standards of justice), and untruthful. In early days such faults might pass in the character of a superhuman tribal chief, magnificent in courage and might, loyal to his clansmen, royally generous in his gifts, stern in discipline and crafty in counsel. Civilized times and a settled social order demanded something more. Melkart of Tyre no more than the Baals of Canaan could hold out any hope of a higher morality.

The prophets of the classical period brought the overdue advance in ideas of Jehovah's character. As they led religion out of the twilight of fantasy into the wholesome light of rational values, it was clear to them that God must Himself be at least as good as they saw He expected men to be, however difficult it might be to recognize human standards of conduct in a superhuman person.

The prophets' remoulding of the idea of God is indeed, as we must frankly confess, partial. There is more perhaps in their conception of the divine character which we should wish to correct than in their ethical ideals for human society. Yet certain dominant conceptions they did once for all establish.

[1] Amos ii. 11–12; Judges xiii. 5, xvi. 17: the regulations in Num. vi. are a perpetuation of ancient custom in modern ritual forms.

[2] Jer. xxxv. 2–11; 2 Kings x. 15–17.

First, the prophets tell us that God is not capricious but consistent in His actions. It seems to have been extremely difficult for men to conceive of a really consistent divine character. We can partly understand why. If the divine is simply the "completely other", we may give up the attempt to find any principle in its actions. If it represents mere power raised to a high degree—ancient peoples are familiar with power in their chiefs, asserting itself characteristically by way of irresponsible and arbitrary action. The literature which antedates the great prophets is full of examples of divine caprice. Thus Jehovah accepted Abel's sacrifice and rejected Cain's, just because He so chose.[1] He called Moses in the desert, and gave him the most signal tokens of His favour and confidence, and then before he reached Egypt, "Jehovah met him and sought to kill him".[2] David was puzzled to account for Saul's malignity towards him. "If it be Jehovah", he said, "that hath stirred thee up against me, let him smell an offering, but if it be the children of men, cursed be they before Jehovah!"[3] Elijah had to reproach his God for causelessly killing the son of the good widow to whom He had sent him, and by mingled expostulations, appeals, and "symbolic" practice induced Him to reverse His action.[4] In the pre-prophetic literature such non-moral traits appear alongside of those higher conceptions of the character of Jehovah which were present from an early stage of the religion of Israel.[5]

In contrast to all this the prophets make the sublime assumption that God does act on principle. It may be difficult to discover and define the principle of His action in particular cases, but He is never merely capricious, and never inconsistent with Himself. He has a settled purpose, and will not be moved from it. "He also is wise," says Isaiah, "and will not call back His words". The idea is

[1] Gen. iv. 4–5 (J). [2] Exod. iv. 24. [3] 1 Sam. xxvi. 19.
[4] 1 Kings xvii. 20–22. [5] See chap. II, p. 54.

finely expressed in a phrase put into the mouth of Samuel by his seventh-century biographer: "The Strength of Israel is not a man that He should repent".[1] The "otherness" of God is here invoked in a remarkable way. Contrary to general belief at the time, God is unlike man, *not* in exercising a royally irresponsible power, but in being perfectly self-consistent. He is too far above human variableness to be moved from His course by "smelling an offering". So averse are the great prophets from the idea of mollifying an offended Deity and persuading Him to change His plans, that they sometimes speak as though prayer and intercession were in vain.[2] In fact there is an unresolved tension between the thought of the unchangeableness of God and the reality of repentance and forgiveness. Yet on this consistency of the divine character is ultimately built up that conception of His trustworthiness or "faithfulness" which is the only sure ground of intelligent faith.[3]

Next, if Jehovah is consistent in His action, there must be some discoverable ground for the "wrath" which He was believed to express in the infliction of misfortune. The idea of the "wrath of God" plays an important part in all religions at a certain stage of development. Behind it lies the primitive conception of the terrible or awe-inspiring manifestation of the "holy"—the *mysterium tremendum*. It is neither personal, rational, nor moral. At the anthropomorphic stage this reaction of the "holy" is conceived as the devastating anger of a tremendously powerful Being, who is naturally prone to just such unreasonable tantrums as one knows in one's tribal chief. One hastens to propitiate Him.

The prophets never think of questioning the general

[1] 1 Sam. xv. 29.

[2] Isa. i. 15, xxxi. 2; Micah iii. 4; Jer. vii. 16, xiv. 11–12, xv. 1–2.

[3] The faithfulness of God is one of the recurrent themes of the Psalms; cf. also 1 Cor. i. 9, x. 13; 2 Tim. ii. 13.

belief that misfortune is the result of the wrath of Jehovah. But they cannot allow that He is ever angry without reason. No good man is so. There is a principle in His wrath—the principle of retributive justice. This is the central theme of prophecy in the eighth and seventh centuries. It arouses the most intense emotion in the prophets, and spurs their imagination to its boldest flights. Writing at a period when the outlook was increasingly gloomy, they proclaimed the misfortunes they saw around them to be Jehovah's just punishment for the sin of men—for sin not in the sense of any breach of *tabu*, but in the sense of such well-defined moral wrongs as inhumanity, injustice, and falsehood. Thus Amos reviews a series of recent misfortunes—famine, drought, vegetation-pests, plague, and earthquake. Other observers no doubt agreed with him in attributing them to the wrath of God—and they redoubled their devotion to the sacrificial ritual. Amos announces that Jehovah sent these troubles to warn Israel of His disapproval of their wrong-doing, and that since the warning has brought no improvement things will grow worse until utter destruction comes.[1] Isaiah perhaps had this prophecy of Amos in mind in writing that sombre poem[2] which celebrates present and imminent disasters, with the recurrent refrain,

> "For all this His anger is not turned away,
> But His hand is stretched out still".

Here is the basis of the "eschatology of woe" as we find it in the great prophets. Those may well be right who think that a certain shuddering dread of some ultimate disaster was an element in Hebrew religion from a very early date,[3] though our extant sources do not justify us in saying so definitely. But if it was so, it was no more

[1] Amos iv. 6–12. [2] Isa. ix. 8–x. 4.

[3] So H. Gressmann: *Ursprung der israelitisch-jüdischen Eschatologie.* 1er Teil.

than a mythological form of recording the "numinous" terror of God's irrational "holiness". For the classical prophets it is a "fearful looking for of *judgment*"—the inevitable issue of a just God's resentment of continued wrong-doing. Their visions of appalling catastrophes are an imaginative apprehension of what to them is intuitively certain—that God will visit sin with exact retribution. For their powerful and elemental thinking the issue is as simple as it well can be. Since God is just—do good and all will be well; do evil and destruction will follow.[1]

> "If ye be willing and obedient,
> ye shall eat the good of the land;
> But if ye refuse and rebel,
> ye shall be devoured by the sword—
> for the mouth of Jehovah hath spoken it".

It has been said above that the prophetic imagination, like that of all true poets, is not fantasy, but a function of reason in its widest sense. And here we see that some of the most highly emotional and most imaginatively wrought passages in prophet after prophet are controlled by a central idea which, if we grant their premises, is simple "horse-sense".

The relentless following out of this idea led some of the prophets into almost unrelieved pessimism, which seemed only too fully justified by their nation's fate. Yet the pain of exile raised questions whether the correspondence of desert and punishment were really so exact as the prophetic theology assumed. Moreover, the development of the idea of individual moral responsibility made the doctrine of exact retribution still more difficult to square with facts.[2] Isaiah had stated the principle of retribution very simply and quite generally, having in view the destinies of peoples as corporate wholes. In that sphere it is not difficult to see a broad rhythm of historic movement, which does

[1] Isa. i. 19–20. [2] See especially Ezek. xviii.

exhibit something of that inherent justice of things. Ezekiel applies the principle with characteristic rigidity to the fate of individuals:[1]

"When the righteous man turneth away from his righteousness and committeth iniquity, he shall die because of it; . . . Again when the wicked man turneth away from his wickedness that he hath committed and doeth that which is lawful and right, he shall save his soul alive. . . . Yet saith the house of Israel, The way of the Lord is not equal. O house of Israel, are not my ways equal? are not your ways unequal? Therefore will I judge you, O house of Israel, every one according to his ways."

In the next age, thinkers like the author of Job and some of the Psalmists felt with increasing force the difficulty of justifying that position by the facts of this life—and of course no other life is as yet in view. Indeed, Jeremiah, a clearer though a less rigid thinker than Ezekiel, had himself confessed the difficulty: "Wherefore", he asks, "doth the way of the wicked prosper?"[2] But apart from that painful problem, the religious spirit can never rest content with a bleak "Pelagianism" like Ezekiel's. Even when it cannot see its way to consistency, it insists that God does something more than recognize and duly recompense the goodness or badness of men. It is to the credit of the prophets that they did not let a logical insistence on the justice of God obscure the witness of experience to other sides of His character. To these we shall turn immediately. Yet let us place on record the epoch-making importance (in the strict sense of that abused epithet) of the discovery that a principle of justice is somewhere embedded in the

[1] Ezek. xviii. 26–30. Compare here the Hindu doctrine of Karma, which is the result of a perfectly logical application of the doctrine of retribution, protected from any interference by ideas of the "grace" of God, and extended to an infinite series of lives instead of being confined to one.

[2] Jer. xii. 1. See further chap. VIII, pp. 181–182

divine dealings. The mind of man will not willingly let that discovery drop, however the notion of justice may need to be modified.

If Amos is the pioneer in proclaiming the justice of God, Hosea has the credit of enunciating the complementary truth of the grace of God. He is indeed as sure as Amos that Jehovah is just and that disaster awaits the guilty people of Israel. Yet when he contemplates the execution of the sentence he feels a "stop in his mind". He had loved a woman. They married and she bore him children. Then she left him for another man, and fell into degradation. And yet he found he loved her still.[1] How then could Jehovah abandon His people? "When Israel was a child, then I loved him".[2] If that is true, and if a good man could not throw over the wife he loved, there must be something eternal in the love of God, and the maintenance of His justice could not demand that He should ever hate the sinner.

> "How shall I give thee up, Ephraim?
> How shall I deliver thee, Israel? . . .
> I will not return to destroy Ephraim,
> For I am God and not man—
> The Holy One in the midst of thee."[3]

Once again we have the idea of the "holy"—the mysterious "otherness" of the divine—interpreted in a rational and ethical sense, within the sphere of value. As the author of Samuel appealed to that "otherness" against any thought of human caprice in God, so Hosea appeals to it against any suggestion that God could love more feebly than a man. Just because He is holy, God must needs love beyond the poor capacities of a human heart. Holiness is again being reinterpreted in

[1] Hos. i., iii. 1–3. That this is a true story and no symbolic fiction seems to me, as to most interpreters of the prophet, self-evident, though it is not easy to be sure what the precise facts of the story were.

[2] Hos. xi. 1.

[3] Hos. xi. 8, 9.

terms of the highest human values. It is worth noticing that this process takes place by way of a " sublimation ", as the psychologists say, of sexual experience, and by way of reaction against the sexual degradation of Baal-worship.[1] It would perhaps not be too much to say that we have here the one positive outcome of the disastrous experiment of Israel with that form of worship. There was little trace of " tender emotion " in Jehovah of Sinai. The divinities who competed for His people's worship found a place in their cults for those softer, more feminine elements which his original stern masculinity excluded. Their degraded eroticism was bitterly denounced by the prophets, and by none more bitterly than by Hosea. Yet the conflict with the Baals challenged religious experience to find in Jehovah himself something corresponding to those tenderer elements in man which though they may lend themselves to gross perversion yet provide the stuff for the noblest of human relations.

It is the nature and property of love to have mercy and to forgive ; and through the stern proclamations of Jehovah's relentless justice runs a strain of wistful belief in His mercy. Isaiah was initiated into the prophetic office through an experience which included the sense of forgiveness,[2] and though the message he was then bidden to deliver held out no hope for the guilty nation,[3] yet he never ceased to call for repentance, and he pinned his faith to the watchword, " A remnant will repent ".[4] He gave it as a name to his son, Shear-jashub ; and saw in the little group of his own family and disciples the nucleus of a people on whom Jehovah would yet have mercy. Similarly Jeremiah, with an even more absolute and well-grounded pessimism about the corrupt generation to whom he spoke, nevertheless falls back, when all seems lost, upon the hope of a " new

[1] Hos. ii. 2–8, 12–14, etc.
[2] Isa. vi. 7.
[3] Isa. vi. 9–12.
[4] Isa. x. 21, vii. 3, viii. 16–18, xxxi. 6, etc.

covenant", by which sin will be forgiven, and God's law written on the heart of His people.[1] In both prophets the belief in God's mercy is so imperfectly harmonized with the dominant conception of His justice that it has sometimes been thought necessary to excise the more optimistic utterances as later interpolations, but this is probably going too far. The prophets are not logicians bound by a mechanical consistency. Ezekiel's rigid "Pelagianism" might seem to have left no loophole for unmerited mercy, and yet he cannot rest in it. There is no possible hope of mercy, he thinks, unless men repent and do good. This is indeed the general prophetic belief. But what if they will not repent? Then God (not for their meriting, but "for His own name's sake") will intervene and create in them a "new heart", so that they *will* repent.[2] This is conceived in a crudely supernatural way, but it testifies to the conviction that there must be something in God beyond mere retributive justice. Ezekiel's younger contemporary, the "Second Isaiah", is most definitely in this matter the successor of Hosea. Like him he finds in Jehovah something corresponding to the "tender emotion" in man.

"But Zion said, 'Jehovah hath forsaken me,
  And the Lord hath forgotten me.'
Can a woman forget her sucking child,
  That she should not have compassion on the son of her womb?
Yea, these may forget,
  Yet will I not forget you.[3]

Remember these things, O Jacob,
  And Israel, for thou art my servant:
I have found thee; thou art my servant
  O Israel, thou shouldest not forget me.
I have blotted out as a thick cloud thy transgressions,
  And as a cloud thy sins.
Return unto me,
  For I have redeemed thee."[4]

[1] Jer. xxxi. 31–34.
[2] Ezek. xxxvi.
[3] Isa xlix. 14–15.
[4] Isa. xliv. 21–22 (R.V.).

The mercy of Jehovah is thus in some sort prior to repentance and grounded firmly upon the "faithfulness" of the perfectly good God. As in the earlier prophets the thought of retribution most kindles the imagination, so in this prophet the idea of a righteousness revealed in saving men clothes itself with the emotion which finds imaginative outlet. And it is thoroughly characteristic of the whole prophetic outlook that this merciful and "saving" righteousness is conceived as the chief part of the "otherness" and (as we may fairly call it at this stage of development) the transcendence of God.[1]

> "Let the wicked forsake his way,
> And the unrighteous man his thoughts;
> And let him return unto Jehovah, for he will have mercy upon him,
> And to our God, for he will abundantly pardon.
> For my thoughts are not your thoughts,
> Neither are your ways my ways, saith Jehovah.
> For as the heavens are higher than the earth
> So are my ways higher than your ways
> And my thoughts than your thoughts."

It cannot be said that the prophets of the classical period reached a completely unified conception of the divine character in which justice and mercy find a satisfactory reconciliation. Nor did their successors in Judaism substantially advance the matter. They bequeathed the problem to Christianity to solve. Yet it is a permanent contribution of the prophets to the knowledge of God that they saw with the utmost clearness that if God be other than man He is so in nothing so much as in being more completely just, more utterly loving, and withal more self-consistent than frail humanity can ever be. This they saw, and they have given their vision to the world in imaginative utterance which makes us sharers in their experience.

The prophets then led the way in a reinterpretation of the nature of religion, by moralizing the idea of the holy;

[1] Isa. lv. 7-9 (R.V.).

and in a reinterpretation of the character of God through ethical values. We must now add that they led the way in a new estimate of the scope and range of the divine action. They became in a word the founders of ethical monotheism.

Jehovah was a tribal deity with a local habitation. Yet the fact that He was believed to have adopted His tribe at a point of history by a "covenant" made with them at Sinai, meant that from the outset there was something that transcended a merely natural relation; and His early migration from Sinai to Canaan left Him somewhat freer from strictly local ties than many other gods. But it was still obvious to David that if he went into exile from Canaan he must needs "serve other gods".[1] Even within Canaan the God of Israel had to fight for His position. When Elijah claimed for Him the power to give and withhold rain within Israelite territory,[2] it was a definite encroachment on the province of the Baals. But that belief was still struggling for acceptance in the time of Hosea[3] and later. Nevertheless from a period before the great prophets functions were attributed to Jehovah which had a more than local significance. National legends represented Him as displaying His power even in the land of Egypt, turning the holy Nile itself into blood and drying up the Red Sea.[4] Not only so, but at least in the southern kingdom He was before the eighth century made the subject of creation-legends,[5] and represented as "the judge of all the earth".[6] It is possible that something is due to the fusion of Jehovah of Sinai with the El of Abraham, Isaac, and Jacob,[7] who is thought by some to have been a heavenly Father-god like those of many

[1] 1 Sam. xxvi. 19.

[2] 1 Kings xvii. 1, xviii. 1–2, 17–18, 36–45. It seems clear that after two and a half years of drought the rival deities are called upon to give rain, and Jehovah beats the Baal on his own ground. *See* J. G. Fraser, *Folklore in the O.T.*, p. 340.

[3] Hos. ii. 5, 8–9, 12, 21–22 ; vii. 14 (R.V. mg., cf. 1 Kings xviii. 28).

[4] Exod. vii. 18, 20–21 (JE) ; xiv. 21 (J).

[5] Gen. ii. 4–25 (J).

[6] Gen. xviii. 25.

[7] Exod. iii. 13–15 (E).

primitive religions, such as the Baiame of the Australian aborigines, or at a higher level the Chinese Shang-ti.[1] However this may be, there was latent in the religion of Jehovah the possibility of wider activities than those of a mere tribal god.

But, however wide His sway might be, His interest was bound up with His own people, and whatever powers He possessed were used for the benefit of Israel and the confusion of their enemies. Other nations belonged to other gods, whose existence and might it never occurred to the early Israelites to deny, though they trusted that Jehovah was stronger than they. If temporarily the enemies of Israel prevailed, it was because Jehovah was "wroth" with His people; but certainly He would save them in the end, if only for His own name's sake, since a god without a tribe is in a woeful case. The Day of Jehovah would come, in which He would finally vindicate His power by the destruction of foreigners and the humilation of their gods. Along this line it is possible to arrive at a certain kind of monotheism, but to reach an ethical monotheism a fresh start must be made.

It cannot be doubted that such prophets as Elijah and Elisha held this antique view of the scope of Jehovah's interest and power. Amos made a revolution in religion when he repudiated it.[2]

> "What are you more than Ethiopians,
> O Israelites, Jehovah asks.
> I brought up Israel from Egypt? yes,
> and Philistines from Crete,
> from Kir the Aramæans."

The Day of Jehovah is coming; yes, indeed; but Israel has no cause to welcome it. It will bring the vindication of Jehovah's power, not on behalf of Israel but on behalf of

[1] Söderblom, *Das Werden des Gottesglaubens*, pp. 305–307.
[2] Amos ix. 7 (Moffatt).

righteousness, to Israel's cost.[1] With artful irony the prophet calls the roll of the nations—Damascus, Gaza, Tyre, Edom, Ammon, Moab,—and predicts destruction for their sins at the hands of Jehovah: and then just as his hearers are applauding the prowess of their national God, he turns upon them with the startling words—

> " After crime on crime of *Israel*, I will not relent . . .
> You alone of all men have I cared for,
> Therefore I will punish you for your misdeeds ".[2]

It was extraordinarily bold; but bolder still for Isaiah to proclaim actually in time of war that the Assyrian invader was Jehovah's instrument to do justice upon sinful Judah;[3] boldest of all perhaps for Micah to predict that Zion should be ploughed as a field;[4] and for Jeremiah to declare, in the last crisis of the war of independence with Babylon, that it was Jehovah's will that Judah should go under.[5]

It is doubtful if any government in Europe (or America) during the late war would have been more clement than was Zedekiah in dealing with such blatant *défaitisme*. Yet Zedekiah and the *nabis* who supported the war honestly believed, as had all their fathers, that God had as a matter of course exclusive care for His own tribe, and that nothing could matter to Him so much as the triumph of their cause.[6] We on the other hand recognize (when war fever abates) that God is in fact essentially a God of righteousness, and must care more for Right than for the " rights " of any particular nation. That was first taught by the prophets of Israel. The fact that after 2700 years the conviction is still far from secure in the minds of " Christian " peoples indicates how amazing a discovery it was in the eighth

[1] Amos v. 18–20.
[2] Amos i. 3–ii. 16 (ii. 4–5 being by general consent an interpolation. The translation is Moffatt's).
[3] Isa. x. 5.
[4] Micah iii. 12, cf. Jer. xxvi. 18.
[5] Jer. ix. 11, x. 22, xviii 13–17, xxiv. 8–10, etc.
[6] Jer. xxxvii. 3–xxxviii. 28.

century B.C. It is no wonder that not all prophets were so ruthlessly consistent in drawing out its implications as were Amos and Jeremiah. The wonder is that any of them should have conceived so revolutionary an idea in the world of their time.

It was by this route that the prophets of Israel approached monotheism. Elsewhere one God might attain a lonely supremacy either through the victory of his people over other peoples with their gods ; or through fusion or identification with other gods ; or through the sacrifice of a vividly personal identity to a vague and abstract pantheism. Hebrew monotheism arose through the intuitive perception that a God who is righteous first and last must be as universal as righteousness itself.

In taking the view that God cares first and last for righteousness, the prophets did not mean to deny that " mighty acts " of the living God had indeed been wrought in the history of Israel. There was an overruling Providence in their stormy destinies, serving the purpose of eternal Right. The same Providence had guided Philistines and Aramaeans, and by the same principle of justice Assyria and Moab were judged. Yet the course of Israel's history had represented the main line of providential action. Israel had a certain intimacy with Jehovah, which meant that they were more directly exposed than other folk to His righteous judgments, but also that when they were loyal to Him and to the right, they would experience the most signal tokens of His saving power. Isaiah had an intense conviction that Jehovah, whose glory filled the earth, was enthroned on Zion ; and when he gave to King Ahaz the watchword " Immanuel—God is with us ",[1] it was with the sense that the immediate presence of the righteous God of the whole earth was there, to judge and to save. Again, he proclaimed that Jehovah had brought the Assyrian into

[1] Isa. vii. 10–14, viii. 10.

the land, an irresistible foe to a corrupt people, sunk in luxury and injustice. Entangling alliances and expensive military preparations were all futile.[1] But let the people only repent and do the right, and the holy Presence, a terror to ill-doing, would be their surest shield against calamity.[2] "The Assyrian shall fall with the sword—not of man".[3] It so happened that the Assyrian forces unexpectedly retreated. The fact is certain; the reason remains obscure. Isaiah was remembered, ironically enough, chiefly as the patriotic prophet who had declared the inviolability of Zion[4] —a doctrine against which Jeremiah had to protest with all his might[5], in vain.

Jeremiah indeed was sure that Jehovah was God of the whole earth; and he broke through all local limitations when he assured the exiles in Babylon that they could still worship Jehovah in the fullest sense away from the Holy Land.[6] Yet he too held that the religious community of the future would be continuous with historic Israel.[7] Though that people had contumaciously broken the ancient "covenant" with its God—a covenant so recently renewed with every circumstance of solemnity under Josiah—yet Jehovah would grant a "new covenant", upon a new basis of inward and individual knowledge of God, and it would still be true, in a deeper sense than ever before, that "they shall be my people and I will be their God".[8] In that glorious future pagan peoples also would come to the knowledge of Jehovah, and in some sort be incorporate in His people.[9] Yet a renovated Israel is still the focus of His providence.

There is here an undeniable limitation to the universality

[1] Isa. xxii. 1–14. [2] Isa. xxviii. 16, xxix. 1–8. [3] Isa. xxxi.
[4] Isa. xxxvii. (from a seventh-century biography of the prophet, cf 2 Kings xix.). [5] Jer. vii. 3–15.
[6] Jer. xxix. 1–15, cf. Ezek. xi. 16.
[7] Jer. xxiv. 4–7, xxxii. 6–16, 36–44.
[8] Jer. xxxi. 31–34. [9] Jer. xvi. 19–20.

of God. His rule indeed is universal, and His interest in mankind is universal; yet He works in history primarily through His relations with a particular people. The limitation was inevitable and even salutary at that stage. Monotheism is indeed the ideal form of religion; but even monotheism can be too dearly purchased at the expense of a vivid sense of the personal dealings of God with man in actual history. History is always particular and concrete. If God is a living God whose purpose works in history, then He must have particular relations with a human society. The conception of humanity as one family was not within the range of thought at that period. The idea of a community formed purely upon the basis of individual response to the love of God was only adumbrated by Jeremiah. Thus if the love of God was to remain an effective religious idea, there must be a people in whose history His love for men could in the future, as in the past, be manifested.[1]

> "Yea, I have loved thee with an everlasting love
> Therefore with loving-kindness have I drawn thee."

There was something here too precious to be lost, and Jeremiah served the truth well in holding firmly to his confidence in the loyalty of Jehovah amid the faithlessness of men, a loyalty which for him could only mean that despite all its sins Israel would be granted forgiveness and a renewed opportunity of becoming serviceable to the divine purpose.

Ezekiel was so persuaded of the truth of this that he set forth in exile the outlines of a policy of reconstruction, which indeed in many ways involved a reaction towards ways of religion repudiated by the greatest prophets. His picture of the future is a dramatization of the conception that Jehovah is Lord of the whole world, reigning, however, through His own people, who have direct access to

[1] Jer. xxxi. 3

Him.[1] He was probably the first of the prophets whose names are known to us to give a recognized place in his scheme to the popular hope of an ideal Ruler, or " Messiah ".[2] The " Messianic " prophecies found in the books of Isaiah and Jeremiah are widely held to belong to the period of the Exile ; and we can well understand that when the national dynasty was brought to an end the hope of restoration should have been embodied in the ideal figure of a great King, whether a " righteous Scion " of David, or a superhuman personage. The whole Messianic belief must be understood as an imaginative expression of the conviction that the great God has purposes yet unfulfilled which He must accomplish in and through His people. According to the level of religious belief and experience the idea might become subservient to the most vulgar kind of chauvinism, or to a high ethical monotheism.

This peculiar combination of a belief in the universal sovereignty of God with a highly concrete conception of His particular Providence in history, is found most fully developed in the prophecies which announced the close of the Exile, incorporated in the second part of the Book of Isaiah (commonly referred to as the " Second Isaiah "). It is indeed in these writings that we first recognize monotheism in the strict sense, that is, the belief that Jehovah is not merely the only God whom Israel may rightly worship, and not merely the supreme God of the pantheon, but actually the only God there is. Other so-called gods are mere illusion. " Thus saith Jehovah the King of Israel, and his redeemer Jehovah of hosts : ' I am the first and the last, and beside me there is no God ' ".[3] He is " the everlasting God, the creator of the ends of the earth ".[4] He made man ; He orders the destinies of all peoples, sets up and pulls down their rulers. He used Babylon for His purpose,

[1] Ezek. xl.–xlviii.
[2] Ezek. xxxiv. 23–24, etc.
[3] Isa. xliv. 6–20, cf. xlv. 21–22, xlvi. 9.
[4] Isa. xl. 28.

and when Babylon in pride outstepped the limits of her divine mission, He raised up Cyrus to punish her and to carry further His righteous design.[1]

This righteous design, however, is to be understood by reference to the destinies of Israel. From of old Jehovah chose that people to be the object of His special providence. From the days of Abraham, the Friend of God, He has led Israel.[2] When the people proved false and rebelled against His purpose He "hid His face" in righteous wrath, and gave them over to their enemies for punishment. But He was faithful still to His people, and now that the punishment is complete His ancient kindness reasserts itself, and He will prosper them once more.[3] This hope of restoration is not the unethical self-confidence of the "false prophets". On the contrary, the promises are addressed to them "that know righteousness, the people in whose heart is my law".[4] The righteousness of God is manifested not merely in delivering His people from their foes, but in making them a righteous nation. The whole national history is subordinate to the purpose of eternal right. And the purpose itself extends beyond Israel.

Here a twofold strain reveals itself in the prophet's thought. At times he speaks as though Jehovah's purpose would be fulfilled in the establishment of an Israelite empire superseding the empires of Babylon and Persia, when the nations shall "lick the dust" before the chosen people.[5] But at other times his thought soars higher. He sees Israel as God's "servant" for the enlightenment of the heathen.[6]

> "I Jehovah have called thee in righteousness,
> and will hold thy hand,
> and will form thee and give thee for a covenant of the people,
> for a light of the Gentiles;

[1] Isa. xliv. 21–xlv. 7.
[2] Isa. xli. 8–14.
[3] Isa. xlii. 18–xliii. 11.
[4] Isa. li. 7.
[5] Isa. xlix. 22–26, cf. xliii. 3–4
[6] Isa. xlii. 5–9 (R.V. mg.), cf. li 4–6.

to open the blind eyes,
  to bring out the prisoners from the dungeon,
  and them that sit in darkness from the prison house.
I am Jehovah ; that is my name ;
  and my glory will I not give to another,
  neither my praise to graven images ".

Here the implications of monotheism are clearly drawn. Since Jehovah is the only God, His purpose must be to make Himself known to all peoples. And the reason He called Israel to be His " servant ", and trained him through history in the way of righteousness, was that ultimately Israel might be a missionary nation, bearing witness to the righteousness of God among all peoples. For it is Jehovah's will that all nations shall be saved.[1]

" There is no God else beside me,
  a just God and a saviour.
Look upon me and be ye saved,
  all the ends of the earth ;
for I am God, and there is none else.
By myself have I sworn,
  the word is gone forth from my mouth in righteousness
  and shall not return,
that unto me every knee shall bow,
  every tongue shall swear."

This is the high-water mark of prophetic religion. Obviously there is still a tension between universalism and nationalism, and the Jewish religion never wholly succeeded in resolving it. The two tendencies are in manifest conflict throughout the post-exilic period, and on the whole the narrower tendency is winning. It remained for Christianity to reveal the full implications of monotheism.

The achievement of the prophets is, when all is said, a most remarkable advance in religious ideas. They discovered a God whose divinity is consummately revealed in personal relations with men upon principles intelligible

[1] Isa. xlv. 21–23 (R.V.).

in the light of the highest human values—a God who is both righteous and loving. They saw that as a "living God" He manifests Himself in concrete historical processes. And this righteous and living God they saw to be necessarily universal in His activity. There is but one righteousness, and there can be but one God, if the will of God be indeed the moral absolute. Holding firmly to this belief they were also convinced that His righteous will is the sole finally effective force in the universe. Such an idea of God, emerging from the confusions of antique superstition in early Hebrew religion, we cannot but regard as a revelation of truth itself to the seeking mind of man.

CHAPTER V

THE PERSONAL RELIGION OF THE PROPHETS; THEIR HISTORICAL RELATIVITY

WE have now before us the main creative ideas by which the prophets were inspired. But no estimate of their achievement would be complete which leaves out of account their own personal religious life as a contribution to our knowledge of God. That prophecy is a form of religious experience is not something that goes without saying. Inspiration of a kind may exist apart from anything that we could recognize as religion. The psychic "medium" may display extraordinary powers of suggestibility and automatism, not unlike those of some prophets, without any sense of personal communion whether with God or with the lesser spirits supposed to exercise the control He is as far as may be a passive, impersonal instrument. Not so the prophet. What he speaks is the utterance of a truth that has entered deeply into his own soul first of all, as an element in personal religion.

It is indeed with the great prophets that we first come into direct touch with personal religion. Behind the stories of such ancient leaders as Moses and Elijah we can divine authentic religious experience, but it is a different thing to meet the prophet in his own writings and follow the movings of his spirit in communion with God.

Enough has already been said of the imaginative form in which the prophets apprehended God, of its vividness and of the intense feeling of reality which lay within it. It is true that no intensity of feeling is a guarantee of objectivity; yet our study of the intellectual content of their experience would dispose us to believe that they were indeed in touch with a Source of truth beyond themselves; for the ideas they discovered are of a freshness, importance, and universality congruous with the divine origin claimed for them. The truth of their message is one thing, the touch with God which the message implies is another. The latter is the central factor in personal religion, and it is with this that we are here concerned.

We may start with that consciousness of vocation which we have already recognized as one of the foundation factors in the prophetic experience. It separated the prophet from other men, as one who acknowledged himself to be specially dedicated to a mission. The mission, however, had always a reference to the people of God as a whole. The great prophets felt themselves to be in a succession which had had historic significance for Israel from of old; and however they might wish to dissociate themselves from the unworthy *nabis* of their day, they yet saw in prophecy a national institution divinely ordered for the training of God's people. Micah speaks for them all: "I truly am full of power by the Spirit of Jehovah, and of judgment and of might, to declare to Jacob his transgression and to Israel his sin".[1] Through the severely impersonal language of the earlier classical prophets we can discern the travail of their own souls in the fulfilment of their public calling. Jeremiah and Ezekiel let us a little more deeply into their private feelings. In Jeremiah particularly we recognize a sensitiveness which makes the sins and sorrows of his people an intimate personal concern. It is as though in his own experience the tragedy of Judah were finding conscious expression. And when Ezekiel tells how he lay first on his left side and "bore the iniquity of the house of Israel" and then on his right side and "bore the iniquity of the house of Judah", through all that is

[1] Micah iii. 8.

bizarre in his description we can discern the overwhelming sense of responsibility for his people's sins.[1] " Son of man ", he heard the Voice say to him, " if the watchman see the sword come, and blow not the trumpet, . . . and the sword come and take any person, . . . his blood will I require at the watchman's hand. So thou, son of man, I have set thee a watchman unto the house of Israel ".[2]

Under stress of this public calling the prophets exercised an almost ascetic suppression of individual feeling. What to most people is private experience of the most intimate kind became for them the vehicle of divine lessons to the people. Hosea's domestic tragedy must have stirred private emotions at which we can only guess. The whole emotional content of the situation has been translated into a sublime apprehension of the divine love. Ezekiel gives us the poignant episode of his wife's death in exile. " Son of man, behold I take away the desire of thine eyes with a stroke ; yet neither shalt thou mourn nor weep nor cause thy tears to run down ". So spoke the Voice, the prophet tells us ; and he proceeds, " At even my wife died, and I did in the morning as I was commanded ".[3] Private grief is at once absorbed into the larger tragedy of national disaster. Some who suffered loss in the late War will understand.

Yet it was impossible altogether to suppress evidence of individual reaction to the truth which came to the prophet first as a message for others. Isaiah's vision of God brought him, besides a public calling, a personal sense of forgiveness and of the power and nearness of God. His maxim, " In quietness and in confidence shall be your strength ",[4] was the principle by which he lived. When his message was rejected, he records the resolve, " I will tie up the testimony and seal it in my disciples, and I will wait for Jehovah, who hides His face from the house of

[1] Ezek. iv. 4–6.
[2] Ezek. xxxiii. 6–7 (R.V.).
[3] Ezek. xxiv. 15–24 (R.V.).
[4] Isa. xxx. 15 (R.V.).

Jacob; and I will look for him".[1] Through good report and ill the prophet gave an example of quiet, heroic faith in God which is no less a treasure for mankind than his teaching.

But it is Jeremiah who most "unlocks his heart", in a series of intimate confessions to which the Bible affords no parallel until we come to the letters of Paul. For him the personal problem became most acute because in the conditions in which he lived his work was almost foredoomed to failure. His ruthless analysis of the public situation made it impossible for him to utter any message with the smallest chance of acceptance by the majority of his contemporaries. He was alone.

> "With the merry crew I sat not rejoicing;
> Lonely I sat because of Thy hand:
> For with spleen Thou hast filled me.
> Why is my grief perpetual?—
> My wound mortal,
> That will not be healed?
> Wilt Thou be to me like a winter brook,
> As waters that fail?"[2]

Then comes the divine answer:

> "If thou return I will restore thee;
> Thou shalt stand before me:
> If pure thoughts thou utter, unmixed with base,
> Thou shalt be as My mouth."[3]

He looks into his own heart; how can he be sure that the thoughts he utters are "pure thoughts unmixed with base"; for

> "Deep beyond sounding is the heart,
> And sick beyond cure:
> Who can know it?"

Again there is a reply:

> "I, Yahwe, search the heart,
> And try the reins."[4]

[1] Isa. viii. 16–17 (G. B. Gray).
[2] Jer. xv. 17–18 (Skinner).
[3] Jer. xv. 19 (Skinner).
[4] Jer. xvii. 9–10 (Skinner).

His need and perplexity make him turn in prayer to God :

> "Heal me, Yahwe, that I may be healed ;
> Save me, that I may be saved ;
> For Thou art my praise ! . . .
>
> Be not a terror to me,
> Thou, my trust in the evil day !
> May my foes be put to shame, and not I :
> May they be dismayed, and not I !
> Bring on them the day of evil ;
> Destroy them with double destruction."[1]

It is not altogether Christian in sentiment, but what authentic converse of the soul with God ! Here we can see prophecy bringing forth a distinctive type of piety, which became the norm for Judaism and Christianity. Friedrich Heiler, in his treatise on Prayer (*Das Gebet*, 1919)—a work of great learning and also of unusual insight—distinguishes two main types of piety, that of mysticism and that of the prophetic-evangelical tradition. Christianity has found a place for both, but its dominant note is the prophetic-evangelical ; and indeed Christian mysticism has come powerfully under its influence, and to that extent differs from all other mysticism. Some sentences from Heiler will serve to characterize the type of personal religion which begins with the prophets[2] :

"The fundamental psychic experience of mysticism is the denial, born of satiety, of the normal life-impulse. . . . The fundamental psychic experience in *prophetic* religion is an unrestrained will-to-live, a steadfast impulse towards the affirmation, reinforcement and elevation of the life-feeling, a sense of being conquered and possessed by values and tasks, a passionate striving towards the realization of these ideals and ends. . . . Mysticism is passive, quietist, resigned, contemplative ; prophetic piety is active and ethical, it makes claims and demands. . . . In the

[1] Jer. xvii. 14, 17-18 (Skinner).
[2] The translation is my own ; the italics are Heiler's.

prophetic experience the affections blaze forth, the *will* to live asserts itself, conquers and triumphs even in the utmost defeat; It defies death and annihilation. Out of the deepest need and despair *faith* breaks through at last, born of the fierce will-to-live—faith, which is unshakable confidence, rock-firm trust and reliance, bold and daring hope. The mystic is one who gives up, renounces, and rests; the prophet is a fighter, who perpetually struggles from doubt to assurance, from torturing uncertainty to absolute certainty of life, from weariness to fresh courage, from fear to hope, from the crushing sense of sin to the blessed consciousness of grace and salvation" (p. 255). "The mystic has a tendency to turn prayer into contemplation and absorption; in prophetic piety the naïve prayer of primitive man awakes afresh with the realistic power and vitality proper to it. On the highest levels of religious experience of the great prophetic personalities the original creation of prayer is achieved anew. The occasion to pray is usually supplied, as in the naïve man, by some momentary, concrete need. A menace to the healthy will-to-live, to the elementary life-feeling, a conflict between experienced value and the actuality which contradicts that value, gives the motive for the appeal to God in prayer" (p. 348).

We may now report the most essential things we have learned from a study of the prophets regarding the character of their inspiration. Though it often appears to have been accompanied by psychical phenomena such as we observe in the "medium", it is not to be identified with any form of unconscious automatism. So far from involving a "dissociation of personality" it is a function of personality integrated in its purest activity, which is communion with God. In such communion the prophets received an enhanced power of insight and criticism, turned upon their inherited beliefs and the problems of their times. Its outcome is seen to be continuous with the best in earlier religion, and yet not readily to be explained as a mere unfolding of latent elements in it. Their criticism is radical and their ideas are new. Not only so, but they commend themselves to the reason as essentially worthy of the God whose "word" they seemed to the prophet to be.

Their inspiration did not make the prophets independent of the historical conditions of their time. They did not desire or conceive any such independence. The notion of them as mystical dreamers brooding in a realm above space and time, and forecasting the remote future in riddles to be deciphered by an amazed posterity, is wholly misleading. They were intensely men of the hour. They believed that God had shaped the past of their people, and that He had given them a word relevant to the present in which that past had issued. When they spoke that word they expected it to be a decisive factor in determining the course of the immediate future. Their interests were particular and not general, concrete and not abstract.

Yet they spoke eternal truth. We do wrong to suppose that in order to speak a word for all time a thinker must be detached from the special conditions of his own time. On the contrary, those who are deeply implicated in the problems of real life, which are always particular and never general, must "speak things", as Oliver Cromwell said, and it is the man who "speaks things" whose words posterity is apt to heed. In the realm of imagination certainly—and to this realm prophecy psychologically belongs—it is those who live vividly in their own immediate situation who attain the universal. "I suppose it will be generally admitted", writes Sir William Watson,[1] "that any deliberate and self-conscious effort after universality of temper and views is the one hopelessly ill-fated means towards such an end. Indeed it would often seem as if the opposite method were more auspicious. To be frankly local, in the sense in which Burns and Béranger—yes, and one may add Homer and Virgil—

[1] Preface to Alfred Austin's *English Lyrics*, 1896, p. viii.

are local, has not seldom been a direct road into 'the general heart of men'. Dante, the poet of a city, a church, a political faction, and a but newly consolidated language, would appear to have done his best to de-universalize himself; and we know with what splendid unanimity the world has baffled that design". Similar language could be used with perfect propriety of the Hebrew prophets. Their discoveries in the realm of the spirit are always orientated towards some actual situation, and that gives them their stamp of reality and urgency. Such discoveries have some prospect of permanence. Opinions may be formed at leisure; convictions grow out of days of stress. And where an absolutely sincere mind wrestles whole-heartedly with the situation as it is, refusing any flattering fallacies that offer immediate comfort, it is in the posture to which God often grants some saving intuition of unsuspected truth. This sincerity is characteristic of the prophets, and their intuitions stood the test of their own time so well that they have become a permanent heritage of the race.

When therefore we set out to read the prophets, it is the part of a decent humility to let them speak for themselves with the help of any imaginative effort on our part which will put us as nearly as may be in their place. To understand Amos we must try to stand with him before the altar of Bethel, "the king's chapel", and put ourselves in imagination in the midst of those hectic years when North Israel enjoyed its fleeting brilliance under Jeroboam II, with the storm-cloud of Assyrian aggression darkening the horizon. Much of what he says will be strange in our ears, but if we have the sense for such things we shall discern among his wild eloquence the tones of a man who saw with the utmost clearness into the real facts of a concrete situation, and uttered truth so conclusively relevant to that moment that it has become historic. When we read Jeremiah, we must imagine ourselves in the beleaguered city of Jerusalem, making its last stand for independence. Everything has gone wrong. Muddle and vacillation are on the throne. Faction-strife rages among the turbulent nobles. A ruined and sullen peasantry is barely loyal to its oppressive rulers. Religion is breaking out into those morbid forms which war-time has made all too familiar. Then we must listen to this lonely man with his unpopular message, which he would suppress did it not " burn like a fire in his bones ". Here is the utterance of one who has stood on the perilous edge of despair, and brings back a word that is spoken once for all, just because it was spoken truly and decisively for the moment.

" I am convinced," wrote Goethe, " that the Bible will grow ever more beautiful the more one understands it, that is to say, the more one looks into it and observes that every word, which we take generally and apply in particular to ourselves, possessed in certain definite circumstances, a special, immediately individual reference of its own, determined by special conditions of time and place."[1] That is the way in which we should approach the biblical writers. In no other way shall we get the whole value of their writings as authentic expressions of real religious experience. They are historically conditioned, and the conditions are essential to their full meaning.

This has an important bearing on the question we are considering—that of the nature of inspiration in the sphere of religion. It is closely bound up with history, and in its utterances the temporary and the eternal are intimately mingled. So far as the mere psychological mechanism is concerned, many scientific discoveries might be described as " inspired ", as when Archimedes in his bath, according to the story, suddenly leapt to the solution of a problem in hydrostatics over which he had long pondered in vain. But

[1] *Maximen und Reflexionen*, VI, quoted as the motto of Johannes Weiss' *Schriften des Neuen Testaments*.

once discovered, the principle of Archimedes holds its place in an abstract scientific system, and the crown of Dionysius, the dishonest goldsmith, and the rapturous cry of "Eureka" are the embroideries of an idle tale. It is not just so with the prophets. They uttered eternal truth—all truth is eternal; but here the eternal cannot be isolated from its temporary conditions by any simple analysis. The eternal and the temporary are together in the unity of an imaginative experience shaped by historical conditions. For the purposes of theology, which as a department of philosophy (or as some would have it, of science) is abstract, we may state the content of prophecy in isolation from its form, as dogma. But religion (which lies deeper than theology) returns to the living unity of experience in its historical conditions[1]. This inseparable interweaving of the eternal and the temporary in an historical revelation has important corollaries in the philosophy of religion, which we must not here consider.

All this means further that we must always allow for limitation and error in the prophets. It should hardly be necessary to state so obvious a proposition, but the doctrine of inspiration has been so confused by the demand for inerrancy that it is necessary. No one not blinded by a superstitious bibliolatry could possibly accept for truth, as they stand, many elements in Old Testament prophecy. Intelligent readers who went to the writings of the prophets convinced that they contained nothing but what, being the directly dictated "Word" of the living God, is eternally true, found it impossible to give full value to their actual words. It was necessary to water down, twist and manipulate, explain away, blunt the edge of trenchant sayings. We now learn that the "sting" of the truth in them is inseparable from their idiosyncrasy, and therefore from their imperfection. We are not here thinking of errors of fact in the narrative

[1] See Wheeler Robinson: *The Christian Experience of the Holy Spirit*, pp. 94–103.

portions of Scripture, but of elements in the religious message of biblical writers which we cannot hold to be true or valid. Isaiah in the bitterness of his soul cries out, "Jehovah will not have compassion on their fatherless and widows . . . His anger is not turned away, but His arm is stretched out still".[1] While we can understand and respect the outraged sense of justice that underlies his words, we may not take them as a true description of our Father in heaven. It is no laudable ambition that is expressed in the words, "The nation and kingdom that will not serve thee shall perish; yea, those nations shall be utterly wasted".[2] Yet they occur in one of the most sublime chapters of the so-called "Third Isaiah". It is unnecessary to multiply examples. Any theory of the inspiration of the Bible which suggests that we should recognize such utterances as authoritative for us stands self-condemned. They are relative to their age. But I think we should say more. They are false and they are wrong. If they were inevitable in that age—and this is an assumption which can neither be proved nor disproved—then in so far that age was astray from God. In any case the men who spoke so were imperfectly harmonized with the will of God. "For even in the prophets", says the Gospel according to the Hebrews, "after they were anointed with Holy Spirit, was found matter of sin".[3] Inspiration therefore does not imply moral perfection or intellectual infallibility.

But it is an unprofitable theme. Certainly the prophets were sometimes mistaken. But in their errors they remain greater than we in our most impeccable orthodoxies. That is why it behoves us to let them speak for themselves, with eyes open to the element of error in their teaching, but in

[1] Isa. ix. 17. [2] Isa. lx. 12.

[3] *Etenim in prophetis quoque, postquam uncti sunt spiritu sancto, inventus est sermo peccati*, cited by Jerome, *Adv. Pelag.* III 2. In a translation from a Hebrew, or Aramaic, original there can be little doubt that *sermo peccati* means "matter of sin," i.e. sinfulness, and not "sinful word."

no wise perturbed by it. The part that error and illusion may play in the gradual apprehension of truth is a question for that branch of philosophy known as the Theory of Knowledge, and is not here to be discussed. We must in any case beware of supposing that there is anything final or absolute about our present apprehension of truth. All knowledge is relative (unless it be in pure mathematics), and in *our* minds, too, illusion may serve the ends of truth. But these are deep matters. What we are here concerned to report is that inspiration does not carry inerrancy, nor is it inerrancy that gives authority. It is the capacity to explore independently the regions of the spirit and to convince others of the reality of that which one has discovered. This the prophets possessed. Their words, without being infallible, carry creative power.

Part II

THE AUTHORITY OF CORPORATE EXPERIENCE

CHAPTER VI

THE BIBLE AS A RECORD OF RELIGION IN COMMON LIFE

WE have now got thus far: the ultimate authority is truth itself. That authority comes home to us when we find that the world of our experience as a whole compels us to certain conclusions if it is to make sense at all. Beyond this immediate authority, in religion as in other spheres, the layman receives guidance from the expert—in religion from the saint or prophet—who thus becomes in a secondary sense an "authority".

The first ground of the authority of the Bible is the fact that it contains within it the utterances of men of the highest religious genius, who rise above the limitations of their age and environment and display the authentic marks of personal inspiration. We have, however, already remarked that the writings of these men are not the whole, nor even the larger part, of the Bible. There is a further kind of authority possessed by the Bible as a whole and in its parts, which the prophets share with writers who can claim no inspiration of the prophetic kind. To define this kind of authority we must go back once more to our account of the primary authority, that of truth itself, brought home to our minds when we find that only by making certain assumptions can we make sense of the world of our experience.

We must now analyse more closely what we mean by speaking about "the world of our experience". Let it be granted that if our religious thinking is to be scientific in any true sense, we cannot assume certain principles as revealed, and deduce a theology from them by pure formal logic. We must ground our thinking on facts of experience. Now in natural science we take " experience " to mean the series of sensible impressions we receive by observation of the world in which we live. Aesthetic experience goes beyond this in that it includes judgments of value which the mind passes upon the world. Religion is akin to art more closely than to science, but the definitely personal element is here even more dominant. We are here dealing, in fact, with personality itself, as it acts and reacts towards its total environment.

When it is said that belief must rest on experience, we are inclined to turn our minds at once to what are called " religious experiences " in the narrower sense, that is, the feelings accompanying certain internal processes of the spiritual life, such as contrition, conversion, peace of conscience, ecstasy, or mystical union. It is thought that a man should look within himself for " experiences " of this kind, and build his belief upon them.

This view is partly a heritage from the pietistic movements of the eighteenth century, represented in this country by Methodism and later by the Evangelical Revival, and partly due to the first attempts to extend the empirical method of natural science to theology. The pietists laid very great emphasis upon personal religious " experiences ", and by that emphasis they redeemed religion in their day from a barren ecclesiasticism. But for the most part they did not think to base Christian belief upon such phenomena, or to throw the individual back wholly upon his own limited share in such experiences. Their belief still rested upon the unquestioned authority of their churches and of Holy Writ. The eighteenth century, however, was at the same time the age of rationalism, which questioned all such authority as it had never been questioned before. It may well be that the widespread new demand for emotionally satisfying individual experiences had as an unconscious motive, the desire to underpin the cracking foundations of traditional dogma. However this may be, when in the following century religious people began to admit that all external authority had lost its old cogency, they had recourse to the immediate testimony of inward experience, and many thought to reconstruct theology upon this basis alone. At the same time the theory of knowledge came to lay more stress on observation and experiment, and there was a tendency to bring into prominence the distinctively religious experiences as "phenomena" to be studied scientifically. Thus the empirical psychology of the late nineteenth century set out to collect these "varieties of religious experience", as one collects butterflies, much indeed to the furtherance of our knowledge of the workings of the human mind. For a time it seemed as though theology would take its place among the empirical sciences in the form of a psychology of religious experience. Recent popular thought has come, under such influences, and in the general reaction against traditionalism, to assume that Christian belief is actually grounded for each individual in such inward phenomena as these.

It is because of this excessive emphasis upon individual "experience" in the narrower sense that so much popular religious thought in these days is defenceless against the latest criticisms of psychology. How is any individual to be certain that any particular set of feelings aroused in him in connection with religious ideas or processes is not the product of psycho-physical stimuli having no special religious significance?

It is necessary to widen the scope of what we mean by "religious experience". In the first place it means the whole of life religiously interpreted, rather than isolated feelings. A religious man is not one who has "experiences" which he can describe with particularity, in class-meeting, or in reply to a psychological *questionnaire*, as the case may be, but one who takes all life in a religious way. That vague statement could be made much more definite, but it is not necessary at the present stage of our enquiry.

Again, when this wider definition is accepted, it becomes clear that to place a ring-fence round the individual and expect him to find within that fence adequate material for religious belief is illusory. We are not so divided from one another in ordinary life, and our religious experience is not so isolated. A recognition of this fact might bring assurance to persons who have come to doubt their religious intuitions because they do not know how far they are the reflection of influences in their environment. That is something that none of us can ever know. But does it matter ? Of course, we owe an incalculable debt to our environment in all possible relations of life ; but if the religious impulses we have received from our environment make life *for us* a religious thing, in the widest sense, then we need not further question their validity.

We may now go further and recognize that as there is no absolute limit to be placed to our individual experience, so no narrow limit can be set to our social environment. It is co-extensive with human history. There is on one side at least complete continuity in the series of events in time into which all our own thoughts, words, and actions fall :

> " Und viele Geschlechter
> reihen sich dauernd
> an ihres Daseins
> unendliche Kette."

Now the religious experience of mankind is a function of this continuous history. It is not the isolated outbreak of abnormal phenomena in this or that individual (though to read some psychological treatments of religious experience one would suppose so).[1] The spiritual intuitions of saints and prophets take their place in the varied life that makes up real history. They are inseparably intertwined with economics and political institutions, with social development and decline, with literature and art and science.

Within this large historical context religion has taken many starts and turns. Whittier, in the first enthusiasm of the modern doctrine of progress, sang :

> " Step by step since time began
> I see the steady gain of man."

To see anything steady about it needs much resolution. Certainly in the religious history of the race there have been many false starts. Whole generations have wandered in the wilderness, and revolutions have come in which it seemed for the time as though the whole of religion would go under. Yet the wandering in the wilderness has not been wholly vain. Over some ways at least the spirit of man has written " No Road ", and that is something gained. And in all the ups and downs of the road, man has been aware of being in touch with something greater than he knew.

Those who would discredit religion as an illusion have to deal not with individual aberrations, but with the stuff of history. It is no doubt possible to dream of a totally different history, but such dreams are wholly unprofitable. An *Outline of History* (as Mr. H. G. Wells discovered when he came to write it) is to a surprising degree the history of religion. All sorts of crimes may be laid to its charge :

> Tantum religio potuit suadere malorum !

But at least it is one of the creative factors in history, and all the more profound and significant movements have had religion at their centre.

[1] See Selbie, *Psychology of Religion*, pp. 1621, for a pertinent criticism of the narrow field covered by the recently dominant school of religious psychology.

The subject-matter then of religious thinking is not simply what I find at certain times in my own mind. It is the experience that comes to me as a member of the historic society of mankind.[1] What I feel is less important than I am disposed to think it; yet it is important, because I too am a man, and the stream of history is passing through my consciousness on its way to the farther reaches.

Now Christianity accepts in the fullest way the reality and validity of history when it insists that the regulative moment in God's relations with man is to be found in the life of a human Individual who inherited the traditions of a people and founded a society through historic acts of His own. And it is consistent with its own doctrine of the Incarnation when it offers the Bible as the vehicle of our knowledge of God. For the Bible is an historical book. Its writings directly reflect more than a thousand years of the religious history of mankind, and indirectly they reach far back into the more distant past. It is true that even so the history it covers is but a fraction of the whole history of man, whether spacially or temporally considered. Yet the history it reflects is so central, so typical, and so obviously creative beyond the particular places and times in which it was produced, that it has a very wide significance.

From this point of view it is an important fact that the Bible is not wholly composed of the striking utterances of exceptional persons. Its prophets and saints, while they have the unique individuality of genius, do not appear as solitary islands emerging from a barren deep. Such islands might be the peaks of a buried continent, or mere chance eruptions. The prophets appear rather as the towering summits of a mountainous landscape, which from its foothills to its mountain tops shows the same geological structure. The prophets themselves firmly believe that God reveals Him-

[1] See *General Introduction*, p. vii.; also H. Wheeler Robinson, *The Christian Experience of the Holy Spirit*, pp. 105-6.

self in the history of their people from age to age. Scarcely a single biblical writer is of the type of the recluse—interested solely in his own communion with God, and contemptuous of the commonalty. Further, the Old Testament contains not only the epoch-making writings of the great prophets, but legends and traditions which reflect the elementary piety of the common man, historical narratives which show the impact of religion upon the vicissitudes of society, pedestrian laws which attempt inadequately to embody ideals in institutions. In the New Testament similarly we have on the one hand the unique sublimity of the words of Jesus and the revolutionary theology of Paul; but on the other hand we have the quiet, everyday piety of James or Peter, and the plain tale of the Acts of the Apostles.

The layman, when he hears of biblical criticism, is prone to think of discussions (which may seem to him profane, uninteresting, or intriguing, according to his cast of mind) upon details of the authenticity or the historical trustworthiness of certain portions of the Bible. The great positive achievement of the critical method is easily overlooked, namely, that it enables us to read the Bible historically, as perhaps no preceding generation has been able to read it. In its task biblical criticism has been greatly helped by the growth in historical knowledge all along the line. Comparative anthropology, archæology, and the application of economic principles to the interpretation of history have all placed fresh material in the hands of the student of the Bible. But the most important thing after all is the new point of view, which dispenses us from the task of finding verification of dogma in every text, and leaves us free to read the ancient writings in their plain historical meaning.

It is not to be supposed that the use of the Scriptures as historical documents is something for the dry-as-dust antiquary. If history has the significance which Christianity seems to attach to it, the "living past" is a religious factor of high importance in the present. Moreover, psychology is teaching us how permanent are the fundamental traits of the human mind, which are manifested in history. They may be in some sort overlaid or disguised, but they are part of our own equipment, and in this sense history repeats itself.

We may here select for special consideration three aspects of the historical study of the Bible; first, the value of primitive narratives when read in the light of the comparative study of religion; next, the value of those writings which provide as it were a commentary from the spiritual side upon secular history; and lastly, the value of the rich portrayal of all sides of human life in many ages in a way that does justice to the essentially religious quality of it all.

First, then, we put on record the great value of the primitive narratives of the Old Testament, as we now read them in the light of the comparative study of religion. They draw from a very deep *stratum* of the human mind, which was uppermost in remote antiquity and survives half-buried in us all, the substratum of whatever religious feelings we have. In much of its machinery, its "stage-properties" so to speak, the psychologist can recognize the natural symbolism with which the mind in every age tends to clothe its intuitions of mysterious things. Mythology is never arbitrary: it has natural roots. The wonderful tree with its forbidden fruit and the crafty serpent in the garden; the flaming warders of the Gate; the tower to scale Heaven; the great flood-bath from which the world rises new-born beneath the rainbow sign—these and many other mythological images are not wholly strange to our naïve imaginations. They are found by psychologists in the symbolism of our dreams.

Again, in some of the rudimentary religious feelings which the primitive folk of the Bible share with widely separated peoples on a similar plane—such as the haunting weirdness of mountains and of the dark, the sacredness of bread, the awful terror of blood,—we trace something that civilization may transform but does not eradicate. In reading of such things we look into the pit from whence we were digged. They are the raw stuff of human thought everywhere. And out of such raw stuff we see in the Bible the most sublime conceptions of God and life being formed. It gives us a sense of solidity, of being in touch with the good brown soil in which all life is rooted. We feel that we stand

> " . . . mit festen
> markigen Knochen
> auf der wohlgegründeten
> dauernden Erde."

Secondly, it is profoundly interesting to study, in these ancient records of a thousand years and more, the inward or spiritual aspects of movements in history which the secular historian treats from the outside. For example, the migrations of peoples bulk largely in any attempt to tell the story of the human race. Strange stirrings begin from time to time and drive tribes and races from their ancient habitations, to spread them over new regions, upsetting or modifying the system of civilization. The history of classical Greece begins with those sweeping migrations which brought the downfall of Knossos and of Troy, the death of the old Minoan culture and its resurrection in transfigured forms in Hellenism. Modern European history begins with the irresistible sweep of the Teutonic peoples into the Mediterranean basin. Now in the Old Testament we have two cycles of legend referring to periods of tribal migrations—the patriarchal narratives and the story of the Exodus. The relation between the two cycles is not altogether clear, but in both we watch historic migrations in process. What made the Semitic tribes of the desert force their way into the ancient lands of the Syrian culture-zone? We can point to certain facts, such as the periodic excess of population over food-supply, and the pressure of Babylonian civilization upon stocks at a lower level of culture. But there were inward facts as well as outward. "God spoke to Abram in Ur of the Chaldees, saying, 'Get thee out from thy kindred, and go into a land that I shall show thee'".[1] No doubt the voice of God was in part mediated by economic facts, but we may accept also the sense of an irresistible spiritual impulse to adventure—vague and undefined, but real. And so Abraham haunted the fringes of civilization in Canaan, moving his encampment as far as the borders of Egypt under pressure of famine,[2] making an occasional raid into Mesopotamia,[3] seeking alliance with his ancient kin at Haran,[4] and paying awed allegiance to the august priest-king of the holy city of Salem.[5] In the last generation people were sorely agitated by the question, Are the stories about Abraham true? Indeed, did Abraham ever live, or is he a myth? Critics are still not agreed. Perhaps the name stands for some real though pre-historic tribal chief. Perhaps it was originally the name of a deity. Perhaps it is simply the personification of a clan. We now see that this matters little. At least, whether all this happened to one man or not, in a broad sense it is history and it is human experience. When the tribes were on their wanderings, this is the kind of life they led, and this the kind of faith that supported them. The authors of the narratives in their present form were indeed far removed in time from the patriarchs; yet they had the spectacle of nomadic life constantly before them on the fringes of their land, and

[1] Gen. xii. 1–4 (J).
[2] Gen. xii. 10 (J).
[3] Gen. xiv.
[4] Gen. xxiv. (J).
[5] Gen. xiv. 18–20. His name is Melchizedek, i.e. "Zedek is King," Zedek being the local god; cf. Adonizedek, Joshua x. 1 (J). Abd-hiba, king of Jerusalem c. 1400 B.C., is known from the Amarna tablets, which help to give a background to the patriarchal stories.

could interpret the ancient traditions on which they worked with a true sense of their deeper import. The New Testament supplies a richer interpretation. No doubt the author to the Hebrews idealizes these desert wanderers, but essentially he is right: it was "by faith" that they endured, seeking a city whose builder and maker is God.[1] Behind the delight of movement and adventure lies a craving for the permanent, and a deep-grounded faith that the spirit of man is made for something that escapes the flux of things.

The other cycle of migration-legends tells how the nomadic impulse reasserted itself in certain Hebrew clans temporarily settled on the borders of Egypt, how the *Wanderlust* grew to a wild land-hunger, and how at last the tribes burst with fury into the debatable ground between the two great empires of Egypt and Babylon, and claimed it in the name of their God as the "promised land". The thing has often happened: here we are in the midst of it, privy to the thoughts and feelings of the actors in the drama.

Religious people in the past were much embarrassed by having to believe in some way that the fierce impulses which these ancient nomads attributed to their tribal deity were indeed the commands of the eternal God. Their critics scorned a God who approved such atrocities. In the interests of moral sincerity it was necessary for the last generation to say with all emphasis that whatever might or might not be true about the inspiration of the Old Testament, the Christian conscience must indignantly repudiate the horrors of Joshua and Judges. Now perhaps the time has come when we can see things in better perspective. At the stage of human development represented by these books and other passages like them, a certain ferocity is inseparable from any intense feeling. The kernel of the matter is not the bestial cruelty that accompanied the migration into Canaan as it accompanied other *Völkerwanderungen*, but the ideal

[1] Heb. xi. 8–10, 13–16.

impulses which in crude and primitive forms worked upon the desert clans. So the Arabs in later centuries fought in the name of Allah, and the crusaders cried "Dieu le veult!" as they stormed the walls of Jerusalem. But in the Bible more clearly than elsewhere we see how organically these impulses are related to the heroic in religion. We ourselves have within us the liability to such impulses; history repeats itself in the inner life. Well for us if we know that the inward drive to adventure is the purpose of God in us, and can, if the work of the ages has indeed been wrought in us, be sublimated into the motive power of a noble life.

In the same way we may follow in the Old Testament the spiritual aspects of that episode which repeats itself in the life of various peoples, when the rustic, agricultural, locally centred type of civilization gives place to the mercantile type with its international or cosmopolitan orientation. Without going into detail here we may ask the reader to consider under this aspect the conquests of Solomon and his Tyrian alliance,[1] with its sequel in the division between the purely agricultural south and the north with its opportunities for commerce[2]; and to estimate the significance of Elijah's opposition to Jezebel alike in the matter of Baal-worship and of Naboth's vineyard,[3] or of Isaiah's attack on foreign luxury,[4] or Jeremiah's advice to exiled Jews to throw themselves heartily into the social and economic life of the Babylonian Empire.[5]

If we turn to the New Testament we find ourselves in a *milieu* much nearer to ourselves. For the Roman Empire is so much the foundation of our own system of civilization and its culture so intimately associated with our own

[1] 1 Kings ix. 10–28.

[2] 1 Kings xii. 1–20. The cause is given as the pressure of taxation, levied for imperialist and mercantile ventures as well as for luxury-building and the splendour of the court.

[3] 1 Kings xviii. 18–21, xix. 1–2, xxi. 1–20.

[4] Isa. iii. 16–24.

[5] Jer. xxix. 4–7.

education that it can never feel altogether foreign. The Roman authors who are read in school show us something of what Rome meant to its own ruling class. But what did it mean to the much larger and ultimately more important section of mankind composed of the middle and lower sort who were ruled by Rome, with or without their own goodwill? It is only recently that scholars have appreciated how immensely valuable and important the New Testament documents are as materials for the study of the spiritual reactions of Roman rule and Roman ideals upon the subject populations. Take for instance the exquisitely finished miniature of the centurion in the Gospels, with its feeling for the virtues of the best sort of subordinate Roman officer and even of the system under which he worked:[1] "I am a man under authority, and I say. . . ." We need not be militarists to understand why Jesus liked that. And when we have appreciated it, we understand better why Rome with all its faults captured the imagination of the world and endured as an ideal even when its power had fallen. On a larger scale we have the trial scene of the Gospels, which has been worked out dramatically with such skill by Mr. Masefield. It is an illuminating study of the Roman system in conflict with Jewish nationalism, in which the weak points of both turn their virtues to disaster. For here both are confronted with a spiritual fact which neither is able to digest, though in it lies not only the quintessence of the past but the promise of the future of the race. Again in the cosmopolitanism of Paul contrasted with the virulent minority-feeling of the *Revelation*, we have a glimpse of deep issues being fought out beneath the surface of imperial history as it meets us in the Augustan poets or in Tacitus and Pliny.

There are, finally, few aspects of the manifold life of man

[1] Matt. viii. 5–10; Luke vii. 1–10.

which are not reflected in the Bible. If the proper study of mankind is man, not Euripides nor Shakespeare offers richer material for such study than the stories of the Old Testament. Their actors are no faultless types of the virtues, but men whose blood is warm within them. We have here the natural play of motive and action which is after all one of the liveliest interests of the normal mind. The moralist has to his hand a gallery of "characters" for example and warning more living than those of Plutarch or Theophrastus.[1] Yet no narrow moralizing exhausts their interest. For the connoisseur of human nature they are a storehouse of acutely observed types, full of the stuff of tragedy and comedy.

Again it is no accident that since the biblical documents have been critically studied they have provided a rich field for the student of social and economic history. For example, Ezekiel's description of the trade of Tyre is an economic document of the first importance.[2] It surveys with some fulness the sea-going commerce of the sixth century before Christ, and to anyone with imagination it portrays the civilization of the time in the most vivid style. Or by way of contrast we may take the exquisite idyll of rural life in Palestine presented by the Book of Ruth. No doubt the picture is in some measure idealized, yet in essentials this was what life was like in the country districts—not perhaps in the time of the Judges, in which the scene of the romance is laid, but in Judaea after the exile. The strength of the people lay in this simple farming stock, tenacious of the land and its traditions, prospering through unremitting industry, yet never far from the poverty which the death of the bread-winner or two or three successive bad harvests might bring. To put one's best into the soil, to do the right

[1] Alexander Whyte's *Bible Characters* are penetrating studies from this point of view. They ignore all questions of historical criticism; and why not? The value of the character of Macbeth does not depend on researches in an obscure period of Scottish History.

[2] Ezek. xxvii. 1–25.

thing by one's workpeople and one's poorer neighbours, and to stick to the family through thick and thin, these are its root virtues—and no bad foundation for religion, though of religion in the technical sense there is almost nothing said. To take a third example, in view of the association of " Hebraism " in the general mind with a stern renunciation of the Graces, we may well recall that the Canon of Scripture contains in the Song of Songs a sequence of lyrical poems of love, full of a romantic and even voluptuous sense of physical beauty. If the Bible takes an austere attitude to sexual experience, it is not because the life out of which it came was ascetic.

In no part of the Bible is the common life of men more vividly and sympathetically portrayed than in the parables of Jesus Christ. Too often treated as cryptic allegories of theological doctrines, they have not until the other day received justice as artistic presentations of daily life in first-century Galilee. These rapid sketches are drawn with an unerring instinct for the essential points, and the detail that enters in is due purely to the Narrator's interest in the human scene, and not at all, as commentators still stubbornly try to persuade us, to the exigencies of allegory. Indeed, if we read these short stories without prejudice, we shall be startled to see how far the attitude of the Narrator is from any narrowly moralizing tendency. He sets up before us aspects of real life, not asking in the first place whether this or that action is to be morally approved or reprobated, but noting that men do as a matter of fact so and so—the shepherd seeks his sheep[1]; the pearl-merchant knows a good bargain when he sees it[2]; people often do a service not out of pure kindliness but to save themselves trouble[3]; clever rogues use their advantages without scruple and profit by it.[4] We are asked simply to observe

[1] Matt. xviii. 12–13; Luke xv. 4–6.
[2] Matt. xiii. 45–46.
[3] Luke xi. 5–8.
[4] Luke xvi. 1–8.

that life is like that. When we have looked at life as it is, then the meaning of the parable suggests itself to the mind. But there is no mistaking the untrammelled interest in real life, and this gives the parables unique value as historical documents. It may safely be said that the literature of the Roman Empire contains no other such vivid picture of the life of common men under its rule.[1]

The stage is a small town in an agricultural district. Most of the characters are of the middle sort. A typical character is the "householder" who has a vineyard[2] in which he and his sons work,[3] with possibly a gardener to help,[4] and keeps a few head of live-stock which he feeds in the stall (after the French fashion, not at open pasture as we do), and must take to water daily at the pond or cistern.[5] He will have a garden for vegetables,[6] and perhaps a small field which he sows with corn.[7] The soil is mostly shallow, and only too often suffering from the primeval curse of "thorns and thistles", but with luck there will be a corner of good soil that may yield him anything up to a hundred-fold. He attends strictly to business: no social engagement will stand in his way if he is bargaining for a piece of land or trying out a team of ploughing oxen.[8] His wife grinds their own grain[9] and makes the bread[10] which, with eggs and dried fish[11] from the neighbouring lake, forms the staple food of the family. Flesh-meat is a dish for a feast.[12] His house may have but one living-room in which the

[1] The only parallel is the picture of common life in Egypt obtained by a laborious study of masses of accidentally preserved papyri from the rubbish heaps of Oxyrhynchus and other sites.

[2] Matt. xx. 1. [3] Matt. xxi. 28–30. Luke xiii. 6–9.

[5] Luke xiii. 15, cf. Matt. xii. 11, Luke xiv. 5.

[6] Luke xiii. 19; Mark. iv. 31–32.

[7] Mark iv. 3–8, 26–29; Matt. xiii. 24–30.

[8] Luke xiv. 18–19.

[9] Matt. xxiv. 41; Luke xvii. 35.

[10] Matt. xiii. 33; Luke xiii. 20–21.

[11] Matt. vii. 9–10.

[12] Luke xv. 23, cf. Matt. xxii. 4.

whole family gathers in the evening when the lamp is lit.[1] But they live comfortably enough, by dint of a thrift which will patch clothes till the fabric will no longer hold together,[2] and cannot tolerate the accidental loss of a single franc-piece.[3] In common with most peasants he hoards like a magpie, thereby putting temptation in the way of the burglar who digs through the "cob" wall at night,[4] or even robs with violence.[5] It is characteristic, too, that the chance discovery of treasure hidden in the earth—somebody's ill-fated hoard from the time of the troubles—is too much for his habitual caution; he sells up and buys the field as a speculation.[6] His greatest fear is to fall into the hands of the moneylender,[7] or to become involved in litigation, which may end in losing the very shirt off one's back.[8] One knows what these local courts are! Indeed, if the *Cadi* is the wrong sort, the only way to get one's mere rights is the truly Oriental way of making oneself a nuisance until something happens.[9] But the wise man will do anything to get things settled out of court.[10] Officials of all kinds are persons to be avoided; they stand for taxes and the hated *corvée*.[11] To call a man "a friend of tax-collectors" is an insult.[12]

There are more prosperous members of the community—the man whose vineyard is so large that at certain seasons he has to hire extra labour[13]; the big farmer who has slaves ploughing and sowing for him,[14] or a staff of paid labourers

[1] Matt. v. 15; Luke viii. 16, xi. 33 changes the scene to a larger house where the light is in the vestibule.

[2] Mark ii. 21.

[3] Luke xv. 8.

[4] Matt. vi. 19–20; Luke xii. 33; Matt. xxiv. 43; Luke xii. 39.

[5] Mark iii. 27: Luke xi. 21 has altered this commonplace episode of the burglar into a more romantic business of an armed man guarding his castle against raiders.

[6] Matt. xiii. 44.

[7] Luke vii. 41–42, cf. Matt. xviii. 23–34.

[8] Matt. v. 40; Luke vi. 29.

[9] Luke xviii. 2–5.

[10] Matt. v. 25–26; Luke xii. 57–59.

[11] Matt. v. 41.

[12] Matt. xi. 19; Luke vii. 34.

[13] Matt. xx. 1–16.

[14] Luke xvii. 7–9; Matt. xiii. 27

with a bailiff over them.[1] There is the capitalist who deals in wine and oil in bulk,[2] who makes long journeys abroad[3] and expects his slaves to look after the investment of his capital in his absence.[4] There is the *nouveau riche* who has no sense of the traditional responsibilities of wealth, but says to his soul "eat, drink, and be merry"[5] and fares sumptuously every day while beggars starve at his door.[6] A sinister figure is the absentee landlord, who leases his vineyards to tenant cultivators on payment of a proportion of the produce as rent. The system is resented in a district where peasant proprietorship is the rule, and the tenants have been known not only to refuse rent but to attack and kill the landlord's agents. Not that they gain anything by this, for the powerful landlord can get a military force from the government and crush the incipient agrarian revolt.[7]

Other figures make a casual appearance—the shepherd,[8] the fisherman of the lake,[9] the travelling pearl-merchant,[10] the builder, who in a country subject to storms and floods must know how and where to build, if his work is to stand,[11] the doctor,[12] the priest,[13] the pious Pharisee[14], the travelling

[1] Luke xv. 17; (this farmer, we observe, had no difficulty in raising on the spot a substantial sum of money to send his younger son abroad; the elder son worked on the farm.) Luke xii. 42–46; Matt. xxiv. 45–51: Mark xiii. 34.

[2] Luke xvi. 1–8.

[3] Mark xiii. 34–36.

[4] Matt. xxv. 14–30; Luke xix. 12–27

[5] Luke xii. 16–20.

[6] Luke xvi. 19–21.

[7] Mark xii. 1–9. Leases are extant providing for the payment of rent in kind, e.g. Oxyrhynchus Papyri, 1631; and we may recall that Marcus Brutus once applied for a military force to collect moneys due to him in Cyprus, and actually caused the Senate of Salamis to be besieged (Cicero *ad Att.* V. 21, VI. 1).

[8] Matt. xviii. 12–13; Luke xv. 4–6.

[9] Matt. xiii. 47–48.

[10] Matt. xiii. 45–46.

[11] Matt. vii. 24–27; Luke vi. 47–49.

[12] Mark ii. 17; Luke iv. 23.

[13] Luke x. 31–32.

[14] Luke xviii. 11–12.

Samaritan, the innkeeper and the highwayman[1]; and a crowd of loungers, beggars and cripples[2] at one end of the social scale, and at the other kings pursuing in the dim background their arbitrary way, leading armies,[3] sacking towns,[4] or, if the whim takes them, giving lavish banquets to their favoured subjects.[5]

It is in the main a neighbourly little society, where everyone is interested in everyone else's business,[6] and hospitality is free. On a journey you "drop in" on a friend, and naturally expect to be entertained. If he has nothing in the house he can always borrow from someone.[7] Moreover there is a great deal of modest junketing. A home-coming in the family is a good excuse for a feast, with music and dancing.[8] So of course is a wedding, about which all manner of festivities gather.[9] But even without any such special occasion, these sociable folk seem constantly to be giving dinner-parties. At these parties the minute grades of social rank are scrupulously observed. It is the grossest affront to good manners to push into a place which may be reserved for your social superior. Indeed, good breeding demands that you should take the lowest seat until pressed to come up higher.[10] Also, you must dress festively; else you offend your host.[11] To excuse yourself from such a party at the last moment, naturally, is unpardonable.[12]

Such was life in first-century Galilee in the circles in

[1] Luke x. 30–37.
[2] Luke xiv. 21–23; Matt. xxii. 9–10; Luke xiv. 13, etc.
[3] Luke xiv. 31–32.
[4] Matt. xxii. 7.
[5] Matt. xxii. 2. In a certain "far country" (Rome) there is a power that makes and unmakes kings; Luke xix. 12.
[6] Luke xv. 6, 9.
[7] Luke xi. 5–8.
[8] Luke xv. 22–32.
[9] Matt. xxv. 1–12; Luke xii. 36; Mark ii. 19.
[10] Luke xiv. 8–10.
[11] Matt. xxii. 11–13.
[12] Luke xiv. 17–21.

which Jesus moved.[1] There, as everywhere, it took all sorts to make a world. Neighbours were sometimes curmudgeonly or spiteful,[2] masters exacting,[3] servants dishonest or drunken,[4] children tiresome,[5] young fellows dissolute and extravagant.[6] There is no *couleur de rose* about the picture.

The parables are in a large measure typical of the Bible as a whole. For a religious book it is often curiously secular, for a divine book, astonishingly human. It certainly lends no countenance to the view that religion is or should be a thing apart. Here we have life as it has actually been lived in many ages by men like ourselves. We look more deeply into the picture, and we see it shot through and through with religion. Religion is there not as a separable addition to life, but as a quality belonging to its very nature.

We come back therefore to the question from which we started, What is that world of experience which in religion must provide us with the authoritative *data* for all our thinking ? Our experience, we said, is not purely individual. The hopes and fears, faiths and aspirations, struggles, endurances and achievements of mankind are ours. The Bible makes us partakers in many centuries of human experience, and invites us to appropriate to ourselves the rich religious meaning of it all.

[1] We can define broadly the position of the family of Jesus in this society. Two of His grand-nephews were taxed on 39 *plethra* (= about 10 acres, the size of a typical smallholding on Evesham tenure) which they farmed by their own labour (Eusebius, *Hist. Eccl.* III, 20). He Himself, as an independent craftsman, probably held a rather better position, like His closest friends, the sons of John and Zebedee, who formed a small firm owning a few fishing-boats and employing labour.

[2] Luke xi. 5–8 ; Matt. xiii. 25.

[3] Luke xvii. 7–9, xii. 47–48 ; Matt. xxv. 24 ; Luke xix. 21.

[4] Luke xvi. 1–8 ; Matt. xxiv. 48–49 ; Luke xii. 45.

[5] Matt. xi. 16–17 ; Luke vii. 32. Jesus was fond of children, but not sentimental about them.

[6] Luke xv. 13.

This does not yet tell us why, under this head, we should attach *unique* authority to the Bible. Any historical literature, equally sincere, equally broad in its outlook and profound in its knowledge of human nature, would bring us this communion with the life of our kind. Perhaps we should have to look very far for a literature equal in these respects to the Bible. But its specific authority for us rests upon further considerations.[1]

[1] See in particular chap. XII.

CHAPTER VII

THE RELIGION OF THE PROPHETS IN THE LIFE OF THE COMMUNITY

WHEN we turn from the exceptional works of genius which represent most purely the authority of sheer "inspiration", to consider the Bible in its broader aspect as the record of religion in the general life of men, our attention is claimed by the period following the Babylonian Exile. The emphasis rightly laid on the prophets in the historical criticism of the nineteenth century, which may almost be said to have rediscovered them, has tended to make all that followed appear less interesting. And even apart from this, the fact that the historical books of the Old Testament end, as a continuous record, with the Exile, and have nothing to tell of any events after the middle of the fifth century, has given an unconscious bias to our minds when we attempt to assess the history of Israel as a whole. The post-exilic period is apt to appear as a mere epilogue, or a barren waiting-time till the rise of Christianity. But here our perspective is at fault. These five centuries of a nation's life were very far from insignificant. If the age of the prophets saw the rise of creative ideas, it was in the post-exilic period that they became effective in the life of a community. Then for the first time a religious system was established upon the prophetic foundation of ethical monotheism. Its documentary basis is the canon of the Old Testament. Indeed the Old Testament as we know it is the corpus of religious literature of post-exilic Judaism. The Jewish legend that Ezra miraculously restored the ancient writings after their destruction[1] is not all untrue. Not only was a very large proportion of the canonical scriptures actually written in this period,—far larger than we commonly realize—but whatever of earlier literature has survived has done so because the scribes of the sixth and following centuries judged it worthy to survive; and all has come down to us with their mark upon it.

The canon of the prophets was itself the creation of the post-exilic community. Probably there is not a single book which has escaped some revision in the light of the dominant ideas of the period, and in some cases the revision is substantial. The wonder is that so much was preserved by the scribes which is in imperfect harmony with those ideas; just as at a later time the early Christian Church preserved words of its Master by which its own faith and works are judged. It is a task of nice critical discrimination to recover the original thoughts of the classical prophets from the skilfully edited books in which their utterances were preserved for posterity; and it is a task in which complete success is never attainable. But while exacting critical analysis is necessary if we would come face to face with the prophets themselves, the prophetic books just as they stand are a direct witness to the prophetic religion in the form which it took when it became a system. And at bottom it *is* still the prophetic religion with which we are dealing, despite all modifications. The work of the prophets was not done in vain, even though some of the most profound elements in their message were not fully operative until Christianity brought them to clarity and gave them their completion.

The prophetic writings, however, were not, in the estimation of the Jewish Church itself, the central or most important element in the sacred Scriptures. The Bible, as we received it from the Jews, begins with the five so-called "Books of Moses", or the Pentateuch, containing, in a

[1] 2 Esdras xiv. 19–48.

quasi-historical setting, a compilation of the various codes of laws and regulations which formed the institutional basis of the religious life of Judaism. It is not necessary here to discuss in detail the criticism of the Pentateuch, but it will be well to indicate briefly the historical relations of the component parts of this remarkable corpus.

The fundamental document of Judaism is Deuteronomy. The problem of its origin is at present one of the most-discussed problems in Old Testament criticism.[1] Whatever may have been the traditional sources of the laws and regulations which it contains, the setting forth of these laws is permeated with the new ideas which the prophets of the eighth century had propounded—imperfectly assimilated, it is true, but giving life and spirit to the whole code. In some form it appears to have been in the hands of the reformers of the time of Josiah. Their reformation indeed was all but stillborn. But it was a great memory, and during the Exile it came to represent the true religious basis on which the people of Jehovah must stand, and when the community was reconstituted under the inspiration of Ezekiel and the Second Isaiah it was a revised Deuteronomy that provided what we may call its "constitution".[2] The Jews became the people of a book, and that book Deuteronomy. It is a noble manifesto of ethical religion—genuinely devotional, soberly humanitarian,[3] marked with a real sense

[1] For a summary of the situation see J. E. MacFadyen, *The Present Position of O.T. Criticism* in *The People and the Book* (ed. A. S. Peake), pp. 199–204.

[2] This is true in a broad sense, whatever view be taken of the story in Nehemiah viii. Whatever code was promulgated on that occasion, so important in Jewish tradition, so enigmatic historically, during the three-quarters of a century which preceded it, the community must have lived by the code which was authoritative at the close of the monarchy. Malachi, writing as late as the middle of the fifth century, seems still to assume Deuteronomy as the norm of religious observance.

[3] See especially Deut. x. 19, xx. 19–20, xxi. 10–14, xxii. 1–4, 6–9, xxiii. 15–16, 19, xxiv. 5–6, 10–22, and the motive assigned for the keeping of the Sabbath, v. 12–15.

of delight in the ways of God and joy in His commandments,[1] and warmed by a patriotism in which hostility to foreigners is much less prominent than love for the soil and a fine feeling of national vocation.[2] Its theology is simple: God is one, all powerful and perfectly righteous; His will is revealed once for all in the Law; He rewards those who keep it with long life and prosperity, and punishes those who break it with disaster and death.[3]

In the enthusiasm which Deuteronomy aroused, the whole tragic history closed by the Exile was rewritten as a story of God's dealings with His people, on lines first laid down by Hosea and developed by subsequent prophets. The whole historical literature, from Judges onward, comes down to us "countersigned" with the dominant ideas of the Deuteronomic school. The application of these ideas to the facts seems to us often mechanical and artificial, but if the historical corpus consisting of Deuteronomy itself with the Books of Judges, Samuel, and Kings be taken as a whole, it conveys an impressive philosophy of history whose essential truth stands firm, though much of its detail is to us unconvincing. Its interest lies not so much in the detail of events before the Exile—to ascertain these criticism has to look behind the Deuteronomic editing—but in the witness it bears to the conception of God in history which was the working philosophy of the restored Jewish community.

As the life and thought of the restored community developed, other codes came to be added to Deuteronomy. They supplemented or even in part superseded its provisions, particularly on the side of the cult. This marks the most definite departure from the teaching of the earlier prophets. Ezekiel, himself priest as well as prophet, had found a place in his scheme for a reformed and purified ritual, and follow-

[1] Deut. vi. 4–25, viii., x. 12–15, xxx. 11–14.
[2] Deut. iv. 7, vii. 6–11.
[3] Deut. vi. 1–3, xxviii, xxx. 15–20.

ing his lead, the priestly leaders of the people during a period of two or three centuries elaborated a ritual system based on very ancient tradition, but adapted to more advanced ideas of God. The outcome of the process was the "Priestly Code" of Leviticus. And as Deuteronomy prepared the way for a rewriting of history, so the Priestly Code was supported by a revision of the Pentateuchal narrative (or the Hexateuch—since Joshua is included), and by a new version of the history of the Judæan kingdom in the Books of Chronicles.

The priestly narratives in the Hexateuch and in Chronicles are of very small historical value as a record of the events they profess to describe. They have great historical value as representing the assumptions of the established religion in the period after the Exile. The enormous importance attached all through to the cult is astonishing after the protests of the prophets, whose writings the authors of the new code collected and revered. It is indeed ironical that a movement in religion which started with Amos' unsparing attack on ritual should have issued in one of the most elaborate ritual systems ever known. Yet we must not mistake the character of the revived cult. The paganism of the days of the monarchy is gone. Puerile and superstitious as much of the ritual must appear to us (as indeed it would have appeared to Isaiah), there is nothing in it that affronts the moral sense. Ancient practices have been skilfully purged of their grossness and adapted to the worship of the one God whose holiness is at the same time righteousness. If we find in Leviticus a collocation of senseless rules of *tabu* with lofty moral principles, while we cannot but wish for the clear-sighted criticism of an Amos or a Micah, yet it is something that in the revived cult morality has won a definite place. You may still be required to acknowledge the holiness of God by a particular style of hairdressing, but at least you must also acknowledge it by loving your neighbour as yourself.[1] The priestly writers rarely let us into the secret of the meaning they attached to their weird ceremonies, but they certainly intended to express through them their adoration of the lonely and unapproachable majesty of God—of the one God who is good, who from His throne on high spoke the word and heaven and earth were made,[2] and who for His own name's sake revealed to men the way of life which by His inscrutable will He has ordained. This whole literature is an attempt to give rigid and unmistakable form to the religious ideas of Ezekiel and the post-exilic prophets.

Ultimately, the Deuteronomic and later codes were united with earlier traditional codes going back to the pre-exilic period, and the whole given a comprehensive setting in the priestly narrative. The resultant system of life and worship embodied in the Pentateuch in its final form—the Torah[3] —was the most treasured product of the religious movement of the post-exilic period. The prophets whose works were now given to the world in a definitive edition had one and all called upon men to do the will of God. Well, here was His will set forth in concrete detail, unambiguous and inescapable. The comprehensiveness and precision of the code gave great strength and permanence to the social institutions founded upon it, and enabled Judaism to survive almost incredibly the many dangers which threatened its existence. But when we take a long view of things, we must acknowledge that the more precise and

[1] Cf. Lev. xix. 27 with xix. 18. This whole chapter (which mostly belongs to the so-called Law of Holiness, the oldest stratum of the Priestly Code) is an astonishing example of the intermingling of the ethical and the unethical conceptions of "holiness."

[2] The creation-narrative of Gen. i. belongs to the Priestly stratum of the Pentateuch. How it soars above the mythology of earlier creation-stories such as that of Gen. ii.!

[3] The word is much wider in its significance than our word "law," which we use, following the Septuagint νόμος, as its translation. It means etymologically "instruction," and its religious connotation is the revealed will of God.

detailed a code is, the more it is bound up with temporary conditions. The inspiration of the prophets makes them immortal. The studied precision of the "Law of Moses" has made it, as a system, long obsolete. Already before the Christian era Rabbinic casuistry was transforming it and Alexandrine philosophy was allegorizing it. To-day it has, apart from the prophetic ideas underlying it, little more than an historical interest.

The principal value of the "Law" for us is that in it we have the bony skeleton which supported the warm flesh and blood of prophetic religion in the Jewish community. It was the nucleus of their sacred Canon. Indeed some Jewish authorities take the view that no other writings are in the full sense canonical. The prophets are regarded as authoritative commentary on the Law, but so are the Rabbinical writings collected in the Talmud, reaching down into the Middle Ages. But in practice first the prophets and then a selection of other writings came to be placed alongside the Pentateuch and regarded, like it, as Holy Scripture. The threefold Canon is already mentioned by Josephus, and implied in the Ezra-legend referred to above, both late in the first century of our era. It is said to have been officially recognized by an assembly of Rabbis at Jamnia about A.D. 100. The tests for canonicity given by the Rabbis are date and language: to be included in Holy Scripture a book must have been written during the prophetic period (conceived as ending with Nehemiah) and in Hebrew. These tests, however, are mere "rationalization" of a selection which had already been carried out by the general sense of the community, and are quite fallacious.[1] The canonical writings are as a matter of fact those which commended themselves to the religious instinct of Judaism as in various ways formative of its life and tradition. So

[1] *Ecclesiasticus*, for instance was written (and is for the most part still extant) in Hebrew, and is older than *Daniel* and some of the Psalms; yet it is not in the Canon.

far as we can judge from a comparison with extant works of the pre-Christian period which found no place in the Canon, we may fairly say that the selection does in a rough way represent a genuine religious valuation. It is not however, infallible. Who would not give the Book of Esther for Ecclesiasticus ?

But if we regard the classical prophets as giving the spiritual basis of the whole, and the Law as defining the institutional forms within which it developed, the other writings of the post-exilic period transmit to us the living forces of religion, in great diversities of operation, from the prophecies of Haggai and Zechariah immediately after the close of the Exile to the Book of Daniel and the Maccabæan Psalms in the second century B.C. When they are supplemented, as they should be, by the so-called Apocrypha, they bring us into the spiritual atmosphere in which the new religious movement represented by the New Testament comes to us with its utmost fulness of meaning.

The most typical literature of the period is ethical or devotional in character. It is admirably representative of an established religion whose main task is the peaceful penetration of a society in which its principles are already traditional. It is when a religion has become a settled and accepted thing in the life of a people that it is most likely to bring forth a literature of devotion. While new ideas have to be fought for, abuses reformed, false or unworthy notions of God combated, the voices most clearly heard are those of the prophet and the reformer. When the fight is won, and the general conscience of the community is content with its established ways of faith and worship, then the quieter notes of piety and devotion are sounded. It is with good reason that for devotional reading we go by instinctive preference not to the prophets, but to the Psalms. The prophets were concerned to affirm and defend the truth ;

the psalmists assume it and let their spirits dwell securely in it.

The Psalter is the hymn-book of the second Temple. Opinions differ about the amount of poetry of earlier date which may be included in it, as about the date of its completion. It is most probable that the bulk of its contents was composed during the centuries between the Exile and the Maccabæan period ; and that whatever is of earlier date was selected and adapted with a view to the needs of that age. The prophetic religion had won its cause, and had entered deeply into the mind of the people, as well as informing their accepted institutions. A whole community professed at least to live by the law of God. Devout souls could " meditate in it day and night "[1] with a serene sense of satisfaction to be found only in a religion which has become corporate and traditional. The question has often been discussed, how far the piety of the Psalms is individual and how far collective. It is of the essence of the case that it is both. In the prophetic period the individual is set over against the community in passionate protest. In the period of the Psalmists the individual is blessedly conscious of sharing a collective life of faith. The " I " of the Psalmists may often stand for the community (or a group within it), but it is none the less the utterance of a truly personal faith and devotion.

Here personal religion comes to its own. We have observed its emergence in a certain definite form in the prophets, particularly in Jeremiah. It is this prophetic piety which pervades the Psalter. The Psalmists share the prophets' robust faith in a God who, while holy, wonderful, and mysterious beyond telling, has revealed himself unmistakably to men in His works. Secure in the belief in one God, Lord of heaven and earth, they are no longer afraid (as the Deuteronomic writers with their keen sense of natural

[1] Ps. i. 2.

beauty were still afraid[1]) of nature-paganism. For them "the heavens declare the glory of God and the firmament showeth His handiwork".[2] In the spirit of the creation-narrative of the Priestly Code, though with a warmer fancy, they can call the roll of the creatures and cry—"O Lord, how manifold are Thy works; in wisdom hast thou made them all!"[3] But the mighty works of God in history are a still more signal witness to His greatness and majesty. Incongruous in Christian worship, yet still moving in its exultant faith, is that Psalm[4] in which we sing of the destruction of "Sihon king of the Amorites (for His mercy endureth for ever), and Og king of Bashan (for His mercy endureth for ever)!" This and similar Psalms are the poetical counterpart of the Deuteronomic recension of Hebrew history. Their authors, taught by the prophets, sought and found God in what He had *done*.

On that twofold ground of confidence, the works of God in nature and His works in history, the Psalmists take their stand. Times may be bad, and evil strong in the world, but they will defiantly tell it out among the heathen that Jehovah is King, a great God and a great King above all gods.[5] He has chosen Israel to be His people, and He will deliver them out of all their distresses.[6] This is not a mere return to the non-moral optimism of the "false prophets"; for the relation of God to His people has ethical conditions. The Israel of which they sing is the people of the Law, the righteous,[7] whom many of them at least regard as an "*ecclesiola in ecclesia*", the true commonwealth of God within a nation not wholly faithful to Him. Great is His mercy to them; great His demands of them. Sinners,

[1] Deut. iv. 19. [2] Ps. xix. 1–6.
[3] Ps. civ., cf. cxlviii., etc., also Job xxxviii–xli.
[4] Ps. cxxxvi, cf. lxxviii., cv., cvi., etc.
[5] Ps. xcvi. 10, xcv. 3, cf. ii., ix., xxix., xxxiii., xlvii.
[6] Ps. lxviii., lxxvi., lxxxiii., lxxxv., lxxxvii., etc.
[7] Ps. xl., lxxiii., l, cxxv., etc.

though they be of Israel, shall utterly fall, for God will judge the world in righteousness.[1] The apparent prosperity of the wicked is of necessity only temporary.[2] The judge of all the earth must do right. The first Psalm of the corpus sets forth in brief and decisive contrast the inevitable lots of the righteous and the wicked; whatever be the present aspect of facts, it is a necessity of belief that the righteous shall prosper, the wicked perish. Many indeed are the afflictions of the righteous, but the Lord delivereth him out of them all.[3] Acts of faith in God's deliverance, prayers for His help, thanksgiving for mercies received, are the main stuff of the Psalms. Behind it all lies the assumption that the worshippers are, so to speak, in good standing before God; they are righteous. That means that they love and observe the law of God. That pride in the clear, reasonable, beneficent commandments of God which we find in Deuteronomy is shared by the Psalmists.[4] The limitations of the Law had yet to reveal themselves. At this stage we can recognize the well-grounded satisfaction men felt in a religion which associated the worship of God with an intelligent discipline of daily life in social relations. In the main the Psalmists are conscious of keeping the law, and they express this consciousness in terms which sometimes have for us a disagreeable suggestion of self-righteousness.[5] Yet they know too what it is to have a bad conscience. In some Psalms the sense of sin finds most poignant expression.[6] But with it always goes the sense of divine forgiveness[7]—a forgiveness essentially independent of sacrifice and expiation, yet fitly mediated by the ritual.

[1] Ps. l., lxxxii., xciv., cxlvi.
[2] Ps. xxxvi. 1–4, 11–12, xxxvii., lxxiii., xci., etc.
[3] Ps. xxxiv. 19.
[4] Ps. cxix., xix. 7–14, xl. 8, etc., cf. Deut iv. 5–7, xxx. 11–20.
[5] Ps. xxvi., vii. 8, xviii. 20–24, etc.
[6] Ps. xxxviii., li., xxv. 7–11, cvi. 6, etc.
[7] Ps. xxxii., lxv. 3, lxxxv. 1–2, ciii. 10–12, cxxx. 7–8, etc.

Indeed the position of the cult in the Psalms may give us a juster view of its actual significance in the working religion of the early post-exilic centuries than might be gained from an exclusive study of the legal writings of the time. We may fairly read the Psalms as indicating that devout men had experience of divine forgiveness and communion with God in the most inwardly real and direct way, but that it was perfectly natural for them to associate such communion with the cult, as its fitting medium of expression.[1] Thus in some Psalms which breathe the most intense yearning for communion with God, an attentive scrutiny reveals the fact that the form of communion desired is that of mingling with the crowd of worshippers flocking up to the Temple hill on a day of festival.[2] It is not for that less truly inward communion. All the heights and depths of spiritual life are experienced within the forms of a traditional and corporate religion.

We found the authority of the prophets to be essentially that of religious genius, which by virtue of individual "inspiration" apprehended intensely and uttered compellingly fresh and creative ideas. The Psalms too have their authority for religious minds, but it is of a different kind. We do not find here towering individual genius, but a high level of corporate religion maintained through many generations. We are made aware of the immense range of religious experience covered by those few ruling ideas which the prophets had at last made current coin. Genius is never altogether normal; but there are few phases of normal religious experience which are not represented in the Psalter. There is here nothing extravagant, nothing fantastic or exotic, nothing smacking of an artificial and cloistered religiosity. The emotions expressed are simple, true, and

[1] Ps. xx., lxv. 1–5, lxvi. 13–15, lxxiii. 16–17, lxxxi., c., cxvi. 12–19, cxxxiv., cxxxv. 1–3, 19–21.

[2] Ps. xlii., xliii., l. 14–15, lxiii. 1–2, lxviii. 24–26, lxxxiv., cxxii., cxxxii. 13–14.

strong, without a trace of the sentimentality which is the bane of all but the greatest hymns. All is honestly felt and given lyric utterance in language of the utmost purity and sincerity.[1] There is no part of the Bible where scholarship finds it so difficult to define the precise historical setting of the various compositions. There is no part of the Bible where such criticism is less needed. For the situations contemplated are those in which most men find themselves who, in a world like this, try to live by a religion making the large and simple assumptions of the prophetic faith. The Psalter has in all ages nourished the inward life, not of specialists in religion alone, but of those who do the work of the world, and feel the stress and need of ordinary daily life.[2]

The piety of the Psalter implies a definite moral standard as an inseparable element in it. There are some Psalms which have morals for their express theme,[3] and from the collection as a whole it would be possible to get a fairly good idea of the ethics of Judaism on broad lines. But there is also a specifically ethical literature to be considered. Typical examples are the Book of Proverbs in the Canon, and Ecclesiasticus in the Apocrypha. The former contains the work of many authors, mainly of the fourth and third centuries; the latter is the work of Jesus ben Sirach, who wrote early in the second century. All these writers ranked among "the Wise", who according to Jewish tradition were the successors of the prophets. Their claim to the succession is so far justified, that they take with absolute seriousness the principle that to serve God one must live a good life, and make it their aim to define what a good life is, even beyond the written rules of the Torah. As they began by

[1] "The saint when he tries to express himself is no saint unless he is an artist. He must be ascetic in words no less than in life."—A reviewer in *The Times Literary Supplement.*

[2] See R. E. Prothero, *The Psalms in Human Life.*

[3] Ps. xv., ci., and in part xli., lxxxii., etc.

accepting the doctrine, taught by the prophets and laid down with mechanical rigour in Deuteronomy, that good is rewarded and evil punished in this life, their ethics have a utilitarian and prudential cast. They are sure that to be good is the only sensible course in a world like this, and that the sinner is a fool. "Wisdom" is the all-inclusive virtue, and "the fear of the Lord is the beginning of Wisdom".[1] We have seen that the prophets valued highly the intellectual qualities of insight and judgment, and here "the Wise" are their true followers. It was a great thing to state religion in terms of a reasonable morality, where clear common sense keeps fanaticism and superstition at a distance. If a good deal of their teaching has the air of moral commonplace, it is not necessarily the worse for that. The moralist can hardly dispense with the commonplace, since so much of the groundwork of his subject belongs to the unchanging qualities of human nature. It is for him to recommend such fundamental virtues as kindliness, honesty, diligence, sobriety, temperance, chastity, truthfulness, modesty, and to discourage their contrary vices, with such arguments and inducements as he has at his command. Such are the prevailing themes of the "Wisdom" writers. They handle them with the freshness and vigour which spring from conviction and wide experience. Their criticism of life is shrewd, based on a cool and humorous observation, pointed with wit and adorned with a pretty fancy. Their praises of Wisdom often rise to the level of great poetry.[2] Their moral outlook has its limitations. They rarely reach out towards such heroic ideals as self-sacrifice and forgiveness.[3] Yet in their pedestrian way these writers often get far on the road. It is to one of this

[1] Prov. ix. 10 (cf. Ps. cxi. 10); Ecclus. i. 14 (cf. 16, 18, 20, 27) *et passim*.

[2] Prov. i. 20–33, viii., etc.; Ecclus. xxiv., etc.

[3] Yet see Prov. xxiv. 17, xxv. 21; Ecclus. x. 6, xxviii. 1–7. Ben Sirach's more usual attitude is that of xii. 4–7, xxv. 7; cf. also Ps. lxix. 19–28, cix., and many other passages in the Psalms.

school that we owe the fine ethical ideal embodied in the character of Job. His "oath of compurgation" is the classical expression of the ethics of post-exilic Judaism[1]:

"If I did despise the cause of my man-servant
  Or of my maid-servant, when they contended with me,
What then shall I do when God riseth up?
  And when he visiteth, what shall I answer him?
Did not he that made me in the womb make him?
  And did not one fashion us in the womb?
If I have withheld the poor from their desire,
  Or caused the eyes of the widow to fall;
Or have eaten my morsel alone,
  And the fatherless hath not eaten thereof . . .
If I have seen any perish for want of clothing,
  Or that the needy hath no covering;
If his loins have not blessed me,
  And if he were not warmed with the fleece of my sheep;
If I have lifted up my hand against the fatherless,
  Because I saw my help in the gate;
Then let my shoulder fall from the shoulder blade,
  And mine arm be broken from the bone! . . .
If I have made gold my hope,
  And have said to the fine gold, My confidence!
If I rejoiced because my wealth was great,
  And because my hand had gotten much; . . .
If I rejoiced at the destruction of him that hated me,
  Or lifted up myself when evil found him; . . .
If among men I covered my transgressions,
  By hiding mine iniquity in my bosom;
Because I feared the great multitude,
  And the contempt of families terrified me,
  So that I kept silence and went not out of the door—

Oh that I had one to hear me!
  Lo, here is my signature; let the Almighty answer me!"

There is no doubt that Job stands in the succession of the prophets as humane moralists. A public that could accept such a moral ideal as its common standard—and this is necessary to the argument of the book—had certainly not failed to assimilate one side at least of their teaching.

[1] Job xxxi. 13–35 (R.V. slightly altered).

This ethical tradition was continuous in Judaism, and is represented beyond the canonical period in such literature for example as the Testaments of the Twelve Patriarchs, belonging substantially to the second century B.C. It would be difficult to find anything in the whole Old Testament quite up to the level (in its own line) of the counsel put into the mouth of the Patriarch Gad (!)[1], though it is a direct development of that humane tendency that we have observed all through :

"Love ye one another from the heart ; and if a man sin against thee, speak peaceably to him, and in thy soul hold not guile ; and if he repent forgive him. But if he deny it, do not get into a passion with him, lest catching the poison from thee he take to swearing, and so thou sin doubly. And though he deny it and yet have a sense of shame when reproved, give over reproving him. For he who denieth may repent so as not again to wrong thee ; yea, he may also honour thee and be at peace with thee. And if he be shameless in his wrong-doing, even so forgive him from the heart, and leave to God the avenging."

The great Rabbis whose words are preserved in the early portions of the Mishna are once again in the same tradition, and even though Pharisaism often obscured the plain lines of "Wisdom" morality by a false emphasis on irrational forms of religious observance, yet it held within it an ethical ideal inherited from the great prophets. This ideal is acknowledged in the Gospels,[2] with all their trenchant criticism of the Pharisees, and it passed with Paul from Pharisaism into Christian ethics.

[1] Testament of Gad vi. 3–7 (R. H. Charles).

[2] Luke x. 26–28 ; Mark xii. 28–34 ; cf. Matt. xxiii. 2–3, 23–24. Jesus accepted from Hillel (with a characteristic modification) the summary of "the Law and the Prophets" which we call the Golden Rule (Matt. vii. 12 ; Luke vi. 31). Hillel said, "This is the substance of the Torah : what thou hatest for thyself do not to thy fellow" (Aboth d' R. Nathan cited by I. Abrahams, *Studies in Pharisaism*, I., p. 23) ; cf. Tobit iv. 15.

It is important to realize that while the post-exilic religion was elaborating the system of rites and ceremonies in the Priestly Code, it experienced also a parallel elaboration of the ethical side of the Torah of which Deuteronomy is the foundation. The "wise" describe their own moral teaching as "Torah" in the wide sense. Ben Sirach expressly identifies Wisdom with Torah, and even with "the book of the covenant of the Most High God, the Torah which Moses commanded us for a heritage".[1] Thus the "Law" in which the Psalmists delight is not a mere code of rules mostly ceremonial and non-rational, as we are apt to think if we have in mind the legal literature of their age, but a comprehensive ethical ideal. When we contemplate this ideal as it is richly illustrated in the Wisdom literature, we must acknowledge the justice of the claim of Deuteronomy[2]:

"This commandment which I command thee this day, it is not too hard for thee, neither is it far off. It is not in heaven, that thou shouldest say, Who shall go up for us to heaven and bring it unto us and make us hear it, that we may do it? Neither is it beyond the sea, that thou shouldest say, Who shall go over the sea for us, and bring it unto us, and make us hear it, that we may do it? But the word is very nigh unto thee, in thy mouth and in thy heart, that thou mayest do it."

[1] Ecclus. xxiv. 23. [2] Deut. xxx. 11–14.

CHAPTER VIII

THE INCONCLUSIVENESS OF THE OLD TESTAMENT RELIGION

THE devotional literature, then, of the Psalms, and the ethical literature of Proverbs, with other kindred writings, represent the religion of the Jews as an accepted system satisfying in the main their spiritual needs. The lofty teachings of the prophets proved themselves capable of being translated into terms of life and faith for a whole society, living in a larger and more complex world than theirs, and exposed to many vicissitudes and disturbing influences. For during these centuries the Jews were no longer a compact and comparatively isolated national state, but were caught up in the wider life of great empires. They were the subjects first of the Persians, the last of the ancient Oriental monarchies, then of the Hellenistic kingdoms of Egypt and Syria, and finally after a brief period of independence were absorbed into the great western Empire of Rome. They were powerfully affected by these foreign contacts, and the fact that their religion was able to assert itself with undiminished force, and successfully to absorb ideas from the environment without losing its character, is a strong proof of its spiritual vitality. At the same time there are evidences of strain and tension within the accepted system, as various unsolved questions are brought into prominence by the pressure of changing conditions. Partly they are due to insufficient assimilation or application of prophetic ideas, partly to defects or gaps in the prophetic teaching itself. But some such tension there must be wherever a high type of religion like that of the prophets is taken seriously by a community of ordinary men and women who try to make it the guide of an active social life in a complex and civilized world. We who read the Bible to-day have to face the like task. Its value to us is all the greater because it not only attests the fundamental satisfaction which these people found in their religion, but also reflects the tensions that arose in it when they faced the complexities of an actual situation.

For example, there is perpetual tension between the priestly conception of religion as cultus and the prophetic conception of it as spiritual and ethical life. As we have seen, the religion of Judaism, while it set out to be prophetic in its main intention, yet found a place for the revived sacrificial system. There was an unsolved problem at its heart. The problem faces every established religion. For it is hard to see how any corporate religion could dispense with cultus, and yet in practice the cultus always tends to become a substitute for religion as the prophets understood it. Post-exilic Judaism found no radical solution of the problem. In the very period when the cultus was growing to unheard-of elaboration we hear echoes of the prophetic protests[1]:

> "Thou desirest not sacrifice, else would I give it;
> Thou delightest not in burnt offering;
> The sacrifices of God are a broken spirit;
> A broken and a contrite heart, O God, thou wilt not despise."

The Psalms themselves are witness that for the finest spirits prayer rather than sacrifice became more and more the heart of worship, even while sacrifice was unquestioningly accepted as a necessary part of it. In other literature of the time we can see a new ideal of priesthood growing up, in which the priest is a man of prayer more than an official

[1] Ps. li. 16–17 (A.V.).

for the punctilious performance of ritual. Judas Maccabaeus saw a vision of the High Priest Onias—"a great gentleman (*ἄνδρα καλὸν καὶ ἀγαθόν*), reverend of bearing and mild in disposition, fair-spoken and practised from childhood in all the ways of virtue"—and he was (not offering sacrifice, but) "with outstretched hands praying for the whole body of the Jews".[1] That priesthood in an ethical religion demands ethical qualifications is implied already in Malachi's imaginary "character" of Levi, the ancestral priest[2]:

> "The law of truth was in his mouth,
> And unrighteousness was not found in his lips;
> He walked with me in truth and uprightness,
> And did turn many away from iniquity."

Three centuries later the same ideal reappears in the Testament of Levi,[3] and on the eve of the Christian revelation Hillel summed up the character of the true "disciple of Aaron"—"one who loves peace, who pursues peace; who loves mankind and brings them near to Torah".[4] It was this sublimated conception of priesthood, divorced from any necessary connection with a material cultus, that lay to the hand of the Christian writer to the Hebrews,[5] who presents Christ as the true High Priest. A long succession of actual high priests who scandalously departed from this ideal must have done more than any argument or denunciation to remove the Temple cultus from the centre to the circumference for men of true and energetic piety. When Jesus, claiming succession to Jeremiah,[6] expelled the sacrificial animals from the Temple, and pronounced it, in the words of the "Third Isaiah", "a house of prayer",[7] He was carrying this process to its natural fulfilment.

Meanwhile so much of the traditional ritual as could be

[1] 2 Macc. xv. 12.
[2] Mal. ii. 6 (R.V.).
[3] Test. Lev. xviii.
[4] Pirke Aboth, i. 12.
[5] Heb. iv. 14–v. 10
[6] Jer. vii. 11, quoted Mark xi. 17.
[7] Isa. lvi. 7.

practised by laymen took a new lease of life in the discipline adopted by the pietists of the time—the Chasidim and their successors the Pharisees. Fasting, Sabbath-keeping, ceremonial purity, and the payment of a burdensome ecclesiastical taxation formed a code of religious observance, essentially no less external than the cultus itself, and yet commended by the post-exilic prophets and their successors as earnestly as the "weightier matters of the law".[1] In somewhat the same way the English Puritans, while denouncing the externalism of the Catholic cultus, devised for themselves a discipline, in part resembling the old monastic rule adapted for persons living in the world, and often maintained with equal moral fervour the practice of the cardinal virtues and a mere religious etiquette. This peculiar combination is very characteristic of the piety which finds attractive expression in such writings as the one hundred and nineteenth Psalm and the "Third Isaiah", and less attractive expression in the Pharisaism of the Gospels or of Paul's pre-Christian days.

The double process by which the cultus became a matter of prayer more than sacrifice, while many of its ritual or ceremonial elements were absorbed into the discipline of daily life, prepared Judaism for the final catastrophe under Titus. The Temple having been destroyed, the religion was re-constituted with prayer and the Commandments as its pillars.

Again, there is acute tension between the idea of religion as essentially universal (since God is one), and the sectarian nationalism of the Jewish system. As we have seen, the prophets did not bequeath a perfectly thought-out or consistent doctrine on this point. Of the two great prophets

[1] Isa. lvi. 2, 6, lviii. 13, lxvi. 23; Mal. iii. 7–10; cf. Tobit i. 3–11 (*c.* 200 B.C.); Jubilees xxxii. 8–15 (2nd cent. B.C.); Test. Jos. iii. 4; Psalms of Solomon (1st cent. B.C.) iii. 9.

who prepared for the restoration after the Exile, one, the "Second Isaiah", is in the main universalist, the other, Ezekiel, in the main nationalist. Both found successors. The Book of Ruth, pleading against Ezra's harsh suppression of mixed marriages,[1] and the Book of Jonah, proclaiming God's mercy upon heathen Nineveh—"wherein are more than six score thousand persons that cannot discern between their right hand and their left hand, and also much cattle"[2]—are outstanding examples of the continued protests made in the interests of a humaner ideal against a hardening national exclusiveness. The "Third Isaiah", while firmly convinced of the superiority of his own people, would have them become missionaries to the nations, and envisages a day when "all flesh" will worship Jehovah.[3] Malachi goes further, and declares, "From the rising of the sun unto the going down of the same my name is great among the Gentiles".[4] But the narrower tendency prevailed, especially when oppression exasperated national feeling.[5] It had some justification, for the preservation of the prophetic religion might well seem to be bound up with the integrity of the nation, and friendliness to the foreigner was too often accompanied by demoralizing compromises with paganism. Hence the Chasidim, who, forming a sort of conventicle within the national "church", were not nationalists in a political sense, lent all their weight to the exclusive tendency, and we find their successors in New Testament times upholders of a narrow nationalism in religion. Thus whether through political nationalism or through a rigorous puritanism, the later books of the Old Testament are deeply

[1] Ezra x., cf. Neh. xiii. 1–8. This policy was in the sense of Dt. xxiii. 3. Contrast Ruth ii. 12, iv. 11–12, 17. Cf. Mt. i. 5–6.

[2] Jonah iv. 10–11.

[3] Isa. lvi. 1–8, lx. 1–6, lxvi. 18–23; cf. Zech. ii. 11, viii. 20–23; Isa. xix. 19–25 (5th century). So also Ps. lxvii., etc.

[4] Mal. i. 11.

[5] Cf. Ps. lx., lxxii., lxxix., lxxxiii., cxxxvii., etc.

scored with a gloomy and rancorous kind of corporate egotism, which shows how difficult it was for the lofty spirituality of the prophets to become a workaday religion for a whole community. The difficulty is perpetually recurrent, for it is inherent in the situation. The patriot who is also a religious man *wants* his country to be "God's own country", goes on to *believe* it such, and ends with "So let all Thine enemies perish, O Lord!" The Puritan, seeing in the discipline of an exclusive society the only safeguard for true religion in an evil world, readily comes to identify religion with his sect, and develops the vices of the minority mind. How is corporate religion, in any concrete expression of it, to be other than national or sectarian? Yet there can be no going back upon the prophetic discovery that God is the God of all men. The Old Testament wrestles with the problem and hands it on unsolved to the New.

But there was a problem that struck deeper into the heart of things. The prophets had done a dangerous thing when in the interest of a spiritual conception of God they had upset the natural equilibriums of primitive religion. We have seen that a certain tension between the aloofness and the nearness of God is inseparable from religion. The plain "heathen" (and the Hebrew people at large before the prophets were hardly more) solves his problem in a rough way by attributing an awful "holiness" to familiar objects, and by mingling mysterious rites at the local shrine with all the operations of daily life. The prophets took away from the common man all those homely reminders of the presence of God "on every high hill and under every green tree". In modern jargon, they emphasized the transcendence of God at the cost of His immanence. For the prophets themselves nothing was lost thereby, for the depth and strength of their religious experience were such that without any dependence on symbol or ritual they found God very near to their own souls and knew Him at the same moment to be infinitely high and mysterious. It is a post-exilic prophet who has given us the classical expression for that reconciliation of transcendence and immanence which belongs to all complete religious experience :

"Thus saith the high and lofty One that inhabiteth eternity, whose name is Holy : I dwell in the high and holy place ; with him also that is of a humble and contrite spirit."[1]

Many of the Psalmists have reached the same level of insight, and there is for them no longer any contradiction between the nearness and the aloofness of God. But it is evident that the tension had not been altogether overcome for the average man. The elaboration of the cultus is itself a symptom. Jehovah, it was now taught, was confined to no earthly spot. The heaven of heavens could not contain Him. Yet of His infinite mercy He had chosen to dwell on the hill of Zion—the one spot on earth where men could find Him near at hand.[2] The awful " holiness " of that hill therefore must be guarded with all conceivable apparatus of rite and ceremony, which must be made to symbolize in the most impressive way the preciousness of such approach to the Inapproachable as He condescended to authorize.[3] This ritual, defined in the priestly writings of the Old Testament, has had an influence on liturgical practice and language which still survives. It is the cult of a God who is far away, and its anxious scrupulosity betrays an unsatisfied craving for some more direct sense of God's nearness and accessibility such as a cruder religion had given. The idea of intermediaries between God and man begins to be important. Popular imagination makes great play with " angels ".

[1] Isa. lvii. 15 (R.V.).

[2] Isa. lxvi. 1–4, looks at first sight like a prophetic declaration of the utter transcendence of God, but is found to be a protest against a schismatic temple with a syncretistic cult (probably with reference to the Samaritan temple on Mt. Gerizim).

[3] See e g. the ritual for the Day of Atonement, Lev. xvi.

It is thought that we may here recognize influence from the Persian religion, beginning in the period when the Jews were subjects of the Persian Empire, though even in pre-exilic literature the idea of angels is not unknown. "The angel of Jehovah" is a convenient form of speech to avoid the anthropomorphism of the older ways of thinking, and an "angel" has sometimes evidently been substituted for a god in the primitive tradition, as when Hosea says that Jacob prevailed over "the angel",[1] alluding to the very ancient tale of his wrestling with a river-god.[2] The more extravagant developments of the doctrine of angels are found in non-canonical literature, but it is clear that even within the Old Testament some functions of the providential government of the universe are being delegated to subordinate powers—and that not only in apocalyptic contexts, where the activity of angels is an essential part of the scheme,[3] but also in the literature of personal religion.[4] But where the discarded gods of polytheism—for that is what angels really are—have to be brought back to safeguard the transcendence of God, it is clear that the root-problem of religion is not solved.

Deeper thinkers treated the problem of the mediation of the divine in a more interesting way. The conception of Wisdom, as a sort of half-personal emanation of the Divine, mediating between God and the world, is one of the most fruitful products of the contact of Judaism with the outer world. For although we cannot mistake the native Hebrew lineaments of this Wisdom, yet the doctrine would hardly have developed as it did without the influence of Egyptian mysticism and Greek philosophy. For the Hebrew, wisdom was primarily the practical right judgment by which

[1] Hos. xii. 4. [2] Gen. xxxii. 24–32.
[3] E.g. Zech. i. 8–17; Dan. viii. 15–16, x. 11–21.
[4] E.g. Ps. xxxiv. 7, xxxv. 5–6, xci. 11, etc.; Dan. iii. 28, vi. 22. Cf. also Tobit v. 4 *et passim*.

a virtuous man guides his conduct, and the Wisdom-literature is full of common sense precepts for daily life. But since Judaism was a religion of revelation, all wisdom was conceived as the inspiration of God, and its standard form was the revealed Torah, as an all-sufficient expression of the will of God for men. The Wisdom-morality is the Torah on its more humane and rational side. In a system which tended more and more to emphasize the aloofness of God, the Torah, as His revealed will, came to take the place of supreme intermediary between God and man. In its aspect as Wisdom it could more readily be thought of, especially under the foreign influences already mentioned, in relation to the works of God in Nature as well as in relation to His Law for man. Already in the more poetical parts of the Book of Proverbs Wisdom is half-personified as the Companion of God in creation[1]:

> "Jehovah formed me as the beginning of his way,
> The first of his works of old.
> I was set up from everlasting, from the beginning,
> Or ever the earth was. . . .
> When he established the heavens, I was there,
> When he set a circle upon the face of the deep;
> When he made firm the skies above,
> When the fountain of the deep became strong . . .
> Then I was with him as a master workman,
> And I was daily his delight."

A century later Jesus ben Sirach[2] carries the thought of Proverbs a step further, making Wisdom say:

> "I came forth from the mouth of the Most High,
> And covered the earth as a mist.
> I dwelt in high places,
> And my place was in the pillar of the cloud.

[1] Prov. viii. 22–30 (R.V.). The rendering "master-workman" in 30 is not certain; a possible meaning is "foster-child," but LXX supports R.V., and it was clearly so understood in traditional exegesis before the Christian era. Cf. Wisd. vii. 22.

[2] Ecclus. xxiv. 3–6.

Alone I compassed the circuit of heaven,
And walked in the depths of the abyss.
In the waves of the sea and in all the earth,
And in every nation and people, I got a possession."

Finally in the Wisdom of Solomon, which brings us down practically to the Christian Era, we have a fully developed doctrine of divine immanence in terms of Wisdom[1]:

"Wisdom is more mobile than any motion;
Yea, she pervadeth and penetrateth all things by reason of her pureness.
For she is a breath of the power of God,
And a clear effluence of the glory of the Almighty;
Therefore can nothing defiled find entrance into her.
For she is an effulgence from everlasting light,
And an unspotted mirror of the working of God,
And an image of his goodness.
And she being one hath power to do all things;
And remaining in herself reneweth all things:
And from generation to generation passing into holy souls
She maketh men friends of God and prophets."

In such a doctrine there is the possibility of a valid reconcilation of transcendence and immanence, and doubtless it was a possibility realized by many in their experience. But as a philosophy of religion it has inherent weaknesses. The poetical half-personification of Wisdom evades rather than answers the question whether in religious experience one is in direct touch with a personal God, or only moved by a cosmic force. The doctrine was perhaps at once too intellectualist and too nearly mystical to strike deep root in Judaism, except in so far as Wisdom could be kept strictly identified with the concrete Torah as the form of a national religion. The ultimate phase of Wisdom-philosophy is to be sought in the Christology of Paul and the Logos-doctrine of the Fourth Gospel, in both of which the fictitious personification of Wisdom is carried into the realm of reality by the conception of God incarnate in a human Person.

[1] Wisd. vii. 24–27 (R.V.).

But once again, behind the difficulty raised for religious experience by the new emphasis on divine transcendence lay a more radical doubt. Could the prophetic assurance of the government of the universe by a good and all-powerful God stand in the face of facts ? The theodicy of the prophets,[1] at least in the form in which it reached the mind of the ordinary man, was simple and rigorous : because God is just, the righteous prospers in this world, the wicked is punished. Throughout the Old Testament this belief is " orthodoxy ". The prophets had mainly had in view the destiny of peoples as historical units. In that sense their doctrine obviously meets many of the facts. At least, the most profound observers of many peoples and ages have seen reason to regard history in its great rhythms as a moral order. *Die Weltgeschichte ist das Weltgericht.* But any application of the principle in particular detail is confessedly difficult. The Jews very naturally did not find it easy to admit that they were so vastly more wicked than other nations as to account for their repeated calamities on straightforward principles of justice. The problem became far more difficult when, under the influence of teachers like Ezekiel, the doctrine of exact retribution was extended to the individual lot. There is no question more perpetually recurrent in the Old Testament than that of the undeserved sufferings of the righteous and the undeserved prosperity of the wicked.[2] It besets the later prophets. In the Psalms it crops up with pathetic insistence. It is in the minds of writers of the Wisdom school. The astonishing thing is that the doctrine of exact retribution should have been so tenacious of life. Many partial solutions of the problem are offered. The wicked may prosper in life, but their " latter end " will be terrible ; or their sins will be visited on their posterity.[3] The righteous suffer by way of moral discipline.[4]

[1] See chap. IV. pp. 100–104. [2] Jer. xii. 1–2 ; Ps. lxxiii. *et passim.*
[3] Ps. xxxvii., lxxiii. 17–19, etc. ; Ecclus. xxvii. 25–29, xl. 15, xli. 6.
[4] Ps. cxix. 67, 71 (R.V.).

> "Before I was afflicted I went astray,
> But now I observe thy word . . .
> It is good for me that I have been afflicted,
> That I might learn thy statutes."

There is no mistaking the genuine experience that lies behind such confessions. Profounder still is the suggestion of the "Second Isaiah" that the sufferings of the righteous may have vicarious value for the redemption of the nations,[1] but it was a suggestion that did not, apparently, carry much weight in the biblical period.[2] The most elaborate treatment of the whole problem is in the dramatic poem of Job, in which the orthodox doctrine is expounded with persuasive eloquence, only to be decisively rejected as untrue to the facts of life. The traditional theology is in ruins, and no theory is offered to replace it. The author offers only his own unshakable certainty of God, and his acceptance of a purpose too vast for his understanding.[3]

> "I had heard of thee with the hearing of the ear,
> But now mine eye seeth thee".

There is, of course, nothing more to be said. It is no small part of the value of the Old Testament that it faces these ultimate problems of human existence simply and frankly, without having recourse (with exceptions which we shall presently notice) to the hypothesis of a future life. That hypothesis too easily becomes a mere way of escape from the pressure of the problem, and it may be said at once that a belief in immortality which is adopted *merely* as a way of escape is of small religious value. Not when it is made to buttress up a dogmatic interpretation of the world, which would fall apart without its support, but when it springs out of a religious experience of life as a whole, already secure on its own ground, is the belief really valuable for religion. Only this latter kind of belief in immortality is

[1] Isa. liii. [2] See chap. X, p. 215. [3] Job xlii. 5 (R.V.).

likely to hold its own in our time, when so many people cannot accept it as a dogma. Those who accept it and those who do not will profit by the intellectual discipline of following out the lines of Old Testament thought, and seeing how with no help from any doctrine of immortality such as most surrounding peoples possessed, the men of the Bible found themselves able to maintain all the religious values through a penetrating experience of God in life. All the more significant then become those passages in which we are brought to the threshold of belief in another life. A late Psalmist sings of his communion with God in these terms:[1]

> "Nevertheless I am continually with thee:
> Thou hast holden my right hand.
> Thou shalt guide me with thy counsel,
> And afterward receive me to glory.
> Whom have I in heaven but thee?
> And there is none upon earth that I desire beside thee.
> My flesh and my heart faileth;
> But God is the strength of my heart and my portion for ever."

A reader with a Christian background is naturally inclined to take such a passage as referring directly to a future life; but no such reference, apparently, was in the writer's mind. Nevertheless, such an experience of God carries within it its own eternity. Similarly Job, although he will not solve the problem of his suffering by positing a future life in which it may be redressed, yet gives utterance to the famous passage "I know that my Redeemer liveth", which has been translated in closer agreement with the true original text as follows[2]:

> "I know One to champion me at last,
> To stand up for me upon earth.
> This body may break up, but even then
> My life shall have a sight of God;
> My heart is pining as I yearn
> To see him on my side,
> See him estranged no longer."

[1] Ps. lxxiii. 23-26. [2] Job xix, 25-27 (Moffatt).

The exact implications of this rather obscure passage are still disputed, but at least the poet asserts that it is unthinkable God should lose interest in His servant after his death. From this it is a mere step to a real doctrine of eternal life in communion with God. As Mr. H. G. Wells once said that there is "a God-shaped blank" in the heart of some atheists,[1] so we might say that the religion of the Old Testament has within it a blank which more and more closely shapes itself to the form of a belief in a future life.

Where even faithful men felt so bitterly the difficulties of faith, it is not surprising that in many minds a deep scepticism arose about the whole prophetic religion. Was it at all true that the world exhibited the moral government of a righteous God? Some of the Psalmists allude to such scepticism as being rife in their times, or even confess to having once shared it.[2] Its best representative within the Canon is the anonymous writer of about 200 B.C. who calls himself "Koheleth", the Preacher—in our version Ecclesiastes. The dangerous questionings of this writer have been in some measure cloaked with a decent lip-service to orthodoxy—by some pious interpolator, no doubt, rather than by the man himself. But the main lines of his commentary on life remain clear. He is no atheist, or scoffer at holy things, but he has observed life coolly, and whether as a whole it justifies the assertions made by contemporary teachers of religion, he takes leave to doubt.[3]

"All manner of things have I seen in my fleeting life, the good man perishing by his very goodness and the evil man flourishing upon his evil. Be not over-good; be not over-wise; why expose yourself to trouble? And be not over-evil either, do not play the fool; why die before your time?"

[1] *God the Invisible King*, p. 99.
[2] Ps. xiv. 1, liii. 1, lxxiii. 11–17, lxxvii. 7–10, xcii. 6–7, xciv. 7.
[3] Eccles. vii. 15–17 (Moffatt).

As a criticism of the ultra-pious Chasidim, with their theology of exact retribution, it is admirable. No less admirable is his comment on their overdone devotions[1]:

"God is in heaven and you are on earth; so let your words be few."

From this unexpected quarter we seem to hear preludings of that devasting criticism of conventional religion that meets us in the Gospels: "I came not to call the righteous" . . . "They think that they shall be heard for their much speaking!" No fanaticism or high-falutin could live before the penetrating satire of Ecclesiastes. A religion that could tolerate his book in its sacred Canon must have been very sure of itself—or sure of something deeply real in it that could survive fallacies in its theology and trivialities in its practice. But Ecclesiastes cannot himself offer any positive valuation of life beyond the repeated maxim[2]:

"There is nothing better for a man than to eat and drink and enjoy himself as he does his work";

Nor, in spite of his genuinely reverent spirit, can he find in God more than a vague over-ruling power, whose rule is a blind fate[3]:

"Whatever happens has been determined long ago, and what man is has been ordered of old; he cannot argue with One mightier than himself; and lavish talk about it only means more folly. What is the use of talking? Who can tell what is good for man in life, during the few days of his empty life that passes like a shadow."

Here is a portent that for men incapable of the heights of prophetic experience, or prone to analysis rather than to enthusiasm or submission, the religion of Judaism was

[1] Eccles. v. 2 (Moffatt). [2] Eccles. ii. 24 (Moffatt) *et passim*.
[3] Eccles. vi. 10–12 (Moffatt).

failing because it had no adequate philosophy behind its faith and practice.

The pessimism of Ecclesiastes is shared by a group of writers who in other respects stand at the opposite pole, namely, the apocalyptists. While the sceptical mind of the one contented itself with criticism, and fell back into a refined and reverent Epicureanism, the ardent faith of the others "brought in a new world to redress the balance of the old". But they agreed that the traditional prophetic doctrine of an absolute divine justice meted out exactly in this present world did not meet the facts.

Apocalypse was in itself no new thing. The primitive *nabi* had his visions of divine mysteries, and vision is an element in the experience even of the classical prophets. Doubtless, too, such visions had early been concerned with what became the absorbing interest of literary apocalypse, namely, the ultimate issues of the divine purpose for the world, that is eschatology. But apocalypse as a literary form arose as prophecy declined, and although there are apocalyptic traits in such prophets as Ezekiel, yet such typical apocalypses as those which we have in the second part of the Book of Zechariah and in the Book of Daniel, with their numerous non-canonical successors, clearly form a distinct class of literature, differing both in form and in content from prophecy proper. While prophecy is spontaneous, first-hand, and imaginative, and carries the proof of its inspiration in what it says, independently of the psychological forms in which it is cast, apocalypse revives all the primitive respect for the psychologically abnormal, and yet is derivative, reflective, and even pedantic in its methods. Where the prophet gives us personal intuition in an imaginative form which kindles the imagination of the reader to respond and understand, the apocalyptist gives an artificial allegory to which he must provide a key.

The "interpreting angel" is a standing character in works of this sort. The material of the "vision" frequently has a literary history of its own, and certain features recur so constantly that they come to be common property, rather like the stock plots of an Elizabethan theatrical company. Thus Daniel's vision of "one like a son of man" (a figure which, as many authorities believe, was already traditional when the Book of Daniel was written) provides material which is variously utilized in the Parables of Enoch, in the Apocalypse of Ezra, and in the New Testament *Revelation of John*[1] (a work deeply Jewish and only superficially Christian). This is not to say that these authors did not "see" the vision for themselves in an abnormal psychical state ("in the spirit", as the Christian writer says[2]). The "subconscious" is capable of curious processes, and the presentation of material, originally learnt from tradition, as a fresh "vision", lies by no means outside observed psychological facts.[3] However that may be, it is characteristic of apocalyptic to work upon derived material. Much of this material can in fact be traced to earlier prophecy, and the apocalyptists regularly turn the poetry of the prophets into prose, taking what the prophets meant as imagery for literal prediction. This is directly connected with the outstanding difference between prophetic and apocalyptic eschatology.[4] The events to which the prophets look forward, though they are supernatural in the sense that they are the direct act of God, and on a scale unprecedented in human experience, are yet not different in kind from the work of God as known to us in nature and history. Apocalyptic eschatology, on the other hand, includes events which mean the break-up of the whole order of Nature. The stars fall from their places, the moon is turned into blood, the sea gives up its dead, and so forth.

[1] Dan. vii. 13–14; 1 En. xlvi. 1–6; 2 Esdras xiii. 1–6; Rev. i. 13–20.
[2] Rev. i. 10, iv. 2, xvii. 3.
[3] See B. H. Streeter, *The Sadhu*, chap. V.
[4] T. H. Robinson, in *The Psalmists*, ed. D. C. Simpson, p. 88.

We have seen that the post-exilic literature of Judaism reveals an increasing tension between the current doctrine of divine justice and the observed facts of life in an increasingly complex world. Job and Ecclesiastes boldly deny the current doctrine. Apocalyptic gives up the attempt to show that the fortunes of men and peoples in the present world are directly governed by God. This order of space and time is under the rule of a power or powers of evil, which God, for reasons best known to Himself, permits to hold temporary sway. Here it is almost certain that we must again recognize influence from the Persian religion. The Old Testament as a whole knows no " devil ", in the sense familiar to traditional Christianity. Even in the Book of Job the Satan, however unwelcome his attentions may be to men, is a faithful servant of the will of God. But the Persian system sets the evil Angro-mainyu and his minions over against the good Ahura-mazda. Similarly in the apocalypses evil spirits and rebellious angels oppress the people of God. Thus sin, and the suffering of the righteous and the prosperity of the wicked, are no longer a problem. What else would you expect in an age given over to the powers of evil ? But the sovereignty still belongs *de jure* to the God of heaven,[1] and in His own good time He will assert that sovereignty *de facto*, passing judgment on all evil and giving to merit the recognition denied to it in the present. Thus all the blessings promised to the righteous are postponed to the good time coming, and they endure the light affliction of the moment in the hope of an exceeding weight of glory in the future. As for those who died without receiving the promise, God will by His illimitable power raise them up at the end to enjoy the reward of their good deeds.[2]

[1] Dan. iv. 17, 25, 32, vii. 22–27.

[2] Dan. xii. 2–3. Note also that the other clear reference to resurrection which the Old Testament contains (Is. xxvi. 19) is found in a late apocalypse (Is. xxiv–xxvii).

In the hands of its greatest exponents, as notably in the Book of Daniel, apocalyptic is capable of becoming the expression of a splendid faith, and of suggesting what may fairly be called a philosophy of history. But it opened up a realm of fantasy full of dangers. Not only could the most sublime faith in the ultimate supremacy of right clothe itself in this fantastic guise, but also the baser passions, repressed in the real world by conscience or fear, could find unbridled license in a world where nothing was too extravagant to be true. Thus it comes about that the typical apocalypse is full of a vindictive gloating over the downfall of national enemies, and an unhealthy indulgence of personal and corporate pride and cupidity. The New Testament apocalypse is tainted with these vices no less than some of its Jewish congeners, and perhaps it would have been well for Christendom if those great scholars of the Eastern Church who disliked its presence in the Canon had had their way. Yet it must not be thought that apocalyptic is no more than an outlet in fantasy for the repressed passions of a deeply injured people. In spite of its defects it was an adventure of faith into unfamiliar regions. It established the principle that the issues of the providential order of history lie in the unseen, and it made current coin the sublime doctrine of a future life, which when a fresh outbreak of prophetic experience gave it richness of content and purged its crudity, made its way into the very centre of religion. Apocalyptic profoundly influenced the writers of the New Testament. Where they are most true to the distinctive Christian outlook they criticize its ideas by the light of reason and experience, and restore to the realm of poetry its misused symbolism, thus revealing how great a service it rendered towards the ultimate resolution of the inner tension within the religion of Judaism.

If now we survey the Canon of the Old Testament in its

complex unity, we must report that there is no finality in it. It represents a process, and an unfinished process, rather than an achievement. It could carry no authority, if authority belonged only to that which is fixed and final. But the religious life is itself a process rather than an achievement. In the minds of all of us a few great affirmations contend with doubts and speculations as widening experience puts them to the test. The Old Testament sets this process before us on the large scale of history, and bears impressive witness that through all uncertainties faith advances towards something surer and finer. If at moments in our own pilgrimage we are as much in doubt as Job or Ecclesiastes, we can stand back and see that such moments belong to a process which taken as a whole reveals God. Thus the process at large in history bears directly on the process in little in our lives, and our faith is confirmed by the authority of corporate experience through the centuries. Nevertheless, to see clearly whither the process is tending we must look beyond the Old Testament to the New, without which its witness remains incomplete.

Part III

THE AUTHORITY OF THE INCARNATION

CHAPTER IX

THE NEW TESTAMENT AS THE LITERATURE OF A DECISIVE MOVEMENT IN RELIGION

IN the New Testament, as in the prophetic literature of the Old Testament, we are once again in the presence of religious genius, authenticating itself to the mind that has the sense for such things in the inspired quality of being "first-hand". In Paul at his best, here and there in the minor epistles, certainly in the Fourth Gospel, most of all in the parables and lyrical sayings recorded in the Synoptic Gospels, no one can miss the prophetic note. The "inspiration" of such writing is not in question; this *is* inspiration, the *datum* of any argument about its nature. Nor is its authority dependent on any tradition or theory of authorship. Even where the ultimate authorship of sayings attributed to Jesus is in question, the primary religious value is not affected. For some purposes it is extremely important to ask whether the Parable of the Prodigal Son, or the fourteenth chapter of John, was or was not actually spoken by Jesus Christ; but the answer to that question is not the measure of the authority we feel in such utterances. They possess inherent truth, which was once apprehended in experience, it matters little by whom, so passionately that its utterance makes us sharers in the experience.

The claim, however, is put forth that the Scriptures of the New Testament have a specific authority going beyond their general and intrinsic authority as religious classics. The tradition of the Church indeed makes no distinction between the inspiration and authority of the two Testaments; but the hesitation of many people to-day to allow in the field of the New Testament the freedom of criticism they allow in the Old issues from a feeling that in the documents which record the beginnings of Christianity there must be found somehow a final authority which remains when the authority of Church and Councils, and the authority of the Bible as such, have been given up. Jesus Christ, the Lord and Master of Christians, must surely be absolutely authoritative for them. The Gospels, therefore, which record His words, and report the "saving facts" of His life, death, and resurrection, must have unique authority. The epistles, though less directly deriving from Him, must surely be held to proceed from a point so near to the source of the Christian tradition that they retain binding force even for minds prepared to treat the older Canon with critical though respectful detachment.

If any apologetic is offered for this attitude, it usually takes the form of argument for the early date and historical accuracy of the Gospels, and for the "genuineness" of the epistles, as writings of the early and venerable teachers of the Church to whom they are traditionally attributed. This line of defence, however, wears thin. Its upholders, if their minds are at all open, are apt to find themselves defending a diminishing nucleus of writings. Even a moderate criticism leaves few epistles beyond nine or ten of Paul's to their reputed authors, and makes large deductions from the material offered in the Fourth Gospel as a direct record of "the historical Jesus". If in addition to this we should be obliged to admit that there are elements in the genuine epistles of Paul which are rather inherited from Judaism or borrowed from Greek thought than learned from Jesus, and that even in the Synoptic Gospels the tradition of His words and acts is not entirely pure, the ultimate body of authoritative New Testament writings may reduce itself to quite insignificant dimensions.

In this book the view is taken that the New Testament as a whole does possess a specific authority going beyond the general authority which would be allowed by a discerning mind to parts of it, as to any such religious classic whatever its source. But in order to recognize and define it we must not try to show that when criticism has done its worst there remain at least a few sentences of such immediate and infallible authority that they outweigh all the other religious literature of the world, and lay private judgment to rest. Nor must we attempt to draw an absolute line between the scriptures of the Old Testament and the New, any more than we can draw an absolute line between these and other sacred books. The uniqueness of the Bible in both Testaments is the uniqueness of the particular historical process it represents; and the specific character of the New Testament is due to the unique intensity of the process within its field. That unique intensity proceeds from the central Figure of the New Testament, in Whom the whole history finds its climax and its interpretation.

The New Testament consists of twenty-seven writings, about twenty of which were already collected into a Canon recognized in practically all parts of the Church by the end of the second century. Later additions to the Canon came slowly; they were few and relatively unimportant. In the fourth century Eusebius[1] counts as "acknowledged" Scripture the four Gospels, the Acts of the Apostles, fourteen Pauline Epistles (including Hebrews), 1 John and 1 Peter, the *Revelation* being added with a note of doubt. This may be taken as representing the old second-century Canon. He gives a second list of "disputed" writings, namely, the Epistles of James and Jude, 2 Peter, and 2 and 3 John. These complete our own Canon. His third list contains books which had claimed canonicity at some period in one

[1] *Hist. Eccl.*, III, 25.

church or another, but were not ultimately accepted as Scripture. Among these he would like to include the *Revelation*, but is clearly aware that he has the general opinion against him. The rest are still known to us in whole or in part, and three of them are commonly read among the "Apostolic Fathers", namely, the Shepherd of Hermas, the Epistle of Barnabas, and the Teaching of the Twelve Apostles. The exclusion of these and the inclusion of their competitors which form Eusebius' second list resulted from a long process of discussion and balancing of claims. The original Canon on the other hand came into being by a process which we can no longer trace in detail. The grounds of canonicity alleged by the Fathers are not always convincing, and as in the case of the Old Testament canon we may suspect that they were rather "rationalizing" an existing selection than freely applying tests. At bottom the selection was instinctive. The Church read as Scripture those writings which it felt to be most vitally related to the spiritual impulse that created it. It did not at first regard these writings as specially authoritative because they were canonical; they became canonical because they had already made good their authority. So far as we are able to compare the writings of the original Canon with their competitors, especially with those which were ultimately excluded, there can be no doubt that as a whole they stand, spiritually, intellectually, and aesthetically, on an altogether higher plane.

By about A.D. 200, then, there existed a New Testament which substantially is ours. Now by that time the Christian Church had come to hold a "strategic position" in the spiritual life of the world, and was quite conscious of it. For three or four centuries in the lands which inherited the ancient civilizations of Egypt, Mesopotamia, and Greece the spirit of man had been on the move. Alexander's conquests had brought the old order to an end. There was a mingling of cultures, a cross-fertilization of East and West. The old forms of communal life provided by the tribe and its civilized analogue the city-state were broken, and the individual soul was astray in a world to which there seemed to be no limits. Philosophy sought to give him a foothold in it. New religions arose and old ones were transformed to meet fresh needs. Judaism, now widely diffused through the new Greek-speaking world, played its part in the spiritual adventure. The Old Testament was done into Greek. The first translation, the so-called Septuagint, is already a Hellenistic document in more than language. It was read by pagans, and as Greek thought had profoundly affected the religious outlook of the Jews, so the influence of the Septuagint was felt beyond the borders of Judaism. But in the end Judaism shrank, or was forced, into its shell again. By the time of which we are speaking it had reorganized itself after the revolt of Bar-Cochba on the rigid and exclusive lines which have persisted until our own time. All round in fact we see evidence that things were settling into new lines within the stable organization of the Roman Empire. The greater mystery-religions, particularly Mithraism, were emerging from the general mass, and ministering to the religious needs of whole classes of worshippers. In philosophy, Stoicism had by this time reached its final form, and had shaped the moral ideals of the age, and the later Platonism, uniting philosophy with religious experience, was preparing for its classical expression in the next century.

While out of the chaos and ferment of the earlier Hellenistic period these various tendencies defined themselves, it gradually became clear that the destined leader of the central advance was the Christian Church. Consciously the heir of the most powerful religious tradition of the ancient world, that of the Jews, it found itself able also to interpret and even to incorporate the deepest elements in

Hellenistic philosophy and religion. The Judaism from which it sprang had already responded, to a greater degree than it intended or admitted, to the influences of the wider world, especially among Jews resident outside Palestine and speaking the common dialect of Greek.

How far the influences present in this Hellenistic Judaism had power in Palestine itself, the scene of the Gospel history, is uncertain, but in Samaria at least, and likely enough in "Galilee of the Gentiles", they were stronger than we commonly realize. In any case the majority of the New Testament writings were produced in the environment of the Græco-Roman world, where the Judaism of the Dispersion was of a type better represented by Philo of Alexandria than by the tradition of the Talmud. But in asserting its independence of Judaism, Christianity naturally became more hospitable to thoughts which were in the air of the Græco-Roman world it set out to win. Thus it comes about that the New Testament largely speaks the language and answers the questions of that cosmopolitan civilization which is in so many ways the forerunner of our own. The historian of Greek thought can trace a true continuity running through all its stages, in which the New Testament forms a vital link. It is in fact even more than the Septuagint a department of Hellenistic literature.

To pursue this theme in any detail would lead us too far afield, but the following points may be considered :—

First, the principal conceptions employed by the New Testament writers to signify the religious status of their Master are such as would carry their full meaning only to a reader who had learnt in some measure to "think Greek". The purely Hebrew "Messiah" (chiefly in its Greek dress as "Christ") is indeed freely used, but it is hardly ever left to explain itself, and indeed its Christian meaning departs far from any sense it had borne in Judaism. The titles "Lord", "Saviour", even "Son of God", though they all have a Hebrew ancestry, get the distinctive shades of meaning which fit them to express Christian experience largely from their non-Jewish religious associations. "Logos", or "Word", had been naturalized in Hellenistic Judaism by Philo, who owed a great debt to Plato and the Stoics. No other titles given to Jesus are of greater weight than these. Thus the New Testament implies that the divine Person whom it sets forth meets the spiritual demands of the changing world-civilization of the time, and claims to dominate it.

Secondly, the sacramental ideas of early Christianity, especially as presented by Paul and in the Fourth Gospel, have undeniable affinity with those of some contemporary Hellenistic cults, as Paul himself confesses when he compares and contrasts "the Table of the Lord" with "the table of daemons".[1] This affinity should not be exaggerated. The Christian sacraments originated in a Jewish context; they have behind them the prophetic symbolism of the Old Testament[2]; and their meaning for the earliest Christians was knit closely with ideas drawn from Jewish eschatology. Yet Christianity, even in its New Testament forms, is a sacramental religion in a sense in which Judaism never has been. Baptism and the Eucharist answered to a widespread need of the Gentile world, to which the great advance of mystery-religions in the same period also bears witness. The Christian "mysteries" proved finally more satisfying than the others, we may fairly suppose, because while their very simplicity made them the more impressive, they carried a greater power of regeneration and moral cleansing by reason of the Person whose Spirit informed them. But when the historian of the period is surveying the development of the sacramental or mystery-religions in the Græco-

[1] 1 Cor. x. 21.

[2] See H. Wheeler Robinson, *Prophetic Symbolism*, in *Old Testament Essays* (pub. Griffin), pp. 1–17.

Roman world, he is justified in including early Christianity among them, in spite of marked differences.

Thirdly, in many parts of the New Testament, and notably in Paul, the vigorous and ethically progressive philosophy of Stoicism has provided congenial matter for the Christian spirit to work upon. Not only is Paul frequently a Stoic in method and vocabulary, but such important conceptions as those of " conscience ",[1] of the " law of nature "[2] as the norm of morality, and of " contentment " or self-sufficiency[3] as a quality of the good life, are thoroughly Stoical. The resultant Christian ethic looks very different from Stoicism, but there can be no question that a very large Stoic element has been taken up into New Testament thought, not in the least by way of mere copying, but by the absorption and transmutation of essentially kindred ideas in a new philosophy of life inspired by a distinctive religious experience.

Fourthly, the influence of Plato, which Judaism had already found congenial, has entered deeply into the thought of the New Testament, especially in the Epistle to the Hebrews and the Fourth Gospel. In the former, the philosophy of " Ideas ", or eternal Forms, of which all phenomena are copies, dominates the whole argument. In the Fourth Gospel the affinity is rather with that peculiar kind of Platonic thought, modified by oriental influences, which is otherwise best represented for us by the Hermetic literature of the second and third centuries. This Gospel is in fact one of the most remarkable examples, in all the literature of the period, of the profound interpenetration of Greek and Semitic thought. Some critics, approaching it from the side of Judaism, have pronounced it the most Jewish of the Gospels, while others, approaching it from the other

[1] Rom. ii. 15 ; 1 Cor. viii. 7–12, x. 25–29, etc.

[2] Rom. ii. 14–15. This is the original and proper use of the term. Its use in the loose terminology of modern science is improper and misleading.

[3] Phil. iv. 11–12.

side, see in it a thoroughly Hellenistic book. Nowhere more evidently than here does early Christianity take its place as the natural leader in new ways of thought, uniting in itself the main tendencies of the time, yet exercising authority over them by virtue of the creative impulse proceeding from its Founder.

Apologists for Christianity have often thought it necessary to minimize or explain away the presence of such "pagan" elements in the New Testament. Rightly considered, this is one of the most illuminating things about it. It means at least that early Christianity was not a thing "done in a corner". It was deeply implicated in the life of the time. Christian thinkers of the period after the New Testament freely recognize how like many things in their religion were to elements in the "Hellenism" it was to supersede. They offered explanations of the resemblances which were not always consistent. The most profound explanation offered was that the divine Word which was incarnate in the Founder of Christianity had already been active in the world before His coming, preparing the way for the Incarnation. It was therefore nothing to be wondered at if there were many things already in the minds of men whose true meaning became clear only in the light of Christian experience. None of the New Testament writers is a mere borrower of ideas. They have taken up as though by some natural attraction all that was of deep spiritual import in the life of the time and given it fuller significance within the movement of thought started by the impact of Jesus upon men. Thus the historian of ideas in the ancient world can trace them again and again into an ultimate phase which is a Christian phase, true to their original intention, yet creatively new. What such ideas meant merely for the time we may often best gather from non-Christian writers, but what they were to mean for the future was determined by the part they could play in a Christian philosophy.

Looking back we can see that within the frame of the Christian Church a new civilization was forming, which would remain and bring forth its own distinctive life as the old civilization fell away. In the second century this was still hidden in the future; yet the Church of the second century was intuitively aware of its destiny. It looked back upon its own formative period as upon the crisis of the spiritual history of mankind, and made its canon of Scripture out of those writings which most directly represented the spiritual forces active in that crisis.

Thus the New Testament writings, all produced, with insignificant exceptions, within a century of the death of Jesus, are a contemporary record of a great spiritual movement in which the history of mankind took a decisive turn. Quite apart from all detailed questions of authorship, sources, and so forth, in every New Testament writing we are in direct touch with this movement, through the mind of someone or other who shared in it. We, whose world has been shaped by this movement in its ever-expanding waves of influence, may here learn from within what, as a matter of spiritual experience and apprehension of truth, was the secret of the movement, and by sharing the experience and the apprehension may have its central act re-enacted in ourselves.

The principal writers of the New Testament all hold the firm belief that they are living in a "new age". The terms in which they express this belief are for the most part borrowed from the apocalyptic eschatology of the later Judaism. This was for men of that time a natural and not unreasonable form in which to clothe their most energetic religious beliefs. For us it is, as a scheme of thought, too fantastic to be taken seriously. Consequently we tend either to ignore as far as possible the eschatological language of the New Testament, or to give it a hasty "re-interpretation" which leaves out a large part of its vital content. When the New Testament writers tell us that the Kingdom of God has drawn near,[1] that they are risen from the dead,[2] or born again,[3] that they have tasted the powers of the age to come,[4] that the principalities and powers governing the age of darkness have been finally overthrown,[5] and that they have been translated into the kingdom of the Son of God[6]—when they use these and many other expressions of the same order, they are speaking the language of apocalyptic eschatology. Every one of these expressions variously signified, for those who used them, the point at which miracle enters in on the grand scale. Through a long apocalyptic tradition runs the idea for which they stand —that after the tedious centuries God would awake and act, and an age of supernatural bliss would dawn for His " elect ". Always the day of miracle had been postponed to the future, and it was not expected to come without a shattering of the whole frame of things as we know them. For the men of the New Testament this awakening of God has taken place, and the age of miracle is here. It is no longer fantasy, but actual experience, and not less truly " supernatural " because the crude supernaturalism of apocalyptic expectation is not justified by the event.

We do less than justice therefore to such language as I have cited if we seek to confine it within the bounds of the " psychology of religious experience ", after the current fashion. No doubt we have before us the phenomena of individual " conversion ", which the psychologist can study with profit. But if these " converted " persons were at all right about what had happened, their " conversion " involved the acceptance of something that had been *done*, in a more " objective " sense. To describe this something

[1] Mark i. 15.
[2] Col. iii. 1–3.
[3] John iii. 3–8; I Pet. i. 2, 23.
[4] Heb. vi. 4–6.
[5] Col. ii. 15; John xii. 31, xvi. 11.
[6] Col. i. 13.

they had at their disposal only the mythological language of eschatology, supported by two significant rites, both originally eschatological in their associations. The sacraments remain to us, rich in suggestion, whatever particular explanation we may give to them when we "rationalize". For the rest, we are perhaps in no better case than the first Christians for describing directly the "new creation" of which they became aware in their "conversion". But on the other hand we have what they had not, an historical perspective down many Christian centuries. We have before us the historical situation briefly set forth above: at the dawn of the Christian Era, a new spiritual impulse, momentous in its issues for the future, entered history, prepared and assisted by many movements beyond Christianity, but finding its decisive point of application in the Christian Church. That is the external account of what happened. The inside account is given by the New Testament writers. Using the language of mythology they bear witness to spiritual facts verified in their experience, and corresponding to facts of the outward order verifiable by historical evidence. A new age has begun for mankind through the coming of the Son of God into the world. In thus referring the new spiritual impulse to a unique Personality entering the world of men, they supply a sufficient cause for the effects observed, and a cause attested by their experience. Everything in fact that they have to say of their Founder falls within this context, and the evidence for His supreme religious dignity is bound up with the evidence for His historical existence.

CHAPTER X

THE NEW TESTAMENT AS THE "FULFILMENT" OF THE OLD

IF we wish to assess the religious significance of the New Testament as "objectively" as may be, we shall do well to view it in relation to its direct historical antecedents; and that means primarily, in relation to the Old Testament and the non-canonical literature of Judaism. The New Testament writers themselves are intensely aware of their continuity with this older tradition. However revolutionary they feel their experience to be, they always regard it as the "fulfilment" of what had been contained in the ancient faith of the Jews. Their frequent references to that which "is written" are apt to be an embarrassment to the modern reader. He rightly feels that the application of the written word is often mechanical and arbitrary. One evangelist, for instance, suggests that when Hosea wrote "Out of Egypt have I called my son", he was foretelling a temporary exile of Christ in that country, instead of alluding to a well-known episode in the early history of Israel.[1] But such aberrations (by no means extravagant when compared with some contemporary rabbinic interpretations) should not blind us to the truth which underlies the appeal to prophecy. No great religion was ever a wholly new religion. Christianity could hardly have made its universal appeal if it had not taken up into itself so much of the deepest religious experience of past generations, and while it laid under contribution the whole spiritual life of the

[1] Matt. ii. 15. The idea is that the Messiah "recapitulates" the history of the chosen people.

ancient world, it found the continuity of tradition which a great religion requires in Judaism ; and this continuity it could never abandon without essential loss. No doubt Christianity still needs to be exhorted to cast off "Hebrew old-clothes". The need was first pointed out by its Founder, and emphasized by its pioneer theologian, Paul. But when Paul's great but one-sided interpreter, Marcion, that eminent non-conformist divine of the second century, proposed to abandon the Old Testament altogether, the Church rightly rejected the tempting simplification. It is not accidental or unimportant to Christianity that it related itself directly to the needs, aspirations, and intuitions of the Old Testament tradition, a tradition embodied in the continuous life of a particular people, yet shaped by contact with the great civilizations of the ancient world, Babylonian, Iranian, Egyptian, Greek.

Pre-Christian Judaism, as we have seen, was an attempt to embody in the whole life of a society the religious ideas of the prophets. The attempt met with a large measure of success, but it also revealed a certain lack of complete clearness and consistency in the ideas themselves, and it raised fresh questions relative to the new world of wider contacts in which the religious society now had to live. Provisional answers were given to such questions, but a thoroughgoing solution waited upon a fresh outbreak of religious genius like that of the prophets themselves. That outbreak came with Christianity, and the answers given to some of the outstanding questions of Judaism in the New Testament will serve to bring out the significance of this fresh step, provided we always bear in mind that the new thing that came into the world was not merely a fresh handling of an intellectual problem, but a new life which included as one of its elements a fresh insight into the whole spiritual situation.

Among the outstanding questions left open by Judaism

we may select five of the first importance which may be formulated as follows :

I. The issue between nationalism and universalism in religion, or the question of the implications of monotheism.

II. The issue between righteousness and grace, or the question of the divine character.

III. The issue between divine justice and the human lot, or the problem of suffering.

IV. The issue between this-worldliness and other-worldliness, or the question of immortality.

V. The issue between transcendence and immanence, or the problem of mediation.

It will not be easy to treat of the Christian answers to these questions separately. It is indeed a mark of every significant advance in thought that questions formerly supposed to be independent are seen to be related, so that in answering them we are led to a fresh synthesis. This is certainly a mark of the movement of thought represented by the New Testament. For convenience, however, we may follow these five headings.

I. If there is but one God, and He wholly good, then all mankind must be His care. But if He has revealed Himself by " mighty acts " in the history of a people, and if His service consists principally in regulating the conduct of men in society by definite and concrete principles of righteousness, what then ? How can the conclusion be resisted that His Providence must be specially concerned with that society which having experienced His " mighty acts " has made His righteousness the fundamental constitution, so to speak, of its body politic ? This was the dilemma. The Christian Church was itself the solution. For almost without meaning any such thing it found itself a supra-national body which nevertheless carried over the traditions of historic Israel. During the early New Testament period there was acute controversy between the party in the Church which wished to perpetuate within it the national distinctions that marked Judaism, and the party which held all this to be superseded. The logic of facts was on the side of the cosmopolitan tendency. Paul gave it its rational justification. The Epistle to the Galatians is its polemical manifesto, claiming the acts of divine Providence in the history of the ancient people for a new and emancipated " Israel of God " in which there is neither Jew nor Greek. In the epistle to the Romans the battle is in substance won, and the whole epistle may be regarded as an exposition of the philosophical basis of the supra-national religious society. In the epistle to the Ephesians the cosmopolitan character of Christianity can be calmly contemplated as an assured fact, and the most signal manifestation of a divine purpose deeply embedded in the structure of the spiritual universe.

But there is a subtler movement in the thought of Paul on this point. From the outset he has no doubt that the Church is in principle supra-national, but in the earlier epistles it is still an exclusive society, over against the bulk of mankind, which will be destroyed at the coming of Christ to judgment.[1] In the later epistles the Church is truly universal, for by an inward necessity it must ultimately include all mankind, and form the centre of a reconciled universe.[2]

It is noteworthy that at every point of the argument the universality of the religious society is related to Christ and His work. At bottom it is because the experience of Christ is experience of a universal Person that national limits are of necessity transcended by His Church. He was a Jew and worked within the religious society of Judaism, yet there

[1] 2 Thess. i. 6–10. The Pauline authorship of 2 Thess. is disputed, but it is probably to be accepted. If, however, it is not his own work, it is now very generally held that it comes from the Pauline circle and belongs to an early period of his mission.

[2] Rom. xi. 32, viii. 18–23 ; Col. i. 20 ; Eph. iii 6-10, i. 10. Ephesians, if not by Paul's own hand, certainly represents the final development of his thought. See this writer's introduction and commentary on the Epistle in *The Abingdon Commentary*.

was that in His personality and His message which necessarily touched men at a level deeper than nationality, and broke the system which tried to restrain Him.

If we turn from the epistles to the Synoptic Gospels we see the conflict between the national and the universal in religion fought out to an issue on the stage of Jewish history at a period of peculiar significance. In one sense the whole scene is local, provincial, particular in the extreme. Yet the universal makes itself felt with growing power. It is not that the Christ of the Synoptic Gospels has the traits of a cosmopolitan sage. The picture is too historical for that. He is " a prophet like one of the prophets ",[1] or He is that intensely national Figure, the Messiah ;—in any case a Jewish Teacher and Leader. Yet even in the Gospel according to Matthew, where the influence of nationalist or Jewish-Christian sympathies is most strong, we are given a report of the teaching of Jesus which at once lifts religion into the sphere of the universally human. In the Second Gospel we are shown more dramatically how the best and the worst elements in contemporary Judaism rally to the defence of the national ideal expressed in law and tradition against One whose universality brought Him into conflict with it, and as the tragedy reaches its climax the veil of the Temple is rent in twain and a pagan centurion confesses the Son of God.[2]

But it is to the third evangelist that we owe the most moving and masterly presentation in historical terms of the theme with which we are now concerned. A man of imagination and insight, he conceived the plan of writing a work in two volumes to show how, in the actual sequence of events, religion ceased to be national and shaped for itself a universal society. This great work loses something of its appeal to the imagination because it has come down to us divided into two apparently independent books—the Gospel

[1] Mark vi. 15.

[2] Mark xv. 38–39.

according to Luke and the Acts of the Apostles. The two should be read continuously. This first history of the beginnings of Christianity opens with two chapters of stories and short lyrics which give a beautiful and sympathetic picture of the best kind of Judaism of the time, full of the deepest piety of prophets and psalmists and warm with apocalyptic hopes. The aged Simeon speaks with the voice of the vanishing old order as he moves from the stage with the words :[1]

> "Lord, now lettest Thou Thy servant depart in peace, . .
> For mine eyes have seen Thy salvation . . .
> A light to lighten the Gentiles,
> And the glory of Thy people Israel ! "

Then the author indicates the wider setting : " In the fifteenth year of Tiberius Cæsar, Pontius Pilate being governor of Judaea. . . ."[2] And so Jesus comes upon the scene, surrounded by those representatives of humanity outside the Law whose need reveals Him as Saviour of mankind—publicans and sinners, Samaritans, heathen, and penitent thieves. The inevitable clash with the national tradition brings the tragedy of the Cross, but leads to Pentecost, where the followers of Jesus, now conscious of His Spirit driving them on, proclaim a " promise to all that are afar off ".[3] Stephen dies for words against the Temple and the Law, with a vision of Christ in glory before his eyes.[4] His defence, in itself a tedious and uninspired composition, gains meaning when we realize that its review of Hebrew history might serve as notes for a fitting prologue to the whole Lucan work.[5] Then through vision[6] and prophecy,[7] through experiment and conference,[8] it becomes plain that the Gentiles are to be admitted to equal

[1] Luke ii. 29–32.
[2] Luke iii. 1.
[3] Acts ii. 39 (echoed in Eph. ii. 13, both being based on Isa. lvii. 19)
[4] Acts vi. 13–14, vii. 55–60.
[5] Acts vii. 2–53.
[6] Acts x. 9–16.
[7] Acts xiii. 1–2.
[8] Acts xi. 1–18, xv. 1–29.

citizenship in the Israel of God. Leadership in the new advance falls, in the strange working of Providence, to Paul, the former pillar of the Law, and after his course is run we take leave of him, dramatically enough,—"in Rome, unhindered"![1] The universal religious society is in being, at the very seat of universal empire.

That the religious society of the one God must be universal is to us perhaps so much a truism that its discovery hardly stirs us. It seems to us, looking back, inevitable that the ideas of the prophets, if they were true, must antiquate tribal and national conceptions of religion. But it is the mark of that which is true to the nature of things to appear inevitable in retrospect. The emergence of the idea of a religious society of mankind transcending all accidental divisions was actually due to the New Testament experience of Christ as Saviour of men in their simply human need. It cannot be said that even yet Christendom has fully realized the meaning of that idea in its practice, or ceased to need the witness of the New Testament to the experience that gave it birth.

II. Amos proclaimed a God of judgment, Hosea a God of grace (as well as of judgment). The tension between these two was never really resolved in pre-Christian Judaism. That God, as utterly righteous, can "in no wise clear the guilty" was as certain intuitively as that forgiving mercy is without bounds.[2] The prophets wrestled with the problem. At the end of the prophetic period the only solution that has emerged is that variously set forth by Ezekiel and by the second Isaiah: in the age of miracle to come God will, by sheer exercise of the prerogative of omnipotence, create that righteousness in

[1] Acts xxviii. 31. The word ἀκωλύτως, with which the whole book closes, is frequent in legal documents—"without let or hindrance."

[2] Num. xiv. 18 (JE).

men which will make it possible for Him to accept them as His people and to be their God. This belief remains part of the general apocalyptic hope. But so far as present experience is concerned the belief in the justice of God and the belief in His mercy live on in uneasy juxtaposition. An occasional flash of insight gave the assurance that these two divine attributes are not in irreconcilable opposition even in this age, as when a psalmist writes, "There is forgiveness with Thee that Thou mayest be feared ".[1] But it is clear that the development of legal Judaism was not favourable to the rise of a thoroughgoing doctrine of God which without weakening the moral imperative of His righteousness should give effective play to His grace. The last of the great apocalyptists, the author of the Apocalypse of Ezra,[2] despairs of any real reconciliation of the antinomy.

Now the New Testament writers lift the whole subject to a fresh plane by declaring that the miracle of grace foretold by Ezekiel and the second Isaiah has taken place. God Himself has justified sinners[3] and communicated to them the Spirit whereby they possess not their own righteousness which is of the law, but the righteousness which is of God by faith.[4] This is just what the prophets had declared God must do. When Paul presents God in Christ as "just and the Justifier"[5] he is not making a combination of opposites hitherto inconceivable, but bearing witness that what was conceived as ideal is now actual in experience. But, of course, that makes all the difference. For Ezekiel the act of God remained not only miraculous but actually irrational, a *tour de force* of irresponsible power. It would happen some day, but that is all that could be said about it. When it has become matter of experience it can be reasoned about, without ceasing to be in a deep sense supernatural. The way Paul sees it is this : the highest form of righteousness,

[1] Ps. cxxx. 4. [2] See 2 Esdras vii. 45–74. [3] Rom. v. 6–11, etc.
[4] Gal. iii. 2–6 ; Phil. iii. 9. [5] Rom. iii. 26.

and therefore the righteousness of God, is love. The kindness of God, being the outflow of pure love, is not bestowed as a reward for human virtue, or even for repentance; it "leads us to repentance", and so to righteousness.[1] While there is a grave difficulty in conceiving how righteousness in the legal sense can be communicated by an act of grace, love is a different matter. Not only does God "commend His love to us", but His love is "shed abroad in our hearts through the Holy Spirit given to us";[2] or as a later writer puts it, "God is love" and "we love because He first loved us".[3] We cannot profess to understand fully what love is, or why it so propagates itself; but we know it as part of a total and reasonable experience of life. If therefore love is the key to the character and operation of God, then it is no paradox that the highest righteousness is displayed in a forgiving grace which anticipates even repentance, as also every other merit on the part of man, and makes possible for him all that is necessary for untroubled communion with a holy God.

It is clear that this apprehension of the nature of God arose in men who had found Him through Christ, in particular through what Christ had come to mean for them after He had made the supreme act of love in dying. Now the Synoptic Gospels once again show us in an historical narrative how Christ came to make this kind of impression on men's minds. They never set out to discuss, as do Paul and "John", the theological problem bequeathed by the prophets; and certainly they do not represent Jesus as discussing it. But the teaching they report as from Him presents the relation of God to men, and indeed to all His creatures, as one of unlimited beneficence—unlimited in particular by any unworthiness on their part.[4] But still more significant is it that Jesus is represented as exhibiting

[1] Rom. ii. 4.
[2] Rom. v. 5.
[3] 1 John iv. 19.
[4] Matt. v. 43–48; Luke xv. 11–32, etc.

precisely this attitude of gracious and forgiving love in His own dealings with sinful people, and finding in their loving response the proof of their forgiveness.[1] While in one way nothing could be farther from the theological arguments of Paul than the simple and natural converse of Jesus with men, it is clear that the arguments are about a spiritual reality manifested in the plain story.

Further, the Synoptic narrative makes plain what is implicit in the whole Pauline argument, that the universalizing of religion is intimately associated with this synthesis of righteousness and grace in the love of God. For it was because Jesus employed with the utmost spontaneity and consistency the divine method of unqualified and gracious beneficence even towards the least worthy, while calling upon men for a righteousness exceeding that of scribes and Pharisees, that His ministry became a revolt against the national religion of the Law, and ended in His death.

III. The prophets had tried to establish a correspondence between the ideal righteousness of God and the actual lot of men by the doctrine that virtue is rewarded by prosperity and wickedness punished by suffering. This doctrine authoritatively laid down in Deuteronomy, became the standard of Jewish orthodoxy in the whole subsequent period. It was challenged again and again, but showed an extraordinary tenacity in face of adverse facts. The dominant theology ultimately took refuge in a visionary future where the balance should be righted, and left the undeserved suffering of this age as something due either to the inherent wrongness of the present order or to some inscrutable dispensation of Providence, in any case something unrelated to any rational conception of human values. The "Second Isaiah" indeed, in his ideal picture of the martyr Servant of the Lord, had suggested that the suffering of the righteous

[1] Luke vii. 41–48.

might have in this age a positive value, as vicarious expiation for the sin of others. He was not without followers, but the doctrine he taught can hardly be said to have effectively asserted itself in Jewish theology, though it was invoked to glorify the Maccabæan martyrs.[1] Jewish theologians perhaps showed a praiseworthy sobriety in refusing to commit themselves to it; for indeed the bare idea of vicarious expiation is not wholly rational, and easily lends itself to fanaticism. After all, if God demands the suffering of one in order that the sins of others may be forgiven, a meaning is found for suffering, but at the expense of the rationality of God for which the prophets contended so vigorously.

Now the New Testament takes up the doctrine of the Suffering Servant into a broad philosophy of life in which its irrational elements are transcended. It avers that "Christ died for our sins according to the Scriptures (of the second Isaiah)",[2] and freely cites the language of those Scriptures in illustration of the fact.[3] But that language receives a fresh meaning from its setting. It is not that God demanded, or accepted, the suffering of a man as expiation. He Himself, as Paul has it, "propounded the expiation"[4]—which puts the whole transaction on a different footing. While the Cross is historically the suffering of a Man, it is the manifestation of something in God, which is the analogue or equivalent of suffering. It may be defined as self-giving under the motive of pure love. "God so loved the world that He gave His only-begotten Son".[5] The expression is evidently anthropomorphic. It is a mythological way of saying that in Christ God gives of his

[1] 4 Macc. xvii. 22 (about contemporary with the life of Jesus).
[2] Cor. xv. 3 (where Paul is citing the tradition that came to him from the first believers); Mark ix. 12.
[3] Acts viii. 29–35; 1 Peter ii. 21–25.
[4] Rom. iii. 25.
[5] John iii. 16.

own Being the utmost that it is possible for humanity to receive of God, and that the giving involves for Him what we can only describe as sacrifice. It is thus that Paul can say that God "commends *His own* love to us in that Christ died for us ".[1] The result of this teaching is that the problem of suffering is placed in a new light, because suffering is seen to have a place in the process whose origin is in divine Love, and consequently to possess a positive value. That value is relative to the existence of evil in the world, for Christian theology does not deny the reality of evil, but suffering now appears not as irredeemably evil, but rather as redemptive from evil, when it takes the divine form of sacrifice. This view of things accounts for the strangely serene and untroubled mood in which the most characteristic New Testament thought faces the facts of suffering —a mood so unintelligible to the impatience of much modern thought.

This is what early Christian theologians made of the revelation that came to them in Christ. The earliest accounts of His life were written under the impulse of thought of this kind. The motive of the Passion is obviously dominant in the earliest of them all, the Gospel according to Mark. Comparatively little of the theology, nevertheless, has got through into the Synoptic Gospels. They tell the story of a bitterly wronged and innocent Sufferer, not, like the Book of Job, to raise the problem of suffering, but as "good news". They show Jesus, conscious of a mysterious destiny as Son of God and Son of Man, accepting the suffering that evil entailed upon Him, in the pure spirit of sacrifice.[2] He accounts for it to Himself and to others by half-veiled allusions to the Suffering Servant of Isaiah.[3] But as he resolves to face death He enunciates a simpler and more profound maxim—to save your life is to lose it: to give it

[1] Rom. v. 8.
[2] Luke xii. 50; Mark xiv. 36.
[3] Mark ix. 12, x. 45, xiv. 24.

up is to find it.[1] That is a law of life as such, and therefore surely has its roots in the being of God Himself. No unbiased reader of these Gospels could understand that maxim as a pessimistic denial of life ; it takes up sacrifice into the idea of life at its highest. As we follow the story we are constrained to confess that the way in which Jesus faces suffering, not resenting it, but accepting it with a redemptive purpose, is inherently divine.

It is to be observed that the Christian reply to the question raised by suffering is not a theoretical vindication of the justice of God, but a challenge to accept as divine a certain attitude to life as a whole, in which suffering comes to be subordinate and instrumental to a positive purpose of good.

IV. The prophets know nothing of any life but the present. The troubles of the period after the Exile raised the question of a future life for the individual, while the influence of other religions with which the Jews now came into close touch suggested an answer. Judaism was, however, strangely slow to accept a doctrine of immortality in any sense, and it is only in the Greek period that the belief became current that those whom God deemed worthy would be raised from death by His power, to share in the blessings of the Age to Come. Only such a strongly Hellenized book as the Wisdom of Solomon inculcates anything like the Platonic doctrine of the immortality of the soul.

The New Testament is full of the assurance of everlasting life. There is indeed no discussion of immortality as a philosophical theory. Paul's argument about the resurrection which we are accustomed to read at the burial of the dead[2] is quite unconvincing if we suppose him to be attempting to prove the immortality of the soul. Actually that is

[1] Mark viii. 35 ; Matt. x. 39 Luke xvii. 33.
[2] 1 Cor. xv. 12–58.

not what he is talking about. His premises are those of contemporary Judaism : that a dead man really is dead and done for unless and until God makes him alive again by an act of creative power, and that this miracle will take place when the New Age dawns. On these premises, the fact that Jesus had been dead and was alive did afford a proof that the age of miracle had come, in which all whom God deemed worthy should receive from Him the supernatural life. In a scholastic sense the argument is sound, though it operates with conceptions strange to us. But what lies behind it is a conviction, based on the religious experience mediated by Christ, that there is now no absolute barrier between this workaday world and the eternal order. The new outlook is not limited by the robust "this-worldliness" of the prophets, and yet it differs from the pessimistic "other-worldliness" of apocalyptic. When Paul had outgrown his early eschatological fanaticism,[1] he saw that the natural values of this world, such as those of the family,[2] of work,[3] and of political order,[4] remain for the Christian ; and yet his real life is "hid with Christ in God"[5] and while living "in the flesh"[6] he is already "in the heavenly places with Christ Jesus".[7] In other words, he has experience of the eternal values in a world of space and time.

For the author of the Fourth Gospel the eschatological framework of the conviction has almost dissolved. He holds that to know God as He is known in Christ, that is through participation in the divine quality and activity of love, *is* eternal life.[8] This is in substance the position of practically all the New Testament writers. For people who have reached this position, personal survival needs no proof, nor is it a hypothesis demanded by the

[1] 1 Cor. vii. 29–31.
[2] Col. iii. 18–iv. 1 ; Eph. v. 21–vi. 9
[3] Eph. iv. 28.
[4] Rom. xiii. 1–7.
[5] Col. iii. 1–3.
[6] Gal. ii. 20 ; 2 Cor. x. 3.
[7] Eph. i. 3, ii. 6.
[8] John xvii. 3. Cf. 1 John iv. 16, iv. 12

attempt to justify the ways of God to men in face of the daunting facts of our mortality. Philosophically, the whole matter is still open to speculation, and Christian thought after the New Testament has often used, quite justifiably, Platonic and other conceptions of the immortality of the soul as the intellectual forms of its faith. But the New Testament outlook is in itself such a liberation from the disabling fear of bodily death as makes it possible to think about it with calm clearness of mind, untroubled by that morbid depreciation of this life which is often the price paid for an emphatic assertion of the life to come. That Christian thought has not always maintained this outlook in its purity goes without saying. We may still return with profit to the witness of the New Testament.

We turn again to the Synoptic Gospels. The early believers, we have said, found in the living Christ the centre and ground of their assurance of everlasting life. What did they see in the story of His earthly ministry to guarantee their faith? There is singularly little discussion of the question. Once only is Jesus brought into controversy with the typical deniers of the resurrection, the Sadducees. On this occasion He dismisses with cool contempt the crude notion of a renewal of physical existence. He pronounces the simple but pregnant maxim—" God is not a God of the dead but of the living ".[1] That saying bases belief in survival upon the consideration that communion with the Eternal must in its nature be eternal.[2] For the rest, He always assumes His own survival of bodily death, declaring at His last meal on earth that He will hereafter drink the mystical " fruit of the vine " in the Kingdom of God.[3] This Kingdom of God, which here stands for the eternal order into which He enters after death, He nevertheless declares

[1] Mark xii. 18–27.

[2] It is thus in direct succession to Ps. lxxiii. rather than in the apocalyptic tradition.

[3] Mark xiv. 25.

to have already come upon men.[1] He lives, in fact, speaks and acts, on the assumption that the manifest rule of God, which contemporary thought often associated with the Coming Age of miracle, is a fact of daily experience.[2] He convinced His followers of it, and they tell His story as that of one who "could not be holden of death",[3] because in Him the Kingdom of God itself lived. Whatever we may make of the resurrection narratives as history, we must conclude that experiences of the risen Christ such as Paul tells us were claimed from the earliest days by personal followers of the Crucified well-known to him,[4] would be unintelligible and irrational if they had not been under the spell of a life which they had come to feel to be in its nature invulnerable by the accident of bodily death.

V. We have seen that the problem of reconciling the immanence and the transcendence of God, which has its roots in the primitive tension between the "otherness" and the familiarity of the Divine, became acute in Judaism, and found a partial solution through various conceptions of mediation. These conceptions range from the crude belief in angels, which is a sort of reduced polytheism, through the idea of the Law as itself a sufficient mediation, to poetical or philosophical constructions in which the immanent Divine is conceived as the Wisdom, or the Spirit, or the Word, of the transcendent God, and these aspects of God are given a quasi-personal existence. In the New Testament angels still figure in popular imagination, but the clearest and most vigorous thinker among its writers, Paul, definitely refuses to regard them as valid mediators of the divine. The place of the Law is taken by the Spirit, as in some schools of Jewish thought the Law was identified with Wisdom as a personified emanation of God. But the thought of the New Testament

[1] Matt. xii. 28; Luke xi. 20.
[2] Matt. xiii. 16–17; Luke x. 23–24
[3] Acts ii. 24.
[4] 1 Cor. xv. 4–8.

takes a decisive step in identifying the Holy Spirit of God with the Spirit of Jesus, and regarding Jesus Himself as the incarnation of the Word[1] or of divine Wisdom.[2] This means that the immanent Divine, instead of being conceived in a manner which remains abstract in spite of poetical personification, is conceived as a Person ; in history as embodied in a real human personality, and in experience as a spiritual presence continuous with that personality. Thus all that was true in primitive anthropomorphism regains its place in religious experience, while the transcendence of the Eternal God, the *Fons Deitatis*, is fully safeguarded. Naturally this bold adventure in faith raised philosophical problems which have occupied the mind of the Church ever since. But it is clear that religiously it proved satisfying. If we review the several problems which we have had under consideration, we can see that the Christian solution of them all came through the discovery of God in Christ.

The faith of the Incarnation is variously expressed in the New Testament writings. Its most developed expression is to be found in the Fourth Gospel. The unique constitution of the distinctively Christian experience of God is here portrayed in conclusive fashion. It is intimately bound up with an historical Person, and yet has all the depth, universality, and immediacy associated with mysticism. That it is the Eternal God Himself who is the Object of experience is not for a moment in doubt, yet He is experienced in and through Jesus Christ, whose every word and act in history is a "sign"[3] of eternal realities. The "otherness" and transcendence of God are asserted, and yet in Christ the Unknowable is

[1] John i. 1–18.

[2] 1 Cor. i. 24 ; Col. i. 15–18, where the terms used all belong to the "Wisdom" theology. Cf. Heb. i. 2–3.

[3] John ii. 11, vi. 26. The contrast here drawn between the physical miracle of feeding and the "sign" which those who had experienced it failed to discern shows that the sense "John" gives to the word "sign" is other than that in which "signs" are repudiated in Mark viii. 11–12 ; 1 Cor. i. 22–24.

Object of experience. "No man hath seen God at any time: the only-begotten Son, who is in the bosom of the Father, He hath declared Him"[1]: "He that hath seen me hath seen the Father".[2] To anyone who has thus "seen" God in Christ, all serviceable and significant things in the world become means of communion with God—light, water, bread, wine. For behind these palpable things lie their eternal archetypes, the "real light", the "real bread", which are elements in the hidden world of the divine mind and purpose.[3] Christ Himself in fact is the real Light, the real Bread, since He is the Logos,[4] the uttered Thought of the Eternal, the ultimate Meaning of the world. Thus for the Christian the common world is as full of the divine (of "holiness") as for the naïve animist; but that immanent divine is experienced through and through in terms of Christ, and therefore in a way which does full justice to personal values, rationally and ethically.

While in this view of religion all things are "sacramental" of the divine Presence, the Fourth Evangelist, like other New Testament writers, finds its sacramental quality most intense in the two sacraments of the Church which were already in his time traditional,[5] and particularly in that Sacrament which is mystically a partaking of "the flesh and blood of the Son of Man". At a time when the living memory of the days of Jesus was fading, the experience of Him as a divine Presence might well have lost hold on history. In that case the decisive value of the Incarnation would have been

[1] John i. 18. [2] John xiv. 9.

[3] John i. 9, etc., iii. 5, iv. 10–16, vi. 26–63, ii. 3–10, xv. 1. Observe that these figures are different in character from the parables of the Synoptic Gospels. The intention is to select an object in the world of phenomena, to direct the attention to the eternal "idea" or "meaning" (λόγος) embodied in it, and then to represent this as an aspect of God as known in Christ. ("John's" *ἀληθινά* i.e. the *real* essences behind phenomena, correspond to Plato's *ἰδέαι* and Philo's λόγοι.)

[4] John i. 1–14. Philo had equated the Λόγος with the Platonic Ἰδέα *τῶν ἰδεῶν*, the highest and most inclusive of "real" or eternal existences.

[5] John iii. 5, cf. xiii. 8–10, vi. 1–59, xxi. 12–17, xv. 1–10.

missed. But from very early times the rite about which the distinctive Christian life gathered was one deeply rooted in the solid facts of history. When Paul visited Corinth, about twenty years after the death of Jesus, he "handed on that which he had received",[1] and this tradition included the statement that "the Lord Jesus, the night on which He was betrayed", had performed certain acts and uttered certain words, by which He had wrought out of the most significant elements in His own historical achievement a sacramental rite of communion.[2] Whether by His express intention or not, His followers had continued to repeat these acts and words "in memory of Him", and to "proclaim the death of the Lord". The sacrament remained, linking indissolubly the deeply spiritual experience of God in Christ with the history that gives it its meaning. In it is decisively expressed the Christian interpretation of life and religion.

[1] 1 Cor. xv. 1–3. The meaning can hardly be different in xi. 23.
[2] 1 Cor. xi. 23–26.

CHAPTER XI

JESUS CHRIST AND THE GOSPELS

THE Gospels have so far been treated along with the epistles as documents of the religious experience of the early Church. This approach to them corresponds with the way in which they actually came into being. None of the four books which we call by that title was written until thirty or forty years after the death of Jesus. In the meantime the first unprecedented outburst of spiritual energy had carried the Christian message far and wide ; the lines of the Christian philosophy had been laid down ; and the new religious society had created its distinctive institutions, at least in their rudiments. The life which was in it all had found characteristic expression in epistles and similar " tracts for the times ", whose pointed brevity and informal freshness transmit directly the living experience of those early days. But the centre of the Christian experience was a Person Who had recently lived, and brought about an historical crisis by the things He had done and said. The Hebrew prophets " experienced God in terms of history " ; so did the early Christians—in terms of the historic life of Jesus, with its great sequel. Paul seems to us moderns curiously little concerned about the Gospel history ; yet when he delivered to his converts " the things which he had received ", these things, we learn, included things that Jesus had said and done and things that had happened to Him.[1] This historical reference is implicit when it is not explicit in all primitive expositions of Christian experience.

[1] 1 Cor. xi. 23, xv. 1–3.

When the events began to fade out of living memory as the first generation passed, the need arose for an orderly written account of " the things that took place among us ";[1] and a powerful sense of the value and urgency of the facts, in the evangelists themselves, provided the impulse to write. Thus the Gospels represent in another form of expression the same experience that lies behind the epistles. They represent it not in terms of interior spiritual states induced by Christ in the believer, but in terms of his memories or imaginations of Christ as acting outwardly on the stage of history. That is in fact why these writings are called, not Memoirs or Histories, but Gospels—or rather, why they were at first called simply " The Gospel ", with sub-headings, " according to Matthew, Mark ", and so forth. " The Gospel ", the Good News, meant the setting forth by a Christian missionary of what Christianity is, as a " power of God unto salvation "[2]; and Mark felt himself to be giving this to the world in writing his story[3] just as truly as Paul did in writing the epistle to the Romans. Neither he nor any other evangelist had any idea that in setting forth " the Jesus of History " he was doing other than illuminate " the Christ of faith ".

It is important to emphasize this point of view at the present time.[4] In the last generation discontent with traditional Christian dogma coincided with a new interest in the historical criticism of the Gospels. It came to be thought that in order to discover the essence of Christianity —*das Wesen des Christentums*—we had only to concentrate our minds upon stripping off everything in the New Testament, and particularly in the Gospels, which might

[1] Luke i. 1.

[2] Rom. i. 16, and so regularly in the N.T. (except where it means the actual preaching, as distinct from the content of the preaching, as 2 Cor. viii. 18, etc.).

[3] Mark i. 1. Cf. his use of εὐαγγέλιον elsewhere, i. 14–15, xiv. 9, etc.

[4] On this point see B. W. Bacon, *The Story of Jesus*, chap. I.

conceivably have come out of the experience or the reflection of the early Church, and getting down to the bare unedited facts. We should then be face to face with "the Jesus of History", and from that point could reconstruct a reasonable Christianity free from the perversions which had unaccountably beset it from the first moment it was preached to the world. There is no doubt of the intellectual and moral stimulus that has come through the discipline of trying to penetrate through all mists of dogma and tradition to Jesus Himself as He was in Galilee and Jerusalem in the early part of the first century. But in fact, the attempt to portray "the Jesus of History" in complete independence of the experience of the early Church has not met with great success. Either the critic imports into the narrative far more of his own ideas and predilections than he knows, or his resultant picture is so colourless that we know instinctively this was not the Jesus who turned the course of history.

The manner in which the story is told by the evangelists is in fact part of the story, as the value Jesus had for those who followed Him is part of what He was. Thus the elements in the Gospels which may have been contributed by the evangelists themselves out of their own experience or reflection have both an historical and a religious value, and are not to be cast aside as so much lumber by those who would understand the Jesus of the Gospels. When we have before us any particular story of Jesus, before we bring into play the apparatus of criticism to answer the question, Did this really happen just so? we may pause to consider that whether it did or no, at least someone found at the centre of a profound religious experience a Person of whom it was natural to tell such a story. We know of course that neither his experience nor his way of relating it to history was perfectly pure, and we shall be quite prepared for an element of error. Here the Christian mind exercises an instinctive criticism of the Gospels. It does not really believe, though the evidence is in the earliest Gospel, that the Lord of its faith was such an one as to "curse" a harmless fig-tree because it failed to satisfy His craving for fruit out of season.[1] Taken as a whole, however, the Gospel stories ring true to Christian experience, and promote it in their readers. That is, they serve the primary purpose for which they were written.

When this has been said, however, we must go on to say that the strictly historical criticism of the Gospels is of importance for their religious value—and for this reason: When the Christian experience is set forth directly in terms of the interior life, it is of necessity largely affected by the individual limitations of the human subjects of the experience, however true may be their claim that they are "in Christ". When it is set forth in a form controlled by memory of external events, though the limitations are never wholly transcended, it is nevertheless possible for much in Christ that was imperfectly assimilated in the experience to find a place in the record. That this is actually the case is patent to any careful reader of the New Testament. We may take an example from one element in the Gospel record where no disturbing influence of dogmatic interest enters in.[2] There are well-known passages in the Synoptic Gospels which express an attitude to little children and to animals very remarkable in that age.[3] There is no evidence that this attitude was appreciated in the early Church. Paul asks incredulously, "Does God care for oxen?"[4] and for him and other New Testament writers the child suggests childishness

[1] Mark xi. 12–14, 20–21. We may take it from Mark that Peter, or some other early witness, saw something, or heard something said, which he interpreted as the cursing of a tree, but what that something may have been we cannot say; perhaps a clue may be found by comparing the fig-tree parables, Mark xiii. 28–29; Luke xiii. 6–9, xvii. 6.

[2] I owe this illustration to Canon Streeter.

[3] Mark ix. 36–37, x. 13–16; Matt. xviii. 1–6, 10–14 x. 29 (Luke xii. 6), vi. 26.

[4] 1 Cor. ix. 9.

rather than childlikeness.[1] Even the evangelists show a tendency to interpret the exquisite stories of Jesus and the children in reference to the treatment of spiritually immature adults in the Church.[2] Yet their faithfulness to historical memory led them to represent their Master as dealing with children and speaking of animals in a way they did not understand, but felt to be characteristic of Him. If this is so in this one instance, it may well be so in others, especially where deeply rooted beliefs or prejudices interfered with the penetration of the new life " in Christ ". It is certainly true that the evangelists have preserved statements about Jesus which neither they nor other early Christian writers appreciated in their full significance. Hence we need not be so sceptical as some recent critics have shown themselves of the possibility of getting behind the early Church to the real Jesus of history.[3] At least, the Church was honest enough to tell stories and report sayings of its Master which transcend its own thought and practice, and remain a challenge to the Church of later days. Here was Someone " above the heads of His reporters ", and the extent to which their best imagination could have invented the words and deeds attributed to Him must be strictly limited.

It is therefore worth while to exercise the most strenuous historical criticism in seeking to recover the earliest and most trustworthy forms of the Gospel tradition. A century of such criticism has not been without result. We may now say with confidence that for strictly historical material, with the minimum of subjective interpretation, we must not go to the Fourth Gospel. Its religious value stands beyond challenge, and it is the more fully appreciated when its contribution to our knowledge of the bare facts of the life

[1] 1 Cor. iii. 1, xiii. 11 ; Eph. iv. 14 ; Heb. v. 12–14.

[2] Even Mark shows this tendency in ix. 42, and the context in which Matthew has placed the sayings about " little ones " in xviii. suggests that this was his interest in them.

[3] See B. S. Easton, *The Gospel before the Gospels*.

of Jesus becomes a secondary interest. This is not to say that it makes no such contribution. But it is to the Synoptic Gospels that we must go, if we wish to recover the oldest and purest tradition of the facts. These Gospels coincide, overlap, diverge, confirm and contradict one another in a way that is at first simply perplexing. But out of these curious interrelations of the three it has been possible to deduce a gradually increasing mass of probable conclusions about the earlier sources upon which they rest. This is not the place for any detailed treatment of what is called "the Synoptic Problem"[1]; but the ordinary reader of the Gospels should be aware of certain conclusions which command a very wide consensus of expert opinion. Mark is the earliest source for the story of the public ministry of Jesus, and preserves a number of narratives, including that of the Passion, which in all probability rest upon a first-hand apostolic tradition.[2] Further, those sections of Luke which have parallels in Matthew but not in Mark represent another source, probably in the main a single written Greek document which cannot have been later than Mark, and in some respects had a more primitive tradition of the teaching of Jesus. This second source, commonly referred to by the conventional symbol "Q", cannot be reconstructed as a whole, but its contents can be sufficiently inferred from a comparison of Matthew and Luke. It can then be compared with Mark, and the two sources can be allowed to corroborate or correct one another. Where they corroborate one another—as they do in some remarkable ways—we can be pretty

[1] See B. H. Streeter, *The Four Gospels: A Study in Origins*; B. W. Bacon, *The Story of Jesus*.

[2] The ancient tradition that Peter was the source of many of Mark's stories is found credible by most critics; for the Passion narrative we must probably find the authority in the Jerusalem circle of the early Church. If the evangelist is to be identified with "John whose surname was Mark" (Acts xii. 12) he was in close touch with this circle; the name, however, was very common. That the Gospel as a whole is anything like a transcript of Peter's reminiscences cannot be maintained

sure of being in touch with a common tradition that is very primitive indeed.[1] Mark and "Q" are (along with Paul) the pillars of our knowledge of the facts of the life and teaching of Jesus. The constant study of both, in and for themselves, and particularly in comparison, is an invaluable discipline for anyone who wishes to read the Gospels as a whole with a critical standard in mind.[2] For while neither Mark nor "Q" is unaffected by the modification, revision, and editing of the tradition during thirty or forty years, the more deeply one studies them the more confident does one feel that in them we are in real though not direct touch with the memory of the early disciples. The other portions of Matthew and Luke no doubt contain material drawn from traditional sources just as old and trustworthy as Mark or "Q", but it is certain that they also contain secondary elements not easily isolated except by applying criteria learnt from the earliest sources.

As has already been observed, we all, if our minds are open, apply a certain instinctive criticism to the Gospels. But such criticism has an element of "subjectivity" which though inevitable is dangerous. We so easily doubt the historicity of that which disturbs us. Through the study of the earliest sources we approach a greater "objectivity" of criticism, and our mere preferences are controlled. The amount of ascertained historical fact that emerges should neither be overestimated nor underestimated. It is small in bulk, but not negligible. What matters most is that the more critical our study has been, the more sure we become that here is a real Person in history, many-sided, often perplexing, certainly too great to be reduced to any common type, and not fully intelligible to us; but, for all

[1] See F. C. Burkitt, *The Gospel History and its Transmission*, pp. 147–168.

[2] For the "general reader," *Q, the Earliest Gospel?* by A. Peel (pub. *Teachers and Taught*), may serve as a tentative reconstruction of the "Q" material.

that, unmistakably individual, strongly defined in lines of character and purpose, and challenging us all by a unique outlook on life. Browning is right:

> "That one Face, far from vanish, rather grows,
> Or decomposes but to recompose."

After the discipline of historical criticism we do know Jesus better, and whatever was faulty in the traditional Christianity that has come down to us, or in our apprehension of it, is confronted afresh with the Reality that started it all.

We now approach the question of the authority of Jesus Christ as we find Him in the Gospels. It must first be said that His authority over the Christian soul can never be simply that of a prophet, however great, who speaks to us through a written record. For Christ in Christian faith is not merely an historical figure of the past. Theologians and simple Christians alike (not that these terms are mutually exclusive) find a mystery in His Person to which historical categories are inadequate. While the former seek formulæ, varying from age to age, in which to express His transcendent religious value, the latter find in Him a "present Saviour", or a "Lord and Master" to whom they are personally responsible, in a sense not applicable to any mere character in historical literature. Many theologians are ill-content with the Christological formulæ of tradition, and still more non-theologians find them unmeaning, but few of them would be content to sum up their relation to Christ by saying that they had read about Him in a book and thought Him admirable and His teaching convincing. Even if we start from that curiously dull development of Protestantism for which the Christian religion is "morality touched with emotion", we may still ask, What do you mean by saying that this or that is "un-Christian"? You do not mean that Christian people do not do it, for they do many "un-Christian" things, and even do them without being conscience-stricken. You do not mean that it is explicitly condemned in the Gospels, for many of our ethical problems do not appear there. Do you not mean that in some sense Christ is One who stands in the midst of the world to-day, representing an ethical standard in advance of common ideals and practice? From this to the lofty "Christ-mysticism" of Paul, which some Christians, though they have never been a majority, to-day as always share, there are many imperceptible gradations of Christian experience. For them all an appeal to a Christ contemporary because eternal is natural and indeed unavoidable, over and above any reference to the New Testament records. At the risk of raising philosophical problems which we are not in a position to solve, may we not say in general terms that for Christians, even for Christians who would hesitate to assent to any traditional creed, Christ is in some way identical with "that of God in us", the inner Light, the indwelling Spirit, whatever it is that we live by at our best? His authority, therefore, is the one and only authority we have declared to be absolute, the authority of truth, the authority of God. There can be no discussion of it.

But it is characteristic of Christianity to find its Christ in history as well as above history. Those who would neglect the Gospels as mythical or obsolete and point us to the eternal "Christ within" as the only object of faith, no less than those who will allow us nothing but a "Jesus of History", are proposing an unreal simplification contrary to the genius of our religion, and missing that in it which makes it a unique interpretation of life—the unity of the eternal with the historical. Thus when we have said that the authority of the eternal Christ is absolute, we have not thereby answered the question of the peculiar way in which that authority is mediated in the Gospel history.

A rough and ready answer which is often given is that the teaching of Jesus, as the utterance of the Eternal Word, has the authority of absolute truth. If by this is meant that the sayings reported as His in the Gospels have this authority, it cannot be maintained. There are sayings (not many, indeed) which either are simply not true, in their plain meaning, or are unacceptable to the conscience or reason of Christian people. Thus according to Mark xiii, Jesus gave an elaborate forecast of events to follow His death, ending with the categorical statement, "This generation will not pass away until all these things have happened". By no legitimate ingenuity of interpretation can it be shown that anything resembling some of these events happened before A.D. 100, when the generation to which Jesus belonged may be presumed to have died out. The common-sense reply to such difficulties is that there must have been some mistake in the reporting. Either someone else's words have been wrongly attributed to Jesus, or His words were misunderstood. But in that case we must take the maxim that the teaching of Jesus is absolutely authoritative to mean not the teaching which we possess in the Gospels but some hypothetical teaching which is not directly accessible to us though it is imperfectly reflected in the Gospels. The maxim therefore is of little use to those who seek an infallible external authority. For we no longer accept a saying as authoritative because it lies before us as a word of Jesus, but because we are rationally convinced that it is a word of His, and that will mostly mean in the last resort, because we are convinced that it is worthy of Him, that is, true and important. For although scientific criticism of the Gospels can do a great deal to guide and correct our instinctive criticism, it can seldom speak the last word. If we have been driven from a belief in the verbal infallibility of the Gospels as a whole, we are not likely to find permanent refuge in the verbal infallibility of "Q".

Jesus Himself, if the Gospels are to be believed, did not wish to dispense His hearers from responsibility for their own convictions. "Why do you not from yourselves judge what is right?"[1] He is reported to have said on one occasion, and that principle governs His whole use of parables in teaching. For a parable sets before the hearer a situation in real life which he is expected to recognize as true to experience, and leaves it to him to deduce the meaning. "He who has ears to hear must hear".[2] Someone asked, "Who is my neighbour?" Jesus gave no authoritative definition but told a story, and asked, "Which of these was the neighbour?"[3] The authority therefore which He claimed, and which contemporaries acknowledged in His teaching,[4] was not of a sort to silence private judgment.

If Jesus Christ was a real human Person—if, in theological terms, there was a true incarnation and not a mere theophany in human form,—then He was an individual living under historical conditions and limitations. His authority, therefore, as a religious Teacher must be estimated on the principle we applied to the prophets.[5] He lived intensely in a particular historical situation, and the relevance of His teaching to that situation is part of its eternal significance. He dealt not with general abstractions, but with issues which the time raised acutely for the people to whom He spoke. He dealt with them not as an opportunist, but radically, and with the profound simplicity that comes only of complete mastery of the problem. We have not to face these identical

[1] Luke xii. 57. The meaning, as indicated by the context, is that reflection upon one's own normal, or even instinctive, behaviour as a rational and social being should reveal the fundamental principles of morality without any appeal to an external authority.

[2] Mark iv. 9, etc. The theory of parabolic teaching enunciated in Mark iv. 10–12 is inconsistent with other words of Jesus and with His manifest practice, and is almost certainly due to theological reflection in the early Church. Nor is it likely that the "interpretation" offered in iv. 13–20 goes back to Jesus Himself. See A. Jülicher, *Die Gleichnisreden Jesu*, 2er Teil, pp. 514–538.

[3] Luke x. 29–37. [4] Mark i. 22, 27. [5] See chap. V.

issues, and we cannot always apply His words strictly to ourselves ; but the response that Jesus made to the issues raised for Him challenges us to be satisfied with no solutions of our own problems which have not the same quality. To attempt to free His sayings from their relativity to the particular situation is often to blunt their edge rather than to bring out their universality.

To take an example : there is a saying reported several times in the Gospels, about " bearing the cross ". Luke, intent on applying it directly to the situation of his readers, represents Jesus as saying that His follower must " take up his cross *daily* and follow me ".[1] That rendering of the saying has largely influenced its application. It has been taken to refer to habitual forms of self-sacrifice or self-denial. The ascetic voluntarily undergoing austerities felt himself to be bearing his daily cross. We shallower folk have often reduced it to a metaphor for casual unpleasantnesses which we have to bear. A neuralgia or a defaulting servant is our " cross ", and we make a virtue of necessity. What Jesus actually said, according to our earliest evidence,[2] was, quite bluntly, " Whoever wants to follow me must shoulder his gallows-beam "—for such is perhaps the most significant rendering of the word for " cross ". It meant a beam which a condemned criminal carried to the place of execution, to which he was then nailed until he died. Jesus was not using the term metaphorically. Under Rome, crucifixion was the likeliest fate for those who defied the established powers. Nor did those who heard understand that He was asking for " daily " habits of austerity. He was enrolling volunteers for a desperate venture, and He wished them to understand that in joining it they must hold their lives forfeit. To march behind Him on that journey was as good as to tie a halter round one's neck.

[1] Luke ix. 23.
[2] Mark viii. 34, and so in " Q " ; see Luke xiv. 27, Matt. x. 38.

It was a saying for an emergency. A similar emergency may arise for some Christians in any age. In such a situation it is immediately applicable, in its original form and meaning. For most of us, in normal situations, it is not so applicable. But it is surely good for us to go back and understand that this is what Christ stood for in His day. We shall then at least not suppose that we are meeting His demands in our day by bearing a toothache bravely or fasting during Lent.

This will illustrate how the historical study of the Gospels, with the criticism that necessarily belongs to it, is of religious value. We want to know how Jesus dealt with an historical situation, for although the situation does not recur, all subsequent history, including our own environment, is different because of the way in which it was faced. The way in which it was faced was the right and true way at that time. Therefore it is relevant to all time. We are not at liberty to take the words of Jesus and insist that they must fit any and every situation in which we may find ourselves. He was too deeply concerned with the critical time in which He lived to be thinking about us. Nor can we finally solve our own uncertainties by trying to copy what He did. Again what He did was directed to a particular situation. We must undertake the harder task of passing through the act and word with their time-relativity to the Spirit in them which is eternal. But the more actual the historical situation becomes to us, in all its particularity of time and place, the more powerfully does the Spirit make itself felt.

It is a part of this time-relativity that Jesus, like the prophets, could not but make use of the thought-forms of His age. Some of His teaching, for example, is cast in the mould of an eschatological outlook which is distinctly that of the first century and alien from our own thought. It is almost certain that this element has been exaggerated by His reporters, and it is highly probable that in various ways our records of His teaching are more deeply coloured by their *milieu* than the teaching itself was. Yet it is not to be thought that even in a perfectly accurate report it would have appeared entirely free from such colouring. We need not doubt that Jesus, as He is represented, shared the views of His contemporaries regarding the authorship of books in the Old Testament,[1] or the phenomena of "demon-possession"[2]—views which we could not accept without violence to our sense of truth. We readily recognize that so far He was a man of His time. But who will venture to define how far, or to say, "Here He speaks as a Jew of the first century; there as the Eternal Word"; as theologians once presumed to distinguish what He did "as man" from what He did "as God"? Enough to affirm on the one hand that He could not have spoken so effectively to His time if He had not spoken in its terms, and on the other hand that as a matter of fact this has not stood in the way of His universal appeal. If it be true that much of the prophetic writings appeals at once even to minds quite outside the biblical tradition, it is far more fully true of the teaching of Jesus. The eternal in it has so permeated and transformed the temporary and local that it strikes home to the sincere and open mind anywhere.

We must further observe that it is easy to be overhasty in attempting to purge His teaching of temporary elements. Thus, a great deal of the teaching of Jesus as we have it in the Gospels is coloured with ideas which we readily recognize as belonging to Jewish apocalyptic—the catastrophe of Doomsday, the coming on the clouds, the miraculous transformation of the earth and its inhabitants. How much of this is original? The earlier liberal criticism said, "None; it

[1] Mark xii. 36. The argument depends upon the assumption of Davidic authorship of a psalm which is, in the opinion of recent critics, as late as the Maccabæan period.

[2] Luke xi. 24–26 (Matt. xii. 43–45). Mark iii. 23–27, however, contains a constructive criticism of such beliefs.

was all interpolated by the evangelists out of current thought ". With some relief we concluded that when Jesus spoke of the Kingdom of God He was talking about something we understood very well—progress towards a social ideal. More mature criticism however showed that no objective analysis of the Gospels gave any justification for eliminating eschatology from the teaching of Jesus, though it showed at the same time that in adopting such conceptions from current thought He modified them more than the evangelists themselves realized. To-day we are distrustful of the superficial evolutionism of the last generation, and prepared to confess that anything worthy to be called the Kingdom of God must be more than immanent and natural. Something mysterious, other-worldly, supernatural is inherent in it.[1] The mythological forms in which Jesus' proclamation of it is handed down, we now see, preserve something essential to the idea, which we were in danger of losing altogether in our haste to modernize what He is reported to have said.

The changed outlook is not due to any reaction from the critical position, but to a willingness to be more objective in our criticism and more patient in our re-interpretation. Jesus knew that His teaching might easily be misunderstood by impatient hearers. We do not do justice to it by a lighthearted criticism which prematurely pronounces this or that to be unauthentic or part of the temporary dress of the truth. If Jesus said a thing, or even if He was understood to have said it, all experience shows that it is worth while to wait with great humility and patience until the truth in it, or behind it, declares itself, and separates itself decisively from any temporary and relative element. Patience is a great virtue in all our study of the Gospels. A wise suspension of judgment is often called for. But patience is more readily exercised if we do

[1] See a series of papers on *The Kingdom of God* in *Theology*, May, 1927.

not feel compelled by piety to accept every word that Jesus spoke, supposing we could recover it with certainty from the records, as true for us independently of the conditions which made it the truth for His contemporaries.

When all this is said we must go on to say two things more. First, the peculiar historical situation in which Jesus lived and taught was such that the questions it raised and He answered were of decisive significance not for that age alone but for all history. The very elements in His teaching therefore which are most particularly related to His time are relevant to every age. We shall return to this point in a subsequent chapter.[1] Secondly, the recorded teaching of Jesus has in point of fact related itself in a quite extraordinary way to the universal needs of men. Its radical and elemental simplicity is such that the eternal in it is but thinly disguised, and meets us still with unescapable challenge. Not only is its impact on the mind of subsequent ages no less than on that of His own, but it has revealed under the stress of problems of a later day meanings which were not and perhaps could not have been discerned by His contemporaries.

So much for the teaching of Jesus as a body of reported sayings. But for a final account of its authority we should have to go behind the sayings to the Personality they reveal, or partly reveal. Fragmentary as they are, they yield to diligent and open-minded study the picture of a Mind greater even than its uttered thoughts, a picture which combines with the story of the Life to bring us into the presence of Jesus Christ as a Person speaking with authority. If we ask for proof of that authority, we are in no better case than those who asked it of Him at Jerusalem. He answered by asking another question: "Was John's baptism of human or divine origin?" As if to say, "If

[1] See chap. XIII.

you cannot recognize what is divine when you see it, I cannot tell you ".

It is in view of the total impression made by the Gospel account of Jesus Christ that we advance to a further point. While we recognize in His teaching the temporal relativity which belongs to whatever is in history, we shrink from attributing to it that other and deeper relativity which affects the words of the prophets because of some defect of moral integrity in themselves. They were great men, in true communion with God, and responsive to His grace. Yet they did not meet *all* their experience in the only right way and react to it with invariable truth. Thus they did not see perfectly straight, and we must acknowledge in them not only the relativity inseparable from time, but also an element of error which is there because they are not wholly reconciled to God. Now the total impression made upon us by the Jesus of the Gospels, is that there was not in Him any such uncertainty or disharmony. This is, of course, not a statement which can be demonstrated by enumeration of instances, nor do we expect to prove the universal negative implied. The statement is indeed not capable of proof at all in the strict sense. But it is a belief which rests on good grounds. First, so far as we are able to understand personality at all, we can see that the attitude of Jesus to God and to life, as portrayed in the Gospels, differs from our own and from that of other men precisely in its wholeness, simplicity, and finality. It is undisturbed as ours never is. Secondly, the effect He produced upon men with whom He came in contact—the effect indeed which He still produces upon men—is such that we cannot think He had any unresolved discords in His own soul.

Thus while we do not uncritically accept what Jesus said because of a prior belief in His " sinlessness ", yet there is something in the record that leads us to believe that in some deep and not fully explicable way His inner life possessed a unique moral perfection, which would account for the unique authority His words have actually carried in spite of all local and temporal limitations. It is ultimately this elusive personal "something" that drives us back again and again to the admittedly imperfect record of His words, to exhaust every resource of criticism in the attempt to recover the most authentic and original form of His teaching and to understand it as He meant it. And the more deeply we study the record the more sure do we become that behind all, even the most primitive, interpretation and application of His words, in the words themselves, lay a unique gift to men from the very Spirit of truth. There for the present we will leave the matter, to return to it at a later stage.

Part IV

THE AUTHORITY OF HISTORY

CHAPTER XII

PROGRESS IN RELIGION

THE idea of evolution, originating as an hypothesis in biology, holds wide sway in contemporary science. How far is it applicable to history? This question is related to the other question, much debated recently, whether history is the field of ordered progress.[1] It is difficult to get such a standard of value as to determine with final precision whether the movement discernible in history is or is not progress. In the history of religion, with which we are at present concerned, the attempts which have been made to construe the process of change in men's beliefs and practices as a process of continuous evolution from simple to complex or from lower to higher have not been wholly successful. It now appears that in many respects the religion of peoples which seem to us primitive is more elaborate than that of more advanced peoples, and that so elevated a belief, for instance, as that in a single supreme God, a Father in heaven, is found at such low levels of culture that it is difficult not to call it primitive.[2]

We may fairly assume that all life, not excluding the life of the spirit of man, is evolutionary in the sense that its movements and changes are continuous and organic, resulting from the reaction of an unexplained spontaneity in the living being to the stimuli of its environment. We shall do well not to make any further dogmatic assumption

[1] The Dean of St. Paul's threw down the challenge to the belief in progress in his Romanes Lecture.

[2] See Söderblom, *Das Werden des Gottesglaubens*, pp. 114–185.

that history can be formulated according to evolutionary laws derived from biology. We do not know that peoples, or civilizations, or religions, follow the course of growth, maturity, and decline which is characteristic, more or less, of biological species.[1] Thus we shall hesitate to assume from the outset that the phenomena of biblical history can all be brought under the formula of "the evolution of religion". Rather we shall start with the facts presented by the biblical documents and ask to what conclusions they point.

Amid the perplexing multiplicity of data for the study of religion we have in the Bible a comparatively limited range of such data. We may place the chronological limits roughly at 900 B.C. and A.D. 100, recognizing at the same time that the upper limit must for some purposes be extended indefinitely[2] (though not infinitely). During this period the biblical writings enable us to follow the religious history of a single culture-unit. This unit is the community originally formed by the cohesion of a number of nomad Hebrew-speaking clans who called themselves *B'ne Yisrael,* or Israelites. They settled in the country then known as Canaan, now Palestine, and, strengthened by the inclusion of sundry other racial and cultural elements, formed two kingdoms which enjoyed a comparatively brief independence and were then absorbed into the empires which in turn possessed the near East—those of Assyria, Babylon, Persia, the Macedonians, and Rome. With the Babylonian conquest the unit ceased to be a nation in the ordinary sense.

[1] See R. G. Collingwood, *The Theory of Historical Cycles*, in *Antiquity*, vol. I, nos. 3 and 4.

[2] The earliest documentary sources which we are in a position to reconstruct, the prophetic narratives of the Pentateuch (J and E) may probably be dated to the ninth century and the early part of the eighth, and no doubt still earlier written material was incorporated in them and in the narratives of Samuel and Kings. Earlier still is traditional poetry like the Song of Deborah. Broadly speaking we have contemporary documentary records from about the beginning of the ninth century.

It became a diffused religious group, with its nucleus in the small community resident at Jerusalem. Ultimately this central nucleus lost all local connection with the ancient capital, and Jewry became what it is to-day. But in the meantime the religious life of the diffused culture-group had found a new centre, and expanded in new directions. Out of Judaism arose Christianity, overleaping almost from the outset the racial frontiers set up by Judaism. The Bible closes at the point at which the religious tradition hitherto preserved within the Israelite community in its various forms breaks away and becomes cosmopolitan.

There is true continuity here. The medley of Bedawin clans that invaded Canaan, the monarchy of Solomon, the two kingdoms, the little centralized state ruled by Josiah and his successors, the Jewish world of the Dispersion looking to Jerusalem under the High Priests, and finally the Christian Church as we meet it in the New Testament, are widely different. The religious ideas informing the life of the community at these various stages are also widely different. Yet there is no complete break in the process of change by which one stage gives place to another. We can say more; if we compare this religious tradition with other religious traditions, as for instance that of Buddhism in the far East, we can indeed discern similarities and parallels, but the biblical tradition as a whole displays certain characteristic marks which distinguish it from others and give it a unity of its own.

The biblical literature, properly treated, gives us fairly full information of the development of this particular tradition. It has been studied by scholars on critical principles well established in other departments of historical investigation, with the help of auxiliary studies which the comparative method puts at the disposal of the student. The results are conclusions scientifically reached, possessing that high degree of probability which satisfies the investigator in all fields where human life and action provide the subject-matter. The biblical writings then lie before us in a chronological order which, though not always certain in detail, gives the general succession of events and the broad lines of development.

The evidence does not suggest anything like a smooth and uniform evolution. There are diverse tendencies, sometimes one leading, sometimes another. These are conflicts and cross currents. To interpret the data we need to have the whole process before us.

It issues in the appearance of Jesus Christ and the emergence of the Christian Church. In the light of the end we interpret and value stages in the process. Theologians of the other religions which inherit the biblical tradition, Judaism and Islam, might value them differently. There is no final court of appeal beyond the religious intuition of mankind and the course of future history. But the Christian claim is that in this particular historical process, culminating in the unique events out of which Christianity arose, the real meaning of all history may be studied. That claim implies, first, that history has a meaning, and secondly that this meaning is disclosed more clearly in some events and series of events than in others. Neither of these assumptions is unreasonable, in view of the nature of history itself, as historians in general have regarded it. On a theistic view of the world, the meaning of history is what God means by it. Conversely, what God means is disclosed by the facts of history as they are experienced by men open to their impact and qualified to understand them. It is claimed that in the Bible we have a record of facts thus understood and interpreted, with an interpretation imposed by the facts themselves upon responsive minds. The whole process, fact and interpretation, forms a part of the objective order of history within which we stand and to which we are subject. The claim that the meaning disclosed in it is ultimately regulative of all history, is an act of faith. It can be no other, while history remains incomplete.

We may now attempt to summarize the facts as the

biblical evidence sets them before us. At the outset the Hebrews must have had a religious life very like that which the comparative study of religion shows in most peoples at a relatively primitive level. As we have seen, the ancient narratives reflect the characteristic ideas of such undeveloped peoples. Already, however, before our written records begin, some strong and original impulse had entered in which differentiated Hebrew religion from the common type. Yet its influence was for centuries precarious. The actual practice of religion down to the eighth century, though it cannot be described as primitive, differed hardly at all from that current among surrounding peoples. The ordinary reader of the Bible scarcely realizes all that is implied in the prophetic denunciations of the contemporary cult. It is evident that the grossest heathenism prevailed. At the holy cities of Bethel and Dan Jehovah was worshipped in the form of a bull.[1] The Temple at Jerusalem was adorned with fetish-poles,[2] one of them in the form of a serpent.[3] Human sacrifice was practised at least in times of stress,[4] and sacred prostitution flourished as it does to-day in the temples of India.[5] Nor did this state of things cease at the protest of the prophets. Jeremiah and Ezekiel still

[1] 1 Kings xii. 25–31. The condemnation of this form of worship in the Books of Kings is the result of prophetic teaching; there is no evidence that it was regarded at the time as reprehensible. According to E (the northern history) it had been instituted by Aaron in the wilderness, Exod. xxxii. 2–6.

[2] 1 Kings vii. 21.

[3] 2 Kings xviii. 4. It was called Nehushtan (probably from *nahash* = serpent), and was believed to have been made by Moses in the wilderness by command of Jehovah (Num. xxi. 9 E); i.e. it was of great sanctity and immemorial antiquity. It was not an ordinary serpent, but of the kind called *saraph* ("fiery serpent" A.V.), probably a mythological creature (a sort of gryphon perhaps); and it is at least curious that in Isaiah's vision the winged attendants of Jehovah are called by the same name. In Isaiah's time Nehushtan was still worshipped, but before his death it was destroyed in Hezekiah's reformation.

[4] See p. 88.

[5] 1 Kings xiv. 24. It was forbidden by Deuteronomy (xxiii. 17) and accordingly abolished (officially) in Josiah's reformation, 2 Kings xxiii. 7.

describe all manner of heathen rites practised as openly, if not quite as shamelessly, as a century earlier.[1] Even in the fifth century, B.C., there was a Jewish temple at Elephantine in Egypt which Jehovah shared with four other deities, two of them goddesses.[2] Its worshippers appealed for support to the High Priest at Jerusalem with no apparent sense that they were doing anything outrageous.

It was out of this morass of paganism that the great prophets arose. A hasty evolutionism was formerly inclined to assume that nothing but this paganism had hitherto existed, and that the earlier prophets represented the first advance from this primitive paganism. But the prophets themselves appealed to an older tradition of a purer faith, and stories certainly older than the eighth century, and probably very much older, consistently assert that this state of affairs was a degradation of something better. How far the religion of the patriarchs as presented in Genesis is really ancient, and how far it represents a phase of prophetic teaching, is not certain. But the oldest literature we possess, such as the Song of Deborah,[3] wild and primitive enough in all conscience, has nothing of this gross and sophisticated paganism. The fact seems to be that the traditions of a great religious movement led by Moses and centred at Sinai reflect a real event. There *was* a revelation of God " by His name Jehovah ", a name which stood already for conceptions of the deity capable of leading to the ideas of the prophets.[4]

The next stage was the adaptation of the Jehovah-worship of the desert to relatively civilized conditions in

[1] Jer. vii. 9, xi. 13, xvii. 2, xliv. 15–19; Ezek. viii., etc. Cf. also Zeph. i. 4–5 (late seventh century).

[2] This surprising information is contained in papyri discovered at Elephantine in the years 1906–1908. See Ungnad, *Aramäische Papyrus aus Elephantine*. An excellent short account in the *Clarendon Bible*, O.T., Vol. IV (W. F. Lofthouse), pp. 212 sqq.

[3] Judges v.

[4] See chap. II.

Canaan. If the evolution of religion were continuous, this should have meant an advance, and doubtless to the majority of those who thought about such things it appeared an advance. When Solomon built his great temple at Jerusalem for Jehovah, as well as chapels for a number of satellite gods,[1] and introduced elaborate rites borrowed from the Canaanites or from his Phoenician allies, his enlightened courtiers no doubt congratulated themselves that now the old barbarous ways were gone, and Israel was a civilized nation. Indeed there was much to justify their view. The most conspicuous representatives of the old ways were crazy dervishes,[2] or at best fanatics like Elijah the Tishbite, who came from their deserts and caves in hairy mantles and interfered in politics about which they knew nothing. Their associates were gipsies like Jonadab ben-Rechab—living in tents, forsooth, in this enlightened age![3]

The great prophets of the eighth and following centuries saw through the sham of progress. Of course, they were not simply reviving a pure Mosaic religion. Yet the half-submerged tradition of the earlier time, which had never wholly died, gave them a starting-point. Gathering up the best in the tradition, they transformed it in their own living experience, and gave forth to the world a new word, which once spoken could not be recalled or ignored. History justified them by showing that there was no future for a pagan Israel.

The prophets stood for the belief that one God, and He first and foremost a righteous God, claimed the undivided allegiance of Israel. He desired mercy and not sacrifice. He cared for Israel, but He cared for justice and mercy more. He cared for Israel, but He also cared for all nations.

[1] 1 Kings xi. 5–8.

[2] See chap. II, pp. 47–49. This was the attitude of the typical army officer in the time of Elisha, 2 Kings ix. 11.

[3] 2 Kings x. 15–16. Cf. Jer. xxxv. 1–10.

Indeed, so they came to say at last, there was no other God. He alone, Whose will was eternal right, governed the destinies of all peoples. If Israel was to be His people that meant that they must be servants of His righteous rule, which would one day cover all the earth.

An attempt was made to embody this ethical monotheism (or monolatry) of the prophets in a legal code. Josiah's reformation had this in view, and his law-book is probably represented in some sense by Deuteronomy. But the attempt never succeeded, and Judah went into exile. The reconstructed community, however, started from Deuteronomy. It aimed at including only those who accepted the prophetic religion in its codified form. Thus while the "people of the land" remained at a semi-pagan level, the main stream of religious tradition now flowed through an artificial community based upon a constitution intended to represent the prophetic religion.

After the Exile we feel ourselves in what by comparison is a modern world. It makes our own fundamental religious assumptions—that there is one God and that He is good and requires and helps men to be good also. It shows also the familiar traits of theological speculation and ecclesiastical controversy. The chief ecclesiastical question is that of separatism and comprehension—still a living question. The chief subjects of theological speculation are the transcendence of God and how to reconcile it with His interest in man, and the perennial problem of providence and suffering. Later the question of immortality and the future life begins to agitate the mind. It is all very modern. It is also for the most part rather mediocre. During the whole period there is little that reaches the religious level of the great prophets. Indeed in many respects we must recognize a decline from their heights of faith. After the tremendous proclamation of a religion rising above all manner of ritual and ceremonial it is a poor business to read in the Priestly Code a revival of primitive ritual sometimes not far removed from magic.[1] Again, from the moral idealism of Isaiah or Jeremiah it is rather a descent to the utilitarianism of Proverbs.

Nevertheless if we compare the achievement of this period not with the elevation of isolated genius, but with the general level of religion, we must conclude that it represents a very great advance. It is an advance accompanied by some loss. Still, if religion is to be a decisive factor in the common life of men and not a prerogative of exceptional genius, then a period of popular assimilation is required. The prayer of Browning's Felix, "Make no more giants, God, but elevate the race at once!" is nearer to an answer in such periods. That the common man is struggling into his heritage of religion in the post-exilic period is clear. His grandfather before the Exile had been little better than a pagan, though with higher aspirations striving for expression in his worship of Jehovah. The grandson in Jerusalem and his successors under the High Priests knew that Jehovah required of him to do justly, to love mercy, and to walk humbly with his God. He tried to walk by the precepts which his spiritual guides called the Law of the Lord, and he found peace and joy in so doing. He believed in his people, the people of the Law, and was generally content with brilliant hopes for its future in which he individually could not hope to share. The one God, he knew, was sovereign in the kingdom of men, and one day His Kingdom would be revealed. He prayed in the language of the Psalms, and let the priests do his sacrificing for him, assuming that they knew best, and following the ritual they prescribed, full of sound and colour as it was.

[1] We must here distinguish. The ritual of sacrifice may, in the primitive stage to which it rightly belongs, be a real advantage to the religious life. To revive it in a sophisticated age, when its primitive symbolism is forgotten and it is performed simply because one supposes it pleases God, is superstition.

Thus there came into existence a society whose lay members had a real religious life and experience of a relatively high order, however limited in outlook. It was being made ready for the next great outburst of religious genius.

"In the fulness of time" Jesus Christ came. Believing Himself called to be the "Messiah" of His people, He gathered up their highest traditions, going back directly and consciously behind the period of legalism to the great prophets, and setting Himself to interpret them to His own contemporaries, men brought up in post-exilic Judaism. But while doing so He cut a path clean through all the uncertainties and limitations of the tradition, and showed God to men in a new and commanding way—"He spoke with authority and not as the scribes".

At first sight early Christianity as represented by the New Testament seems almost entirely hostile to the Jewish tradition. Only a close familiarity with both Testaments, and some acquaintance with the non-canonical literature of post-exilic Judaism, reveal how the piety of Judaism underlies every part of the New Testament. The new departure is firmly based in the religious life worked out by the post-exilic community under the impulse of the classical prophets.

Yet Christianity dealt very drastically with the tradition it inherited. It set out "not to destroy the Law but to fulfil".[1] Yet some parts of it were held fit only for destruction. The sacrificial system of the Priestly Code, already out of vital relation to the best piety of the time, went by the board. If the law of conduct, as represented by the Deuteronomic legislation and its developments, was to be "fulfilled", it was not by the Pharisaic way of casuistry, but by going behind Deuteronomy itself to the prophetic inspiration which its authors had intended to express. In the conflict between separatism and comprehension, the

[1] Matt. v. 17.

close national separatism which had been growing in influence at the expense of the broader tendency represented by "Second Isaiah" and the Book of Jonah, was decisively repudiated. The full implications of ethical monotheism were for the first time drawn out with uncompromising clarity.

Through the whole history of the Jewish community as reconstituted after the Exile we can discern ideas and principles which are the germ of Christianity, in conflict with other tendencies. But it would be a misreading of the evidence to regard the process of criticism and selection carried out by Christianity as merely a continuation of the old controversies. It was the inevitable result of the intrusion of a new factor, the personality and the teaching of Jesus Christ. He brought to men a definitely new conception of God, a definitely new experience of God, taking up into itself the highest elements of past experience, but synthetizing them by the impact of something different.

Taking now a retrospect of the biblical history we may place on record certain observations which have a bearing on the "evolution of religion". First, that within this history there is a development is beyond doubt. We trace a process of change, continuously linked together, and the final product is definitely higher, richer, truer than the beginning, if such terms of value have any meaning at all. Yet at the most primitive level elements are already in existence which enter into the final product.

On the other hand there is no uniformity in the forward movement. Indeed some developments which at a point short of the end seem to be progress are ultimately repudiated. Thus the intense nationalism associated with Jehovah-worship, in its earliest forms known to us, appears to be an essential part of the advance Moses made upon more primitive religion. The patriotic idealism of the Song of Deborah, for instance, is linked to a conception of Jehovah, the God of Israel, which lifts Him above the level of local *Elohim* worshipped at every spring and sacred tree. This nationalism is criticized by several of the prophets, with small effect. After the Exile it develops more vigorously than ever. If a good Jew of the fourth century B.C. had been asked for tokens that his people were "better than their fathers", he would surely have pointed to the fact that the racial purity and the distinctive customs of the Chosen People were more faithfully safeguarded than in the half-heathen days before the Exile. Yet in the end religious nationalism had to be disavowed root and branch in the interests of a truer conception of God and His relation to man.

Again, the earliest Jehovah-worship apparently possessed only the simplest kind of ritual, so much so that Amos and Jeremiah could declare that Moses never ordained any sacrifices at all.[1] The cult grew to great dimensions under the monarchy, and in spite of the denunciations of the classical prophets it continued to develop, until the post-exilic Priestly Code provided a liturgy of sacrifice which for elaboration, splendour, and expense has rarely been surpassed. Nevertheless the most vital religion of the time was largely independent of it, and Christianity and Rabbinic Judaism alike dispensed with it. After seeming for centuries one of the main outward marks of religious progress, it was finally discovered to be replaceable without injury to religion.

We may take a third example, which lies nearer to the heart of the whole matter. The development of the conception of God's character is by no means uniform. Jehovah of Sinai was a God of terror, hurling the tempests of His wrath upon the enemies of His chosen people, not for any moral guilt in them, but because they belonged to other

[1] Amos v. 25. ; Jer. vii. 22.

gods whom He disliked. To His own people, however, He was kindly and indulgent, taking delight in their sacrifices and giving them victory and prosperity. It was the epoch-making discovery of the prophets that the wrath of God is governed by the strictest justice. Fierce and terrible He is in His wrath—against *sinners*, native and foreign alike, and not to be mollified by sacrifices or prayers. Mingled with this, it is true, is a conception of the grace of God, and His forgiveness of sin; but this conception is not organically harmonized with the sterner doctrine. In the main the prophetic doctrine of the justice of God was a definite advance upon earlier ideas of His un-ethical "mercy" maintained by those whom Jeremiah called "false prophets".[1] It remained for Christianity to declare that God is a Father "kind to the unthankful and the evil", a Shepherd who goes after His lost sheep until He find it, one Whose "kindness leads men to repentance", and Who "justifies the ungodly". "The righteousness which is of the Law"—in other words, legal or retributive justice—is transcended in the loving righteousness of God as revealed in Christ, "the Friend of publicans and sinners."

With these qualifications, then, we recognize in the Bible a progressive development of religion. The various writers take their place in a series leading up to a climax in the Christianity of the New Testament. Elements that we have noted as limited or mistaken are to be viewed in relation to the process of which they form part, not as isolated factors to be judged in and for themselves.

We have thus deduced from the facts themselves a conception of development or evolution applicable to the

[1] It is implied in many of the great prophetic passages that false comforters were proclaiming the mercy of Jehovah when the truth demanded a proclamation of His severity, e g. Jer. xxiii. 16–17. It is thought by some interpreters that the "penitential psalm" in Jer. xiv. 7–9 is a quotation from the contemporary liturgy of prayer, repudiated by the prophet as too easily assuming the indulgence of Jehovah.

history of religion as presented in the Bible. We have now to observe that we have here not merely a development of religious *ideas*, but a development of religious *life* in a changing social environment. It is not like the development of ideas in a "school" of philosophers such as the Peripatetic in ancient times or the Hegelian in modern. Its goal is not the formulation of a more valid system of beliefs, but the emergence of a world-wide society possessing a religious life and religious institutions of its own, the Christian Church.

The religious life in so far as it is inward and purely spiritual, is necessarily individual; and the religious individual is only partly to be explained by evolution. The sphere in which religious development, properly speaking, takes place is the community. It possesses a continuous history in which individuals play their part before passing on to that higher plane of being which is beyond history as we know it. Now some religions lay such exclusive stress on the inward and spiritual, and therefore individual, aspect of religion that the social and historical aspect falls away. Christianity has never been content with this. It would, of course, be absurd to suggest that Christianity lags behind any other religion in exalting the inward converse of the soul with God in that "secret place of the Most High" which lies beyond time and space. But it never allows its votaries to abide there undisturbed. It is concerned to make history. Much might be said about the blunders it has made in the attempt; but whatever measure of failure it meets there is something in its genius that keeps it to the task. Thus it is necessarily an historical religion, and that is to say a social religion. There is something of this character about the other two great religions standing in the biblical succession. The Jews to-day form a society which, if it is not exactly a Church, is something other than a nation like other nations. Islam is in some sense an international society—in a sense strange, for example, to Buddhism, which has only its coteries of monks. Confucianism, having some striking similarities to Christianity, succeeded in permeating a national civilization, but it has not created a society like the Christian Church, which amid the rise and fall of civilizations keeps a self-identity not inconsistent with endless adaptability. The Church is a distinct and indeed a unique type of society,[1] and though by reason of its imperfections there are Christians outside the visible Church in any of its communions, yet Christianity without the Church is unthinkable. Divided as it is it remains conscious of its unity, and keeps the sacraments as the principal signs and organs of its continuous life. But behind the sacraments lie historical events, by which indeed the unity they attest was brought about. The history is preserved in the biblical record. And as things are it is probable that the common possession of the Bible by all branches of the Church is a more effectual bond of union than the sacraments themselves. All Christian communions must go back perpetually to the creative

[1] See S. Freud, *Group Psychology and the Analysis of the Ego*, pp. 41–51, 110–111. Freud takes the Army and the Church as the best examples of "highly organized, lasting and artificial groups," and compares their psychological basis. He finds that the former is based upon "replacement of the ego ideal by an object" (viz. the Commander-in-Chief); but "it is otherwise in the Catholic Church. Every Christian loves Christ as his ideal and feels himself united with all other Christians by the tie of identification. But the Church requires more of him. He has also to identify himself with Christ and love all other Christians as Christ loved them. At both points, therefore, the Church requires that the position of the libido which is given by a group formation should be supplemented. Identification has to be added where object-choice has taken place, and object love where there is identification." In view of the importance attached by Freud to these principles of "identification of the ego with an object," and "replacement of the ego-ideal by an object," it would appear to follow that where both are found in such peculiar relations as in the Christian Church, the group is unique in its formation. He adds, "This further development in the distribution of the libido in the group is probably the factor upon which Christianity bases its claim to have reached a higher ethical level" (Authorized Translation by James Strachey).

events to which the New Testament bears witness, and these are themselves of one piece with the whole history reflected in the older Canon. The Bible is indeed not only a history of the revelation of truth, but it is the record of a history which itself, in Christian belief, was a divine revelation. For the Hindu, things and events are a veil of illusion which effectually conceals God from men. The individual can penetrate to God only by cutting himself loose from his social environment, forgetting time and space, and entering eternity through the negation of everything which (as it seems to us) makes human life distinctively human. For the Christian, things and events are a sacramental manifestation of God. He finds God in historical events and in the things about him, and sets out to deal with events and things that fall within his range of activity in such wise as to make them a clearer manifestation of the divine.

Thus the Bible as an historical record of events possesses a truly religious value. For this purpose it must, of course, be read as any other historical record is read, critically in the fullest sense. Until criticism had restored to us the documents in something like their true chronological order, distinguishing where necessary the varying strata of composite writings, the Bible was, historically speaking, a chaos. While, for instance, it was supposed that the Pentateuch in its entirety belonged to the period of Moses, it was quite impossible to appreciate the true significance of the Books of Samuel and Kings, or of the prophetic writings. Again, this source-criticism must be accompanied by the comparative study of the contents, with the aid of all we now know of the period from non-biblical sources such as Assyrian, Babylonian, and Egyptian inscriptions. These will often enable us to correct mistakes or misunderstanding in the Hebrew records. It must, however, be said that these records emerge from the process with credit. In many details they can be convicted of error, but they are none the less historical sources of a high order, quite indispensable as such to the secular historian. In any case the details in which mistakes are demonstrable are not, from our present point of view, of very great moment. When once we have got the documents in their true chronological order the broad rhythms of the history stand out firm and clear, and we may without misgiving follow the sweep of events, and the development of the ideas that interact with them, from age to age, recognizing our records as a true representation, in broad terms, of what actually took place.

Thus we turn to the beginnings of Bible story, and trace the Hand of God in the impulses that drove the clans to wander—natural conditions and economic pressure on the one side, and on the other the spirit of adventure and of quest; the outward and the inward interacting, and both related to the divine purpose for humanity. Their wanderings bring the clans into the orbits of two great civilizations, not without results for their training, which we must regard as providential. Then the strong sense of a divine calling to freedom and a distinctive life, mediated through the genius of Moses, implants the consciousness of national unity rooted in religion. Through generations of "Sturm und Drang" the impulse to unity contends with the clannishness of these vigorous stocks, till desperate peril and the rise of strong leaders who worthily embody the religious ideals of the people bring them together. There is a divine meaning here. The future did not lie with the "short cut" to unity represented by the despotisms of Assyria and Egypt. It was a harder and longer way that must lead to a unity of positive value to mankind. The group of men represented by the names of Samuel, David, Nathan, and Gad created the distinctive type of Israelitish monarchy, and it remained a regulative ideal, however its traits may have become assimilated to foreign models. The Bible is clearly right in saying that, in relation to his fundamental task at the moment, David was "a man after God's own heart" (i.e. purpose).[1] The part played by the prophets at this point, representing the folk-aspirations on their higher side, was determinative.

The national unity and distinctiveness so asserted had now a hard, and in some measure a losing battle to fight. Israel must learn to be civilized, and to do that without sacrificing its essential characteristics was difficult. The kingdoms went under. They had failed to solve their problem. Yet the ideal of the kingdom of the House of David continued to provide a mould for the aspirations of the people. Meantime the great prophets arose, to snatch a "remnant" out of the wreck of the secular Israelitish monarchies. Here, as we have seen, creative religious genius comes on the scene. The sublime utterances of the prophets are for all time, but in *their* time they led directly to the remoulding of the people of destiny. It was in strict fact the result of prophetic teaching that when the monarchies fell a new community was organized on the basis of Deuteronomy. It was a new thing in the world. The national religion might have been expected to fall with the political existence of the state. Instead, it created for itself a new embodiment. The post-exilic Jewish community is a fact of history simply because the prophets had their vision of God. Whatever religious advance we have to record is clearly enough not simply in the realm of unsubstantial ideas, but in the realm of historic fact.

History has thus created a "people of God", and henceforward we trace its vicissitudes. There is to be discerned a certain alternation of driving forces. The spirit of adventure and quest once more sends the people out into the wider world; its strong clannishness, now finding new

[1] 1 Sam. xiii. 14.

forms through the consciousness of religious isolation, drives it back upon itself. Growing civilization tempts it into a larger use of the outward things of life; oppression and persecution force its thought inward, to deeper discoveries. The hard facts of a precarious national existence break down hasty systems of belief and compel the mind in travail to bring forth more worthy conceptions of the largeness and mystery of divine Reality. If when Rome came on the scene she found the Jewish community harder of subjugation and assimilation than any other people she had met, it was not because the Jews were richer, braver, more numerous, or more warlike, but because their national life was moulded into firmness by ideas and spiritual beliefs, Unsubstantial indeed they might seem to the conquering Roman, yet by virtue of them Jewry continued to exist, and its offshoot the Christian Church conquered Rome and turned Rome's animating idea to its own uses.

The emergence of the Christian Church itself as a fact to be reckoned with was one more example of the interaction of outward conditions with spiritual forces. The time had come when in the general situation of the world some such new departure was due. The conquests of Alexander and the triumph of a cosmopolitan civilization had antiquated all narrowly national forms of idealism. The dispersal of the Jewish race, and its immersion in the commercial and financial activities of this cosmopolitan civilization, had gradually drained the local institutions of Jerusalem of their primary significance. The Roman Peace, with its new security and its removal of old economic and political barriers, both facilitated and demanded some fresh expansion of spiritual life. The bankruptcy of the older ethical systems called for fresh inspiration, which for the time Stoicism was seeking to supply, but Stoicism lacked the elemental driving-force which only religious emotion can give. The time was indeed ripe, when Jesus spoke the new Word which emancipated the People of God from the limitations of the past and created its new social embodiment. The Church at once served itself heir to the most vital spiritual ideas of the time, and using to the full the social, political and economic factors which favoured its development, began to lead the spirit of man into the new world to which it was aspiring. The writers of the New Testament and of early Christianity in general are clearly aware both of continuity and of newness; of their glorious independence of outworn tradition and of their subjection to a perpetual providential order now manifest anew in the Church; of the transcendent destiny of the immortal soul and of its calling in this world of time and space. They are aware, in particular, of standing at an historical turning-point, when the past is gathered up and transformed in a mighty present fact which is to determine the future. The Kingdom of God has been revealed, and the Church must live until all the kingdoms of the world have become the Kingdom of its God and of His Christ.

If we ask, Is there progress here? the answer must be in the affirmative for anyone who takes the Christian standpoint, in view of the ultimate outcome of the process. But in a more general way of looking at the matter there is one point which seems worth making. The biblical history is the record of a community which is facing successfully an ever larger area of the total reality with which man is confronted. By this total reality I mean both the inner world of the spirit and the outer world in which we live. Both worlds are presented in experience for the "essential ego" to make into the stuff of personality. As one tract of reality is explored and occupied, another opens to the view. There are periods in history, like the golden age of Athens in the fifth century B.C., when the spirit of man seems thoroughly to have mastered the world of its experience. But by its very success it comes face to face with a larger world, as the success of the Greek city states led them out into the world of "barbarians" and into strange ways of the spirit which this new adventure opened. In some respects such a new enterprise in its first stages often seems to be accompanied by decline, but for the future of humanity the struggle to appropriate a new tract of reality may be of greater moment than the serene equilibrium of a limited achievement.

> "Better fifty years of Europe than a cycle of Cathay".

The biblical history reflects a process of this kind through several crises. For example, we may look again at the emergence of Israel from nomadic and pastoral conditions into the settled life of a civilized state. The nomad lives in a very simple world. He has few ties, only those which bind him to a handful of fellow-clansmen. His occupations make small demands upon intelligence, while he follows his flock to their feeding-ground and trusts to luck. His economic system follows

> "The good old rule, the simple plan,
> That they should take who have the power,
> And they should keep who can".

When he settles down to tillage, he is dependent on new factors in his environment, on the uncertain behaviour of the weather, on qualities of soil, on the goodwill of neighbours. These call for new spiritual resources in himself—technical skill, industry, foresight, faith, tenacity—all those traits of mind and character which make the farmer in all ages a distinctive type. As agriculture leads to other industries, to trade and commerce, the world becomes still more complicated. The attitude to other peoples can no longer be confined to simple defence and offence. Some way of co-operation must be found. The religious conflict between Jehovah and the baals of the land or the great Baal of mercantile Tyre is an aspect of the problem of reconstructing the ideas and institutions of society in relation to a wider environment. When the earlier prophets succeeded in convincing the people that not the baals of the land but Jehovah with His known character and relation to Israel, was the Lord of rain and of crops, and that it was He who "giveth the power to get wealth ",[1] it was, however commonplace it seems to us, an important step in the development of ethical monotheism ; but also, by making it appear natural to centralize worship at a single national sanctuary, it led to a new kind of social and political organization, which was a reply to the challenge of the whole situation.[2] This reorganization was, however, not completed before the horizon widened once again.

When in the last days of the monarchies Israel became involved to its cost in the large "Realpolitik" of the time, it meant once again an expansion of the world, a wider range of facts to deal with, and an answering development of institutions through the reaction of religious impulses upon the actual situation. The organization of post-exilic Judaism was a very remarkable social phenomenon. It was not deliberately planned ; it emerged as the response to the facts of the situation. At the centre was the little community at Jerusalem, inheriting the traditions of the reformed monarchy, but with no visible political head to compete with the world-powers with which the Jews had now to make an accommodation. It even came to be held that monarchy itself had been apostasy from Jehovah. The post-exilic redactor of the early traditions makes Jehovah say of the people who asked for a king, "They have rejected me, that I should not be king over them ".[3] Thus in the post-exilic community Jehovah was regarded as the

[1] Deut. viii. 18. Cf. xi. 10–12.
[2] 2 Kings xxii–xxiii.
[3] 1 Sam. viii. 7. The earlier view is that expressed in 1 Sam. ix. 15–16.

"invisible King", whose deputy was the High Priest. A community which is neither a republic nor the realm of a visible king clearly possesses peculiar elasticity and power of adaptation. The majority of the Jewish people at this time lived outside the limits of the little Judæan state. In the provinces of the Persian Empire, particularly in Babylonia, lived thousands of Jews, including the wealthiest, the most civilized, and many of the most learned members of the race. In Egypt, in the Seleucid colonies of Asia Minor, and later throughout the Roman Empire, Jews played a prominent part in the economic life of the world; so much so that Roman legislation accorded them preferential treatment in many respects. All these were bound to the central body at Jerusalem by the closest ties, religious, legal, financial. The Jewish Dispersion, in fact, with its centre at Jerusalem, was a "far-flung" society of an entirely new type. It was neither an empire nor a federation. In it a strong social solidarity existed apart from political unity or independence. It provided a model for a truly international society. And through and through it was the creation of a religious impulse. The Temple and the High Priest were its visible symbols of unity; the pious pilgrimages were its chief means of communication; the "law of Jehovah" codified in the Pentateuch was the universal norm of its ethical life.

On the other side, the inner life of Judaism was enlarged and enriched by contact with the wider world. The faith of Zarathustra, the philosophies of Plato and Zeno, the mysticism of Egypt, have helped to shape the thought of later Judaism, yet in such a way that these outside influences are completely assimilated and transmuted by the inherent power of the religion of Jehovah. It is doubtless partly as a result of these wider contacts that in this period the conception of a spiritual world and a future life begins to play a part in Jewish thought—partly so, but perhaps more as a result of the shattering blows that the nation suffered. Hard experience revealed the insufficiency of the robust " this-worldliness " of the classical Hebrew religion. Judaism begins to recognize that man must find himself at home in another world besides this world of time and space if his communion with God is to be secure and real.

Thus the post-exilic stage of development, while in some respects it shows a falling-off from the level of the great prophets, comparable to the decline from classical Athens to the Hellenistic culture of the third and following centuries before Christ, yet represents a wider exploration of the inner and outer worlds of experience, and so prepares the way for Christianity, which for the first time exhibits a religious life and religious institutions inherently universal in their scope.

We seem to have here a real criterion of progress, so far as it goes. Whether we will or no we have to adapt ourselves to our environment as a whole, and clearly the more of it we can effectively deal with the better. In the Bible we find a development in religious life and ideas which accompanies a progressive widening of the inner and outer horizons of the spirit of man, and expresses itself in an ever more effective dealing with the expanding world.

CHAPTER XIII

" PROGRESSIVE REVELATION "

THE Bible, we have seen, records a development in men's notions of God, and in the forms of religious life associated with such notions ; and it is a development in which progress can be recognized. How are we to think of this development ? Is it purely a change in men's speculations about God ? or is it (to use a current phrase) a " progressive revelation ", in which God makes Himself gradually known to men ?

The idea of a " progressive revelation " is not altogether without difficulty. Progress means an advance from something worse to something better. In any science it means an advance from beliefs partly erroneous to beliefs corresponding more fully to truth. Now God, if He wills to reveal Himself, may well reveal one aspect of Himself to one person, and another to another person ; but, it may be said, the one cannot be superior to the other, for nothing which is revealed by God can be in any degree erroneous. Thus there may be successive revelation, but can there be in the strict sense progressive revelation ? If, on the other hand, the term " progressive " is allowed its full ordinary meaning, is it not progressive *discovery* of which we are speaking, rather than revelation ? In discovery men do advance from the erroneous to the true.

Now the view taken here is that there is progress, in the full sense ; that is, that the Bible contains, not merely a succession of statements about God, all equally true, and forming a harmonious whole, but a progressive series, including partly erroneous ideas of God, which are in time changed for ideas approximating more and more closely to the truth. We have, therefore, to meet the charge that we are abandoning belief in a real revelation by God of Himself to men, and substituting a gradual process of discovery.

What is discovery, in any field of research? In Mathematics perhaps (though some mathematicians would not agree) it is simply the progressive unfolding of abstract conceptions within the human mind. However that may be, in any science which has regard to a world of phenomena it is in some measure a response to a stimulus from beyond ourselves. Nature provokes us to know her. Whatever "nature" may be, whether the term stands for a world of things ultimately independent of mind, or for a spiritual system, this is certain, that the "given" from which we start is not of our own making. Before we can discover, *something* has revealed itself. Where the object of our investigation is living, this fact becomes of practical importance. The matter studied by the chemist or the mineralogist is (relatively, at least) inert; it "abides his question". He may force it into such postures for experiment as best suit his purpose. But if the thing we study is alive, all is different. Experiment in these fields is a more delicate and difficult operation. Any high-handed method of force destroys the thing we want to observe. The study of stuffed birds in museums, the dissection of dead birds in the laboratory, must yield to the patient observation of birds living their own life, if ornithology is to make real advance.

There is a story of three men who set out to write a book on the camel. The German went to his study, closed door and window, lit his pipe and meditated until he had evolved from his inner consciousness the "*Sein und Wesen*" of the camel. The Frenchman went to the Bibliothèque Nationale and read up the subject thoroughly. The Englishman packed his portmanteau and looked up sailings to where the camel lives. National prejudice apart, it is clear that the last way is the true way of discovery. If we would discover life, we must allow life to reveal itself.

Where life is personal, this is still more obviously true. Every psychologist knows that if he is to go far his subject must be willing to provide the *data* required. The investigator may find a great deal more in the *data* than the subject ever intended to give away, but knowledge of the human mind must await upon self-revelation.

Now if the last Reality is personal, as religious people believe, then Its discovery will certainly wait upon self-revelation. This is the universal postulate of the Bible. From the most primitive to the most advanced stage it is never doubted that God takes the initiative. All knowledge of God starts with His will to reveal Himself. In the most primitive stories it is so. Abraham in his wanderings came to the terebinth of Mamre, and there God appeared to him; whereupon Abraham built an altar, and the terebinth became a sacred place. Jacob sleeping at Bethel, was surprised by a dream which showed him that "this is the house of God and the gate of Heaven". Moses keeping sheep was arrested by a call from God, which call he obeyed with momentous results. The prophets, however one is to explain their experience, were distinctly conscious that a word came to them from beyond the limits of their conscious personality and brought them new truth—"thus spoke Jehovah". Psychology may do much to explain this consciousness; but we should be chary of explaining it away. The experience, after all, as it is given and recorded in history, is an experience of revelation and not merely of discovery.

Now if we take the view that all increase in knowledge is in a real sense revelation—the self-revelation of the universe to men—then we may observe that such self-revelation is necessarily relative to the development of our faculties in time. The child receives true impressions of the world, but in his interpretation of them there is an element of what we must call illusion, inseparable from the undeveloped condition of his faculties. As he grows he records and interprets more accurately the impressions he receives. The facts the universe sets before him do not alter; his perception of them does. Adult knowledge of course is not free from illusion, but it is relatively a more adequate apprehension of the facts.

The analogy between the growth of the individual and the development of the race is certainly not to be pressed too far. Yet it does exist. In the first place, although it is very doubtful whether the essential faculties of human nature have improved since prehistoric times, yet the accumulated knowledge of the past gives a better perspective. Further, in all his views of the world a man is in some measure subject to the stage of development in time at which his society has arrived. Thus the nomadic state carries with it certain relations within society, and certain relations between man and the rest of the world—the soil, plants, animals, the sky and the weather, and so on. These necessarily affect the way in which man interprets his experience. The nomadic may pass into the agricultural state, and then into various kinds of political, commercial, and industrial states, in all of which these relations, among men and between men and the world, are altered, and man's interpretation of his experience alters too. As we have seen, these changes, as they occurred in the history of the people of the Bible, involved relations with an ever widening area of reality. If we believe that the ultimate Reality is revealing Itself to the child as he grows to manhood, we may also believe that this Reality reveals Itself to human society in its changes of condition, "in divers parts and by divers manners", without either over-estimating or under-estimating the element of necessary illusion involved in the process of knowledge. In any historical presentation of the development of the knowledge of God, such as we have in the Bible, these temporal stages are reflected as a matter of course, and we may think of God, if we will, under the analogy of a skilful teacher who proportions his instruction to the development of the child. Any reasonable interpretation of the Bible will take account of this alteration of conditions as time advances.

We must not, however, exaggerate the importance of this; for although all men are to some extent subject to these temporal conditions, it is characteristic of genius, as we have seen, to emancipate itself from them to a startling degree and to utter things which are not for an age, but for all time. Certainly the biblical development as we have traced it is by no means a steady accumulation of *data*, building up a system of knowledge "line upon line, precept upon precept". Great personalities burst upon the scene, with something essentially new in what they have to say, often imperiously setting aside the gains of centuries of "progress". The continuity of human thought is indeed not broken. We can trace with some fulness the antecedents of the prophetic teaching. We can in a measure explain what led to it, what previous ideas entered into it, or affected it by way of reaction. But the precise thing in it that is new—that which constitutes the discovery of the prophets—we cannot so explain. We can only trace it to some kind of insight resident in personality, and raised to a high power in genius. Now these men of genius themselves have some account to give of this unexplained insight. It is for them a result of communion with God.[1] When we further observe

[1] This sense that something "comes to them" seems characteristic of genius in various spheres. The poet's address to his muse was not at first a mere literary convention. A great living architect told a friend of the writer that when he designed a well-known public building he "saw" the

that the thing which they think they received from God acts creatively in human life—enables men to deal more effectively with an ever larger area of reality—then we may fairly conclude that they are not wholly self-deceived in thinking so.

Yet even in these pioneers of the knowledge of God, who in many ways stand so independently of their time-environment, we have found ourselves obliged to admit error. At least, we have instances where the teaching which a prophet gives as from God is contradicted and superseded by some later prophet, whose judgment is corroborated by history and by the general consent of religious people. Is there any sense, in such cases, in speaking of a divine revelation ? Is God so capricious as to say and unsay ?

It has often been observed that man makes God in his own image, as the fish in Rupert Brooke's poem

> " trust there swimmeth One
> Who swam ere rivers were begun,
> Immense, of fishy form and mind,
> Squamous, omnipotent and kind ;
> And under that Almighty Fin
> The littlest fish may enter in ".

There is obvious truth in this. It does not follow that God is a figment of the human imagination. But it is a fact, and an important fact, that a man's notion of God depends largely upon what he is as a man.

God in His full essence cannot be known by a finite being. Upon this there is a general agreement in the Bible. From Moses, who knew he was not permitted to see the face of God, to Paul, who cries, " How unsearchable are His judgments and His ways past finding out ! "[1] the men of

plan as though in a vision, complete in all its parts. A facile explanation about emergence from the subconscious still leaves one feeling that something is unexplained. Men of genius in action have the same sense. We who have no inward knowledge of genius should be chary of thinking we have explained it away.

[1] Rom. xi. 33.

the Bible acknowledge the limitations of possible knowledge of the Eternal. Whatever knowledge we do, by God's own grace, possess, is necessarily relative to human faculties and human needs. That which a man is in himself, by innate endowment and by experience of life, makes him open upon that side to what God has to reveal. The innate endowment is something that always baffles us. It belongs to the "essential ego" which the psychologist has to postulate as a starting-point. We can often see how, given this original endowment, experience of life fits a man for some new apprehension of God. Hosea, when his married life ran to disaster, did not act as the *homme moyen sensuel* has acted in countless similar cases. There was in him a deep, ineradicable principle of loyalty which held him to the woman he had loved. He was surprised at himself, but he could not do otherwise, for a divine voice compelled: "Jehovah said to me, 'Go again and love an adulterous woman, in love with a paramour—as Jehovah loves the Israelites, although they turn to other gods'".[1] His own sense of absolute obligation to a certain course of action, we observe, is at the same moment a revelation to him of what God is. Out of his own experience he dared to proclaim God's loyalty to His people—"How shall I give thee up, Ephraim?"[2] Hosea is making God in his own image. But who made Hosea such a man? His own reply is that the same mysterious act of grace made him such as he was and made him see that God is such as He is. Some of the conditions which went to the making of Hosea and of his prophecy we can recognize. Thus he would hardly have felt as he did if the society in which he was brought up had not developed the institution of marriage to a relatively advanced stage. Nor, probably, would this particular figure of the divine relation to Israel have suggested itself if a degraded sexuality had not been an obsession

[1] Hos. iii. 1 (Moffatt). [2] Hos. xi. 8.

in the religion he attacked. But there remains something explicable only out of the individuality of the man and his communion with God. If we further ask, What reason have we for supposing that this view of God is not just a pleasing fantasy of Hosea's ? the first answer is that we ourselves know, when once it is put to us, that this sort of thing *is* divine, and that if there be a God at all He must be like this. The second answer is that historically, in spite of all temptation to think the contrary, Hosea's conception of God won its way into the mind of man, and made history. Because God was seen to be like this, the Jewish "Church" came into being ; and because that "Church", with all its limitations, gave some expression to this view of God, Jesus Christ appeared within it, and brought Hosea's conception of the divine character to full clarity and consistency.

This is an instructive example of the method of revelation. God reveals Himself by giving a man grace both to see his own life aright and in doing so to apprehend something of what God eternally is, and is always showing Himself to be to those who can perceive it. By grace we do not mean an irresistible power overriding personality, nor merely the gift of an extraordinary faculty unrelated to what a man is in himself. We mean a form of communion between God and man, in which the act of God and the spontaneity of human personality are inextricably interrelated. Into the ultimate problem of grace and free will we need not probe. But if personality remains inviolate in communion with God, as we cannot but maintain, then there is a contingent element in revelation, namely, that which is derived from human freedom; and yet this contingency does not impugn its divine origin. Not even the greatest of the prophets can be supposed to have been perfectly harmonized with the divine will, and yet their response to God's grace in their communion with Him was such as to give them insight beyond common men. Why they did so respond, while other men do not, is a question which cannot be answered.[1]

Our justification therefore for using the term "progressive revelation" is as follows: We observe a process which as a whole must be called progressive. At each stage of the process we observe individuals who gathered up in themselves the tendencies of the process, criticized them by some spontaneous power of insight, and redirected the process in its succeeding stages. That which these individuals contributed was a vision of God, determined by what they themselves were. This they were by grace of God, for we cannot give any other account of their experience. Whether we say that men progressively discovered a revelation which in God's intention is eternally complete and unalterable, or that God Himself proportioned the measure of His revelation to the stages of human progress, is perhaps no more than a matter of verbal expression. That progress is there, and in the progress revelation, is the double fact we wish to establish.

From this point we may approach the consummation of the historical process in the New Testament. One dominant Personality controls the whole of this stage of the "progressive revelation". The other minds of the New Testament revolve like planets round a central sun, and shine with borrowed light. Now a reader who approaches the teaching of Jesus freshly is probably struck first with its originality. When, however, we study its antecedents we are struck with its organic continuity with earlier revelation. This is so far-reaching that some students, intent on similarities and parallels, and distrustful of any claims to "uniqueness" in history, have denied that there is anything in this teaching strictly new. Yet in fact Christianity was a new thing in the way of religion.

[1] See J. Oman, *Grace and Personality*, pp. 145–151.

Perhaps since man began to be religious there has been no such momentous new departure. It would be paradox to deny to the Founder the originality which His religion has actually displayed.

The originality of Jesus and the continuity of His teaching with what had gone before are both facts, and both important. He was conscious of both. Thus in the earliest tradition of His teaching we find sayings which seem to imply the permanence of " the law and the prophets ",[1] and others which imply that they are superseded by something new.[2] Source-criticism does not justify us in setting aside the one or the other. Among His followers, the Aramaic-speaking section of the Church at Jerusalem seems to have emphasized the former, its Greek-speaking section, followed by Paul, the latter. One explanation that has been offered is that the teaching of Jesus was in fact more destructive of the traditional religion than He supposed or desired. The clarity of His thinking makes one feel this explanation unsatisfying. May not the truth be that in the depth and range of His insight He was more fully aware of continuity with the tradition than His most conservative followers, and more aware of the newness of what He brought than the most radical ? His criticism of the Sadducees is very pointed : " You are mistaken because you know neither the Scriptures nor the power of God "[3]—i.e. you are deficient both in understanding of the tradition and in personal intuition of divine things. His own reply to the problem they raised lights up the whole history of religion : " God is not a God of the dead but of the living ".[4] Why did no one think of that before ? is the question that rises to our minds. Apparently no one had thought of it, though as we look back we see that it penetrates to the heart of the

[1] Matt. v. 18 ; Luke xvi. 17 (Q) ; Mark vii. 9–13, x. 17–19.
[2] Matt. xi. 13 ; Luke xvi. 16 (Q) ; Mark vii. 14–15, x. 3–5.
[3] Mark xii. 24. [4] Mark xii. 27.

old religion with a sureness born of fresh intuition. That is a single instance of the way in which Jesus "came to fulfil the law and the prophets", as the first evangelist has it. "Matthew" stands in the main for the more conservative interpretation of Christianity. Paul, the "radical", equally lays stress on the fact that Jesus came "in the fulness of the time",[1] i.e. at an historical crisis when His message and work won significance from what had gone before.

If indeed Jesus Christ is anything like what His followers have believed Him to be, then we should expect to find in His teaching a large continuity with all that the Spirit of God has revealed to men everywhere. And we do in fact find this, not only within the biblical revelation, but, as the early Christian apologists were quick to point out, in other religions also. If Clement could recognize with enthusiasm the Christian element in the teaching of Socrates and Plato, we need never hesitate to do full justice to the affinity of Christianity with the best in Confucianism or Mahayana Buddhism. Within the Bible, however, the continuity is more significant, because it is a conscious participation in a tradition. Jesus is, and wished to be, the true successor of the Hebrew prophets. He gathers up into His teaching the most vital elements in the religion of His people, while He relentlessly repudiates many things sacred to His predecessors and contemporaries. The prophets had done the same.

Nothing in the long history we have briefly traced is irrelevant to the work and teaching of Jesus—the primitive religion of Israel, with its tension between the "otherness" and the familiarity of God; the prophetic movement; the popular piety and social discipline of Judaism after the Exile, with its controversies and its groping after unfamiliar truth; Pharisaism, "Wisdom" books, and Apocalyptic.

[1] Gal. iv. 4.

No less than the prophets He was concerned about problems raised by the outward events of His time, for the "Roman question" is in view in the Gospels just as the "Babylonian question" is in view in Jeremiah. Religious minds among the Jews were grappling with that question, and some of them were offering answers to it which up to a point approximated to the solution Jesus presented, but failed to go to the root of the matter in universal spiritual principles.[1] Tradition and the course of outward events provided the material on which He worked. He spoke the word that shaped it into living truth. As we have seen, the truth came disguised in particular forms. It possesses a high power of throwing off the disguise and reclothing itself in forms native to other times and other places.

Indeed from the beginning the impulse communicated in the teaching of Jesus sought fresh forms of expression. Already in the New Testament Paul is not content to know Christ after the flesh,[2] and John is aware that there were many things that Christ could not say to his disciples in His lifetime, so that His Spirit must still lead them into all truth.[3] The Spirit is indeed *His* Spirit, and when we move forward to remoter periods we find that the same Spirit still speaks in startling ways. Yet it is worth while to go back again and again to the record of what Jesus actually said. He said it in answer to particular questions raised for Him by His environment, and He said it partly in the thought-forms of His age, but this only enables to see more clearly how He consummates the "progressive revelation" in the biblical history. If we believe in the reality and significance of history at all, then these facts go far to provide something like an "objective" ground for the impression of unique authority that His words produce.

But over and above all this there is the unexplained

[1] See V. Simkhovi ch, *Towards the Understanding of Jesus.*
[2] 2 Cor. v. 16. [3] John xvi. 12–13.

spontaneity of personality, which is sovereign over the material that history supplies, and is the ultimate medium of revelation. The new thing that the prophets communicated we found to be essentially something in themselves. Because they were the men they were, and reacted to their experience in the way they did, they were open to certain aspects of God unsuspected by other men. God, who is always revealing Himself as men are able to receive it, imparted something of Himself to these men in personal communion. Because of that grace of God they both became men of a certain sort and saw and uttered truth about God. Now it is even more fully true that the new thing Jesus gave to men was bound up with what He was. It is not to be formulated in propositions about God, but discerned in the whole new outlook, the new attitude, the new essential relation to God and the universe which He possessed.

We saw that in the prophets the personal "somewhat" which made them vehicles of truth could best be described by saying that God imparted to them something of Himself, thereby making them the men they were. This determined their attitude to experience. If now we discern in Jesus an attitude to experience which is unique in quality, we cannot but say that God imparted Himself to Jesus uniquely, and that the whole of what Jesus was expressed that self-impartation of God. This is formulated theologically in the doctrine of the Incarnation. Just what it implies is a difficult, perhaps an impossible, question to answer. Any doctrine which denies to Jesus Christ His place in history as a man of a particular race and age does less than justice to His historical importance. Yet any doctrine which does not express His transcendence of history in a unique relation to God and to life fails to satisfy the religious impression He produces. As this book is not concerned with doctrines of the Person of Christ we may leave it at that. We observe, however, that whatever particular doctrine is held, the authority of Christ is in some sort prior to it. It is, as Father Tyrrell defined it, " the authority that truth exercises over the mind, and goodness over the conscience, and love over the heart and affections ; the authority that true Manhood exercises over men, true Personality over persons ".[1] We cannot find even in Christ an authority so external to ourselves as to absolve us from the inexorable responsibility for our own beliefs. If we ask for anything more " objective " we can find it only in the impressive witness of history—the history in which we ourselves stand, and which indeed we are helping in our measure to make.

For what He said stood the stringent test of " hard facts ". No facts could be " harder " than the disaster in which the ministry of Jesus was involved ; yet instead of going under, His gospel reshaped human history.

The death of Jesus was the crisis of religion. The Jewish religious community, which embodied the results of long centuries of development, rejected the appeal which Jesus made. His disciples found themselves, through following Him, detached from the tradition by which their religious life had been supported. With His death they lost the centre of the new faith into which they had begun to grow. They were adrift in a strange, dark world, in which the light of revelation no longer shone. His resurrection meant to them much more than the recovery of a Master loved and lost. It was a new revelation of the power and the mercy of God, the God who had revealed Himself in divers parts and manners in the law and the prophets. In virtue of that revelation the scattered disciples found themselves united in a " fellowship of the Spirit ", and the Christian Church emerged as an historical fact. The Church was conscious of being " the Israel of God " in its ultimate form. That is to say, it was the same " people of God " whose career in history started far back with the call of Abraham, and had

[1] *Mediævalism*, chap. IV.

led through all the strange spiritual adventures reflected in the Old Testament. The goal of that career had been reached, not by a mere development from Pharisaic Judaism (which refused to take the momentous step forward), but through a crisis in which Israel died to its past and rose into newness of life; for so Paul expresses it.[1]

It was from the far side of this crisis of death and resurrection that the writers of the New Testament looked back upon the Old, and claimed for the Church the whole rich heritage of the past of Israel. It was all summed up, and "fulfilled", in Christ. But that was not all. In the act of fulfilment the local, temporal, racial elements in the old religion were finally transcended, and Christianity emerged as a universal Gospel. Its intrinsic or intensive universality was perceived at least as early as the time when Paul wrote to the Galatians, and its universal character began to exhibit itself extensively in the astonishingly rapid advance of the early mission to the Gentile world. Very soon Christian thinkers perceived that as Christ fulfilled the law and the prophets of Judaism, so He also fulfilled the *præparatio evangelica* which lay in the highest reaches of Hellenistic thought. Thus the experience of the Church in history added empirical testimony to the Christian belief in the universality of Christ Himself, as the embodiment of the Word, or Wisdom, of the eternal God.

The process still goes on. Within Christendom developments in the secular sphere present fresh challenges to the faith, and corresponding developments in Christian thought are recorded. But where real moral and religious advance is made, it would not be true to suggest that it antiquates the Gospel or the teaching of Jesus. On the contrary it presents itself as a fresh unfolding of His meaning. And again, the more His Gospel goes out into the wider world, the more clearly does it exhibit its universal character, and the universality of the Person who stands at its centre.

[1] Rom vi. 3–11; Gal. vi. 14–16; Eph. ii. 1–10; Col. iii. 1–4.

As it once showed its intrinsic continuity with the highest in human thought by taking to itself the finest traditions of Judaism and Hellenism, so in later times it has found ways of laying hold upon Eastern religions. The Christian belief is not all " in the air ", that ultimately Christ will be found to have spoken the Word for all the world and for all time. That is as yet faith, not knowledge. For our present purpose it is enough to record that after many centuries of historical vicissitudes His word is still current, fertile, and powerful.

The relation which Jesus Christ bears to the Bible is a symbol of the relation which Christians believe He will at last be seen to bear to the spiritual history of mankind as a whole. It we take our stand at any point in the Old Testament, we see that the spiritual life there portrayed is tending along different lines towards—something, which does not become clear until in Jesus Christ the various lines reach fulfilment. So the spiritual life of peoples, within and without Christendom, shows anticipations which are fulfilled when Christ comes. The process of history brings about again and again the " fulness of time ", in which the achievements of the human spirit, seeking God and being sought by Him, are confronted by the fact of Christ, and the crisis of the Gospels is re-enacted. Not without a death to the past, and a resurrection, is the lordship of Christ established, but from the far side of the crisis the ultimate continuity of the providential order in history is disclosed. It is the purpose of God, says Paul, in the fulness of the times, to sum up all things in Christ.[1]

We may now bring together the two aspects of the process we have been studying. On the one hand we have the movement of events on a large scale, beyond the control of any individual—the migrations of peoples, the clash of empires and civilizations, and behind them natural factors like population and food-supply,—all these shaping from without the history of a community. On the other hand we have the spiritual impulse in powerful individuals, from the half-mythical Abraham or the legendary Moses to Jesus and His followers, shaping it from within. These two

[1] Eph. i. 10.

factors are seen in the biblical history perfectly interacting. The outward aspect of the process we may call providential, though it is seen to be so only because individuals responded to it in a creative way. The inward aspect of the process exhibits the undeniable spontaneity of personality functioning at its highest, in conscious communion with God. But at each point this spontaneity is both conditioned by the outward factor, and directly reflected in its changes and fresh departures. Through the interaction of the outward and inward factors the biblical community is led into ever more comprehensive relations with the entire world of human experience, and at each widening of the field individuals are raised up to interpret the situation in spiritual terms and to absorb more and more of the data of experience into the religious life in its corporate expression.

This twofold process is even to-day by no means at an end, for the geographical expansion of Christianity in our own time, with the accompanying enrichment of its life and thought, is an extension of the history reflected in the Bible. But in the perspective of the twentieth Christian century we can see more plainly than ever how with the culmination of the biblical process in the appearance of Jesus Christ, and the experience of Him that came to His earliest followers, the conclusive step was taken. It is He who gave to the whole process its absolute meaning, and it is He who shapes and controls its remoter issues down to our own day. For the Christ revealed in the New Testament does shape and control the spiritual movements of our time, even those which cannot be said to have taken their origin from Christianity, as in the first century He shaped and controlled the spiritual movements of the Jewish and of the Hellenistic world.

We take therefore the work and influence of Jesus Christ in their full scope as the climax of that whole complex process which we have traced in the Bible, and we conclude that the process itself is so intimately and dynamically related to all that we cannot but hold to be of the highest spiritual worth, that we must recognize it in the fullest sense as a revelation of God, a revelation whose unique quality is measured by the uniqueness of Jesus Christ Himself and His relation to the human race.

Conclusion

THE BIBLE AS "THE WORD OF GOD"

CHAPTER XIV

CONCLUSION: THE BIBLE AS "THE WORD OF GOD"

WE started from the position that authority in the absolute sense resides in the truth alone, or, in religious language, in the mind and will of God. In so far as the Bible possesses authority in religion, it can be only as mediating the truth, or as "the Word of God".[1] Our enquiry has indicated certain ways in which it does in fact mediate truth: first, through the "inspiration" of individual genius, conferring not inerrancy but a certain cogent persuasiveness;[2] next through the appropriation of "inspired" ideas by a whole community, whose experience through many generations tests, confirms and revises them;[3] and finally through the life of One in whom His followers found so decisive an answer to their needs that they hailed Him as the Wisdom of God incarnate.[4] We further saw that these three stages form a continuous history in which as a whole, even more clearly than in its several parts, a divine process of revelation can be discerned.[5] All through our study it has been clear that anything we can say about revelation is relative to the minds that receive it. Nowhere is the truth given in such purely "objective" form that we can find a self-subsistent external authority. Even where it might appear that if Christian belief is true we should have such absolute authority, namely, in the words of Jesus Christ, we have been forced to

[1] Chap. I, pp. 16–17.
[2] Part I.
[3] Part II.
[4] Part III.
[5] Part IV.

conclude that we must still accept responsibility for our judgments. For the report of His teaching is not inerrant, and the criticism of it calls for spiritual insight in the last resort; and further, even supposing we had before us His own undoubted words, they would need "translation" out of their historical setting before they could be directly applied to our own case, and that again calls for spiritual insight. Nor again does the impressive evidence of history attain to complete objectivity, since for its interpretation we must assume a certain estimate of the end towards which its development tends. Thus in every way we are brought back to the importance of the "subjective" factor. Granted that religious authority somehow resides in the Bible, how does it become authoritative *for me?*

If the Bible as a whole is a revelation of God, and the crown of this revelation is the life and teaching of Jesus Christ, then we may start by asking, How did Jesus reveal God? He seems to have made very few general theological propositions, and those of the simplest, as that there is none good but One, that is God,[1] that all things are possible to God,[2] that He is kind to the unthankful and the evil.[3] Nor does He appear to have imparted ineffable secrets concerning God and the spiritual world, in the manner of the apocalyptists or of Greek mystagogues.[4] Some of His followers, indeed, mistook His parables for allegorical mystifications; but when they had done their worst with them the parables still conveyed their own meaning to simple sincerity. The parables in fact, as we have seen, are pictures of life as it is, and in telling them Jesus challenged men to

[1] Mark x. 18. [2] Mark x. 27, xiv. 36. [3] Luke vi. 35 (Matt. v. 45)

[4] Those who would maintain that He did so must refer to apocalyptic passages; these contain statements (among others) which in their plain meaning are not true (see p. 233). Either therefore the tradition is at fault, or such revelations were not inerrant, or their interpretation remains an open question. Apart from these, it is only possible to refer to a supposed esoteric tradition for which there is no historical evidence.

find God in life. That is characteristic of His method. In a sense we might say that Jesus never told men anything about God but what they could see for themselves—when He had brought them into the right attitude for seeing Him —and this He did, not only by what He said, but by what He was and did, and most conclusively through His death and resurrection.

As we have said, the ability to see and to speak of the things of God is not an extraordinary faculty communicated apart from what a man is, but a function of the personality reconciled to God. The work of Jesus was primarily this of reconciliation. He released men from falsehoods and perversions of affection and will which obscured their view of God—and then they began to know God. Jesus is Saviour and Reconciler even before He is Revealer. The first disciples clearly failed to understand much of what their Master said. But His words lodged in their minds, and after they had been completely reorientated to life through the experience of His death and resurrection, they saw for themselves the truth to which He had pointed.

We may study the process most clearly in Paul and the anonymous author of the Fourth Gospel.

Paul was a man of religious genius and shows in all his work the originality of genius. Like all prophets, he is conscious of being directly guided by the divine Spirit. Yet he is also aware that this guidance has been made possible for him by Jesus Christ. It is not that he habitually quotes Jesus as an "authority". He does indeed so quote Him explicitly two or three times,[1] and in his writings there are more reminiscences of the teaching of Jesus than the casual reader observes. But Christ had "apprehended" him, had given him a new relation to God and to life. Christ

[1] In 1 Cor. vii. 10, ix. 14, and perhaps in other less unambiguous places.

had " saved ", had " reconciled " him. He speaks of his own experience when he says, " If any man be in Christ, he is a new creation ".[1] The phrase " in Christ " is a profoundly theological one, and we must not water down its significance. Yet it means, among other things, that through contact with Jesus he had found a new centre from which to contemplate life and the world. Looking from that new centre he found that God revealed Himself in all experience in new and surprising ways.

John speaks of the way in which Jesus revealed God partly in more intellectual terms. He starts from the highly philosophical idea of the Logos or " uttered Thought " of God: and identifies Christ with the Logos in that He has " declared " the invisible God. But this intellectualism is not the deepest thing in his teaching. He is fully aware of personal and moral conditions which must be present before one can receive a revelation of God. He has faced the question, How can I know that Christ speaks of God with authority? He replies " He who is willing to do God's will can recognize whether the teaching (of Jesus) is from God or not ".[2] That is, a personal reconciliation to God is the condition of knowledge of God; even the authority of the Logos is not independent of that. Further, when he comes to tell what Christ actually does for men, he makes it clear that He does something more than speak to us about God with authority. What would be the use of showing a light to a blind man? His eyes must first be opened. This Christ does for us. He does not ask us to believe on His authority; He puts us in a condition to see for ourselves. To John this is prior to any decision about the Person of Christ: " Whether He is a sinner or not, I do not know; I only know that whereas I was blind, now I see ". Then follows the inference, " If this man were not

[1] 2 Cor. v. 17: the whole context is illuminating.
[2] John vii. 17.

from God, He could do nothing ".[1] The divine authority of Christ is inferred from His power to enable men to see God. Now John accepts in the fullest way the mystic's presupposition that "like is known by like",[2] so that there is no knowledge of God apart from a measure of participation in the life of God. What Christ does for us is to communicate to us the life of God. Through Christ we are "born anew" into a divine life.[3] This may fairly be described as mysticism: yet it is not so far removed after all from experience such as the non-mystic may have. For "God is love: and he who abides in love abides in God".[4] The discourses of the Upper Room set us in the midst of a circle of "friends" of Christ;[5] and we shall not be wrong in concluding that the author had learnt in the company of friends of Christ that way of living by love that He communicated, and through it had found unity with God. When once he had found that, then the demand his soul had been making all his life—"Show us the Father"—was satisfied. "He who has seen Me has seen the Father".[6]

If we are to follow the leading of this evangelist, even to see God in Christ is not the first step in the Christian revelation. That "God is like Christ" is often commended to us to-day as an entirely non-dogmatic statement which anyone might accept as a starting-point. As a matter of fact it is a colossal assumption, for anyone who has not first accepted Christ's attitude to life. We may more modestly and more sincerely start by recognizing, as people aware of disharmony within ourselves, of non-adaptation to our environment, and of estrangement from God, that Christ stands for a thoroughgoing reconciliation, and offers such

[1] John ix. 24–33. Whatever historical event may or may not lie behind the narrative, the evangelist is telling, in his own intention, the story of the illumination of the spiritually blind.

[2] *Corpus Hermeticum* (ed. Scott), XI. ii. 20b.

[3] John iii. 5–8.

[4] 1 John iv. 16.

[5] John xv. 14–15.

[6] John xiv. 8–9.

reconciliation to us. When we accept His way, then we come into a position in which we can begin to see the truth of God in our own experience as interpreted by what He said and what He was.

From what the New Testament shows us of the manner in which Jesus revealed God to men, we may learn something about the way in which the Bible as a whole may become the "Word of God" to us. Jesus was primarily concerned not with delivering "doctrine", but with making men anew, so that they could receive the revelation of Himself which God is always seeking to communicate. Similarly, the most important thing we find in the Bible is not "doctrine" but something that helps us into a new attitude to God and to life. Of course, no mere reading of books could make anyone good or religious, if he did not wish to be such. There are indeed many cases on record where the casual reading of a portion of Scripture awakened a desire for God which seemed to be completely dormant. Perhaps, if fuller *data* were available, it would be found to have been more awake than the subject himself realized. In general we may take it that if the Bible is to do its work it makes certain demands upon its readers at the outset. In the same way Jesus Himself could not save men without their own goodwill. There was a village where "He could not do any deed of power, and He was astonished at their lack of faith".[1] Still less can the Bible do anything for a reader who does not satisfy such minimum requirements, which may be summed up as sincerity, openness of mind, and that fundamental reverence that is a willingness to be commanded. To ask how a man who is radically insincere can become sincere is to raise ultimate questions about personality which cannot here be discussed. No one is born insincere, and probably no one is without his moments of sincerity.

[1] Mark vi. 5-6.

For those who approach the Bible in this spirit (which Jesus described as that of a child), it is capable of awakening and redirecting the powers of mind, heart and will, so that a man's whole attitude and relation to the last realities is shaped anew. It can do this because it is the sincere utterance of men who were themselves mightily certain of God in their own experience, individual and corporate.

The written word is the medium through which we reach the personality and its experience. It is never a perfect medium,

> " For words, like nature, half reveal
> And half conceal the soul within ".

But it is the best we have. In almost all parts of the Bible we can feel ourselves in touch with religious personalities, some of them displaying exceptional inspiration, all of them men of insight and sincerity. They write out of their experience of God in the soul, or of God's dealings in what happened to them and their people. Because they were " men of God ", their experience is a valid representation of divine reality. It profits us as we " live ourselves into it ".[1] As we have seen, the range of experience reflected in the Bible is amazingly wide, and to share it by yielding ourselves to the guidance of its writers is to expose our souls on all sides to the divine action.

The Bible has suffered from being treated too much as a source of information. The traditional theory valued it as giving authoritative information, in the form of dogma, upon matters known only by special revelation. The critical method has too often issued in treating it as a collection of information for the antiquary. Its place as a whole is rather

[1] If we may borrow from the Germans their expressive phrase " *sich hineinleben* "

with the masterpieces of poetry, drama and philosophy, that is, the literature which does not so much impart information but stirs the deeper levels of personality. "Tragedy", said Aristotle, "effects through pity and fear the purgation of such passions".[1] The dramatist has experienced life in terms of the suffering that besets it and the spirit that triumphs over the suffering. The compassion and awe that the experience arouses in him he succeeds in conveying to his audience or his readers. Through identifying themselves with his personages in their pitiful and terrible experiences, they undergo an emotional awakening and cleansing. Thus *King Lear* or *Tess of the D'Urbervilles* does not instruct us in a theory of life, but makes us sharers in an experience of life more intense and profound than our normal level. We are greater men, potentially, for reading such works.

It is here that we find the best analogy to that which the reading of the Bible should do for us. Its writers are men who had an experience of life both deep and intense. They felt with sincerity, and express what they felt with strong conviction. As we identify ourselves with them in our reading, we too may come to a deeper and more intense experience of life. And as God touches us in all great literature, wherein is "the precious life-blood of a master-spirit", so He touches us supremely in the literature of the Bible, because of the intrinsic sublimity of its writings and because the experience they transmit is so organically related to history and to the divine Incarnation in Christ, in which we recognize the supreme act of God in history. The criterion lies within ourselves, in the response of our own spirit to the Spirit that utters itself in the Scriptures. The Reformation theologians, who appealed from the authority of the Church to the authority of the Scriptures, sought confirmation for the latter in the "interior witness

[1] *Poetics*, 1449b. 27.

of the Holy Spirit". This is in effect the "subjective" criterion of which we are speaking.[1]

Thus the religious authority of the Bible comes home to us primarily in inducing in us a religious attitude and outlook. The use that may be made of the Bible as a source of doctrine is secondary to this. It is, however, by no means unimportant. The reaction against the old dogmatic use of the Scriptures has in some quarters gone too far. Anyone, of course, can find in the Bible materials for a "history of dogma". As we have said, the first question we must ask in our study is, What did this writer actually say and what did he mean by it? It is the conscientious putting of that question that has so greatly advanced our knowledge of the actual contents of the Scriptures during the period of critical study. But anyone who takes the matter with full seriousness will not be content to stop there. When he has discovered what the writer actually said and meant, he wants to ask further, Is this what I am to believe about God? Is it *true?* Probably no one who reads this book will think that this question has the self-evident answer, Of course it is true, *because* it is in the Bible. We must take responsibility for our beliefs. But supposing we have found that by approaching the Bible in that "child-like" spirit of openness and sincerity our outlook on life has been altered, our experience deepened, and our sense of

[1] In a sense this may be said to involve a *circulus in probando:* we look to the Bible for guidance towards religious truth; we recognize this truth by reference to our own sincere religious standards. It is in some sense parallel to Aristotle's attempt to define moral good. After all his attempts to find an "objective" or quantitative standard for virtue he has to fall back upon the test ὡς ἂν ὁ φρόνιμος ὁρίσειε—virtue is that which the man of moral insight judges to be such (*Eth. Nic.* 1107[a]). In morals and religion no purely objective evidence is obtainable. But Christianity recognizes a "somewhat not ourselves" in the most inward form of experience: that is the *testimonium Spiritus Sancti internum.* The ultimate "fact" is the unity of experience in which "subjective" and "objective" are one. See H. Wheeler Robinson, *The Christian Experience of the Holy Spirit*, pp. 95–96.

God made stronger, then the beliefs enunciated by the writers to whom we owe this will carry weight with us. We shall not lightly dismiss any theological propositions they may put forth. And after all there are some very dogmatic beliefs indeed which stand out boldly from the pages of the Bible, as for instance the prophetic maxim that there is one God and He is good, and the New Testament definition, " God is love ". Neither is at once self-evident, or always easy of belief. Both are challenged to-day, as they have been in the past, on grounds which no serious person can treat with contempt. In our best moments, it may be, we see that the world of our experience as a whole will not make sense on any other hypothesis. But there are times, it may well be, when doubts are stronger than our faith. It would not be honest at such times simply to silence our questionings with a text. Nevertheless we may well turn away from the narrow scene of individual experience at the moment, to the spacious prospect we command in the Bible.[1] Here we meet with men whom we must acknowledge as experts in life, and find them asserting with the firmest conviction that God is of such a nature. Here also we trace the long history of a community which through good fortune and ill tested their belief in God, and experimented too in varieties of belief, with the result that the " logic of facts " drove deeper and deeper the conviction that while some ways of thinking of God are definitely closed, this way lies open and leads on and on. We can go forward if we will till we come to the great *dénouement* of the story in the evangelical facts of the life and death of Jesus Christ and the emergence of the redeemed society. When we have " lived ourselves into " all that, we may well see our doubts and difficulties in a different perspective ; and so belief raises itself afresh

[1] " Though it is morally certain that we are wiser than our fathers, it is doubtful whether we are more profound than all the ages " (Keith Feiling in *The Times*, Feb. 9th, 1928).

upon a deeper and wider basis. The impressive witness of religious genius and of history has not indeed overborne our individual judgment, but it has delivered us from the tyranny of proximate impressions, made us free of a larger experience, and helped us to a true objectivity of judgment. Such is the "authority" of the Bible in its true and legitimate sense.

The appeal to biblical authority in this sense does not lay Christian thought under the dead hand of the past. Its effect is to associate the Christian mind of to-day with a tradition of life and experience rather than of dogma, of religion rather than of theology. To refuse such an association is to deny something which belongs to the genius of Christianity itself, for an irresponsible individualism in religion is not Christian; and when once the corporate factor in Christian experience is admitted, the factor of historical tradition cannot be excluded. But one element in the life and tradition so transmitted is progressive movement. The attempt to find a static finality in religion, as for instance in the fixing of the Torah, never succeeded.[1] In the New Testament it is the witness to the evangelical facts, as experienced in history by the first believers, that is regarded as constant and unchanging. Their interpretation is subject to development.[2] The last of the great prophetic writers in the canon, the author of the Fourth Gospel, makes Christ take leave of His followers with the words, "I have much still to say to you, but at present you cannot bear the weight of it. When however *He* comes, who is the Breath of the Truth, he will lead you into the whole truth"[3]. We need not confine that leading to the New Testament period. It is not in the nature of an historical religion to be static, and the "faith once

[1] After the Torah was completed, the Mishna was created to bring it up to date, and the Gemara of the Talmud to bring the Mishna up to date!

[2] 1 Cor. xv. 1–11, iii. 10–11.

[3] John xvi. 13.

delivered to the saints "[1] has actually grown and developed as any faith which encounters life and experience in a changing world must develop. Catholic Christianity has its organs for recording and formulating such development, in spite of its traditional conservatism. On the other hand, it was a representative of a type of Protestantism most rigorous in its appeal to the Scriptures who declared, " The Lord hath more light and truth yet to break forth out of His holy word ".[2] If the Bible is indeed " the Word of God ", it is so not as the " last word " on all religious questions, but as the " seminal word " out of which fresh apprehension of truth springs in the mind of man.

[1] Jude 3.

[2] John Robinson to the " Pilgrim Fathers ".

INDEX

(A.) NAMES

(B.) SCRIPTURE REFERENCES

(INCLUDING APOCRYPHA AND PSEUDEPIGRAPHA)

(A.) OLD TESTAMENT

(B.) Apocrypha

(C.) Pseudepigrapha

(References are to *Apocrypha and Pseudepigrapha*, edited by R. H. Charles. Vol. II.)

(D.) New Testament

(C.) SUBJECTS